THE ESSENTIAL WAY OUT IN WEST VIRGINIA

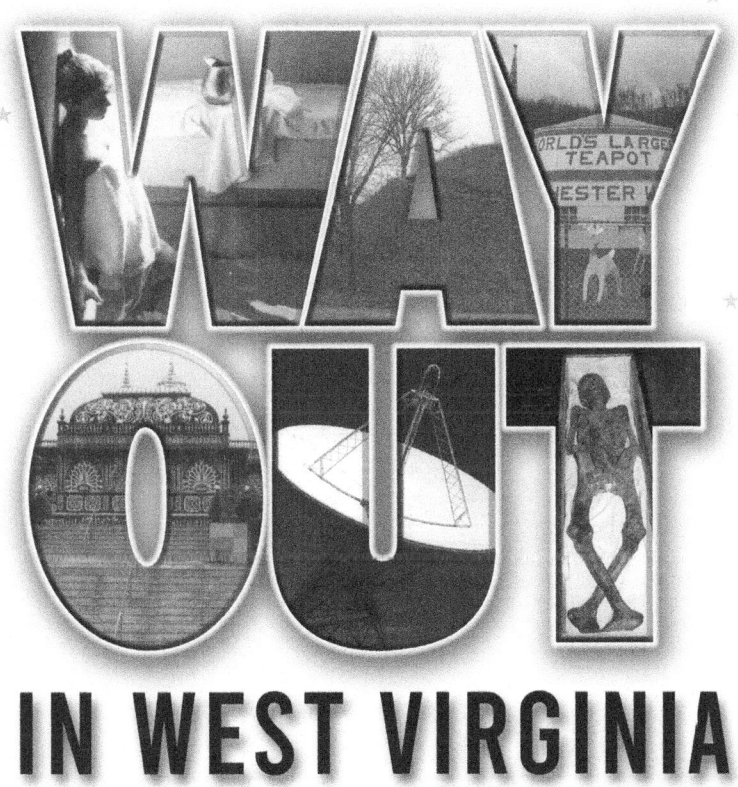

THE ESSENTIAL

FIFTH EDITION

WAY OUT IN WEST VIRGINIA

A MUST-HAVE GUIDE TO THE ODDITIES & WONDERS OF THE MOUNTAIN STATE

JEANNE MOZIER

quarrier press

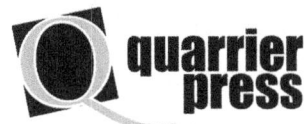

©2022, 1999 by Jeanne Mozier.

All rights reserved. No part of this book
may be reproduced in any form or in any means,
electronic or mechanical, including photocopying,
recording, or by any information storage
and retrieval system, without permission
in writing from the publisher.

Book and cover design:
Mark S. Phillips

Fifth Edition

10   9   8   7   6   5   4   3   2   1

Printed in the United States of America
on recycled paper.

Library of Congress Catalog Number: 2002092271
ISBN 13: 978-1-942294-30-6
ISBN 10: 1-942294-30-1

Distributed by:

West Virginia Book Company
1125 Central Avenue
Charleston, WV 25302

www.wvbookco.com

To my husband Jack,

my personal pilot and

favorite traveling companion.

Table of Contents

A NOTE FROM JEANNE'S HUSBAND, JACK
    ABOUT THIS FIFTH EDITION ix

FOREWORD TO THE ORIGINAL EDITION xi

INTRODUCTION xiii

HOW TO USE THIS BOOK xv

Chapter One: ADVENTURE DRIVING 1

Chapter Two: AMAZING ARCHITECTURE 13

Chapter Three: ART WONDERS 33

Chapter Four: FAR-OUT FESTIVALS & OTHER HAPPENINGS 51

Chapter Five: FAST LIVING 65

Chapter Six: GREAT PLUMBING 75

Chapter Seven: HISTORIC ODDITIES 83

Chapter Eight: LOCAL FOOD SPECIALTIES
    & MEMORABLE EATERIES 107

Chapter Nine: MILLION DOLLAR VIEWS 125

Chapter Ten: MOTHER NATURE'S WONDERS.......................137

Chapter Eleven: REMARKABLE COLLECTIONS......................151

Chapter Twelve: SHOPPING TREASURES 165

Chapter Thirteen: SUPERLATIVES 173

Chapter Fourteen: THINGS THAT USED TO BE THERE 195

Chapter Fifteen: TOURS & TRIPS NOT TO MISS....................209

Chapter Sixteen: TRULY INCREDIBLE 225

Chapter Seventeen: UNUSUAL PLACES TO STAY....................245

APPENDIX..261

INDEX 293

BIBLIOGRAPHY 321

ABOUT THE AUTHOR 323

A Note from Jeanne's husband, Jack about this Fifth Edition

Jeanne thought that one of the best parts of preparing her book about West Virginia's unusual and oft-overlooked features was the opportunity she had to travel to every corner of the state meeting and talking with folks. She felt honored by the affection people demonstrated toward the idea of the book — and all the copies it has sold in multiple printings.

She loved comments like: "My grandmother cried. She said it was the most good things she's ever read about West Virginia in one book." Or: "My father laughed so much as he read it. He said it helped him heal from his heart operation." Some people came back again and again to buy more copies because they loaned them out and the book never returned.

This affection Jeanne had for the marvels of our home state is continued with this newly-revised Fifth Edition through the dedicated and capable effort of her publisher, Bill Clements at Quarrier Press. He, like so many people, recognizes the incredible contribution this book makes to the heart and soul of our state... as well as to its economic development.

To be touched by this book makes us proud to be of West Virginia. It brings people who now live "away" back in spirit. And for those being introduced to West Virginia there is nothing like this book to learn about its attributes and how to navigate them.

So, my friends, do what I do... take this book and sit with Jeanne, who will remind you of your favorite relative — perhaps an aunt or uncle — who knows all the family stories and is eager to tell them to you. She wants you to know the amazing fabric and character of West Virginia.

Enjoy!

Jack

Foreword to the First Edition

No one ever accused me of being secretive, and I'm not about to start now. The intriguing land and friendly people of West Virginia have stayed hidden from view long enough. I want more people to discover that, sometimes, wild and wonderful can be a little weird.

West Virginia boasts pre-historic Indian burial mounds and 18th century mineral spas. You will also find vestiges of frontier life, stories of wild and wooly battles of early industrial development and quirky creations of independent—and eccentric—mountaineers. It is a people's state, with nearly two million acres of land set aside for the public in a remarkable system of state parks, forests and wildlife management areas, as well as two huge national forests.

It was the outline of the state that first struck me as odd. In fact, an early title for the book was *Way Out in West Virginia: It's More Than Just the Shape*. The most irregular of the continental states, it is the easiest puzzle piece to identify. Of its 1,170 miles of boundaries, only 200 or so are man-made and therefore, straight. The remainder wind along rivers and mountain ranges.

The original notion of an "oddities tour" was inspired by personal experience at two extraordinary events staged annually in West Virginia. Beginning with Fayetteville's Bridge Day and the Berkeley Springs International Water Tasting Competition, I moved to collecting other peculiar attractions of my adopted home state. I put the word out on the Internet and the "mountaineer grapevine."

My own tastes range from the merely unusual to the bizarre. I've made the fantastic and supernatural my environment of choice; *Way Out in West Virginia* reflects that point of view. This book is a searchlight for what's different, unique, individual and odd in a state that celebrates those inclinations. Not all the places listed are out-and-out weird; some are conventional but have strange or distinguishing characteristics. Many are on various national registers including Historic Places and Landmarks. All are interesting.

Once you've experienced my list of oddities, whether in real life or vicariously through these pages, I invite you to search out more. The directions are easy—look for anomalies like the sign that announced "Donuts and Pepperoni Rolls" or anything that makes you exclaim "gee whiz"; then explore.

Introduction

Wild, wonderful and occasionally weird West Virginia

From churning whitewater in million-year-old rivers to the galactic ears of the 21st century—it's all a trip in "way out" West Virginia.

The matchless qualities of today's West Virginia began in the mists of time when recurring eons of primeval forces lifted this spot on the planet from the deepest part of a vast inland sea that once covered North America to the state with the highest mean elevation. Our Alleghenies experienced millions of years of erosion before the Himalayas were even born, making today's real estate truly ancient.

Countless shells and watery vegetation from sea cycles have been transformed by relentless geologic pressure over countless ages into the limestone and coal deposits that dominate the present. Marine fossils are regularly discovered on mountaintops. Salt and silica sand resulted from evaporation of a shallow sea period; oil and gas were trapped in eroded sandstone and shale.

Spread out the huge, colorful geologic map of West Virginia and variations in the land are obvious even to the untrained eye, variations "that mean the difference between a gentleman and a bum." The Eastern Continental Divide slices off a strip of the state. To the west, on a great slanted plateau, is the vast majority of West Virginia. Ours is the only state entirely in the Appalachian highlands. The slice to the east is the edge of Atlantis that slammed against the former inland sea, scrunching it into a rippling sheet of jumbled mountains and careening "hollers." Twists, fractures and distortions are commonplace yet distinguishing characteristics of the Mountain State.

Geology is destiny and the mineral kingdom is a high stakes player in the West Virginia game. The state's human history has been a three-century contest of wills between geology and humanity, with the mountains providing obstacles to human constructions as well as endless mineral resources to exploit.

The frontier pattern of independence, self-sufficiency and borderline outlaw nature was established early on in West Virginia and boosted by the constitutionally doubtful steps taken to birth the state. When the area was finally admitted to the Union, decades after all its neighbors, it even had "west" in the name. Wild still remains closer than you think.

The step to statehood had fate adding another peculiar twist. West Virginia began life as the western expanses of the cradle of American civilization—Virginia. The Eastern Continental Divide served as marker point for early treaties between English colonists and the tribes of the Six Nations. The Alleghenies were the first mountains to be conquered, and West Virginia was America's first frontier. Then came the Civil War or the War of Northern Aggression, as it's known in various nooks and crannies of the state. Ripped away from rebelling Virginia as political punishment, West Virginia bears the scars of a child of divorce. As the animated Virginia dandy in the prize-winning film *Gilligan's Appalachia* defines the relationship between the two states: "you'll be the butt of our jokes forever."

Astrologically a Gemini, West Virginia exhibited the duality of that sign in much of its early state history. There were two Constitutional Conventions, two votes for liberation and a capital city that couldn't make up its mind. First the capital was Wheeling, then it was Charleston, back to Wheeling, and finally in 1887, Charleston. Not only is the state's name made up of two words, but it was the second name given. The proposed state's working title was Kanawha until replaced during the second Constitutional Convention.

Trees, mountains, rocks and rapids are found in abundance in this place where Mother Nature chose to express her wildest imagination. Lacking are the cities. There are no true urban areas and the state's ten largest population centers don't add up to half a million people. Geology and terrain have conspired to keep the state a perpetual frontier. Like third-world states all over the globe, even the industrial phase was primarily exploitative. Yet West Virginia's arrested development is proving to be a blessing. It precluded the explosive urban growth of the 20th century and made it a safe, friendly and naturally wild place to be in these opening decades of the 21st.

Life in West Virginia is not all mountain climbing cows and hand painted signs advertising DIRT. There is culture galore, a world famous resort, and man-made wonders to admire on a face-to-face scale unmatched in America today. As noted novelist and maverick candidate for governor Denise Giardinia remarked, "For better or worse, there is no place like West Virginia."

How To Use This Book

Chapters are arranged by category of unique places, events and experiences independent of their location in the state. Each entry is listed alphabetically in the index, which provides contact information and location. To make the book useful for planning trips, there are indexes of each item by county. The ultimate information tool is the toll-free number for visitors: 1-800-CALL WVA. When appropriate, items are cross-referenced in the text to other chapters where there is additional information.

CHAPTER ONE

Adventure Driving

Driving in West Virginia is a constant adventure. Every road is a costly engineering marvel, every scenic overlook offers a million dollar view, and every tree could hide a cunning deer poised to leap upon an unsuspecting driver. The state ranks #1 in the number of cars that hit Bambi each year.

Roads twist, turn, climb and dip through relentless mountains and forests. They hug rivers, skim tree-tops, careen along ridges, and reveal plunging vistas. Tiny jewels of stunning beauty are revealed then disappear around the next curve. Breathtaking rock formations are down-home milemarkers and 200-foot cliffs tower above the roadside. Congested cities and traffic-jammed beltways are nowhere to be found. Breaks in the solid center line are greeted like an oasis in the desert. Driving through sparkling ice-covered hardwoods and snow-laden evergreens is a routine part of the winter sports package. One noted author on a first-time visit observed: "the highways are perfect looking, unstained by wear and tear, and not many people seem to use them."

Two centuries of creative road building in a state full of rivers and mountains have resulted in a treasure-filled inventory that includes not only innumerable hairpin turns, but also countless tunnels, more than a dozen covered bridges, and the highest bridge east of the Mississippi.

West Virginia's topography often demands a package deal of road, river and rail in varying arrangements but usually crammed into a narrow hollow between two mountains. Houses built with a stream between them and the road inspire creatively engineered personal bridges. Some are elaborate, others scarcely more than footbridges.

See "Amazing Architecture" for more on bridges.

Road signs are literal. Mastering the switchback is a driving necessity for Mountaineers and their guests.

"Lay over" roads have a single paved lane down the middle and gravel shoulders to "lay over" if a vehicle suddenly appears from the other direction. This unique highway type is particularly noticeable along the winding, hilly and blind curves in Greenbrier and Pocahontas counties. The narrow, twisting roads that rise and plunge through Wyoming County are marked with "turnouts" at regular intervals to allow traffic to pass.

Rockcatchers are expanses of sturdy netting hung to keep chunks of southern West Virginia cliffs from crashing down onto random motorists.

My special road...

There are skads of special roads throughout the state, and every resident probably has a few favorites.

Although many residents urge traveling south from Wheeling along the Ohio side, I prefer **SR 2**, which closely tracks the Ohio River. Scenery ranges from sheer cliffs and huge industrial complexes with giant mounds of coal, to quaint towns and rolling meadows.

The trip from Wheeling to Bethany on **SR 88** should be a ten-minute commute by mileage. Instead it can take a half hour because of the relentless twists, turns and switchbacks. Except for being paved, it appears virtually unchanged from the road that took students to Bethany College more than 150 years ago.

> **Waving** *to other drivers on most roads in the state is a routine occurrence. Strangers, neighbors, friends or relatives, it makes no difference. Newcomers can be forgiven for thinking that waving must be the law.*

My husband Jack and I were amazed when we stumbled onto **Smoke Hole Road**, hugging the side of North Fork Mountain and Smoke Hole Canyon for eleven heart stopping miles. Carved by the South Branch of the Potomac, the rugged 1,421-foot canyon is a forested treasure house of spectacular views, abandoned log cabins, caves and rare rock formations. The narrow gravel road runs through the Monongahela National Forest from SR 28 west of Petersburg to US 220 at Upper Tract.

It looks like a convulsive snake on the map, but **SR 97** west from Pineville to R.D. Bailey Lake in Wyoming County is a gorgeous drive. The Guyandotte River, about 100 feet below the road, cuts through cliffs of black rock streaked in red and tan, bringing the scene alive with views of rushing water. There are scarcely any signs to mar the view of green mountaintops and only an occasional cluster of giant mine equipment to remind you that humans have made their mark.

The sign warns that **SR 49** from Williamson to Matewan is a rough road. That is an understatement. In a massive road straightening project, a half-mile of dip and drop twists were replaced by a huge dam of dirt with a road over it. It's all part of the near hopeless attempt to flatten and tame West Virginia. Other stretches require 15 mph signs as curves virtually turn back on themselves. Tales abound of huge coal trucks that must back and forward their way around such curves.

For a real challenge drive deep into the southernmost mountains of McDowell County between Welch and Gary on a one-lane dirt road that requires wet creek crossings and rocks that must be dodged. In case your car resists, there is primitive camping along the way.

High Marks

All of Monroe County earns an A+ for pleasure driving with an edge.

The twenty miles along **SR 3** from the Virginia line south along the base of Peter's Mountain, through Sweet Springs Valley, past Gap Mills and the turnoff to Hanging Rock, then on to Union could fill a daylong trip. Way-out scenes along the route include the remnants of Sweet Springs spa, Hanging Rock Raptor Observatory, and Cheese'n More. You'll also find the oldest church west of the Alleghenies, prosperous farms, flocks of wild turkey, covered bridges, countless lived-in log houses, the Eastern Continental Divide, and more than fifty historic buildings in tiny Union.

Cutting across the southern edge of the county, the eleven miles of **SR 122** from US 219 west to SR 12 are awash in pastoral splendor. Cooks Old Mill along Laurel Creek dates to 1797 and still boasts a giant overshot mill wheel. Where SR 122 and SR 12 join is Marie Road, which then twists through miles of park-like scenery on the way north to Talcott and the Greenbrier River. Along the way, you'll see the captivating remnants of **Barger Springs**—a dozen cottages and the pointy-hatted gazebo dating to 1903 that still line the road past the once famous springs.

Even The Interstates

The seventy mph posted speed is often more a challenge than a limit on West Virginia interstates. No two mountains are alike and no engineering solutions are the same. Four-lane highways curve and twist up, down, around and through chains of mountains linked together in an infinite variety of shapes and heights.

I-77 east of Bluefield boasts the twin-tubed, mile-long East River Mountain Tunnel while **I-70** tunnels through Wheeling. **I-64** is thermal Blue Ridge country. The jumbled swirl and bowl of mountain tops is filled with hot and mineral springs' names as the road follows a historic path across the Eastern Continental Divide. Further north, **I-68** cuts through the Divide and is affectionately known as "the tundra" for its predictably hazardous weather.

Highland Scenic Highway

One of the first twenty All-American Roads designated by the U.S. Department of Transportation, **Highland Scenic Highway** is the highest major roadway in the state. More than sixty percent of its 43 miles loom at more than 4,000 feet. Extending from Richwood to US 219 north of Marlinton, the highway passes Cranberry Glades and Wilderness, the Falls of Hill Creek and four scenic overlooks. It passes few signs of human habitation.

Off-highway is an area of unusual honeycombed boulders. When Cecil Underwood was the state's youngest governor, he hiked into the rocks. Forty years later when he became the state's oldest governor, he wanted one of the bigger-than-house-size boulders moved to somewhere more accessible. It was an impossible task. The Forest Service solved the problem and satisfied the governor by opening an easy hiking trail to the rocks. Find the trail entry along the highway eight miles west of US 219.

IN THE KNOW: *For road conditions on major roads call the Department of Highways: 1(877) WVA-ROAD or 1-877-982-7623.*

The twenty-two-mile parkway section of paved, two-lane SR 150 is closed to commercial truck traffic year 'round, and to all vehicles from December through March.

I thought I could manage the trip on March 31, after all the road opened the next day and I had planted garden crops two weeks earlier. At the top of the first peak, with panoramic views mocking me, I had to turn back to Marlinton. Nothing but four-wheel drive could have slogged through the icy slush that covered the roadway as far as the eye could see.

Quintessential West Virginia Highways

In the 1920s—before Eisenhower and the Interstates—the federal government strung together primary highways into a system connecting the forty-eight states. In West Virginia, US 60, US 50 and US 219 all followed ancient buffalo trails used by Native Americans and pioneers. Substantial towns are strung along their route.

US 60 is well documented as the historic **Midland Trail**, running 119 miles from White Sulphur Springs to the State Capitol in Charleston. Interestingly, the trashy part from Charleston to Huntington (*see* "Badlands") is not included on the detailed map of the Midland Trail Scenic Highway.

An ancient buffalo path, the Midland Trail became one of the earliest routes west into the Appalachian wilderness, first as the "old state road" and then the James River and Kanawha Turnpike. It was used by everyone from George Washington and Daniel Boone to Andrew Jackson and Robert E. Lee. It was designated US 60 in 1924.

Climbing to 3,170 feet at its highest point, the Midland Trail snakes along up, down and through the mountains passing by a world class resort, historic

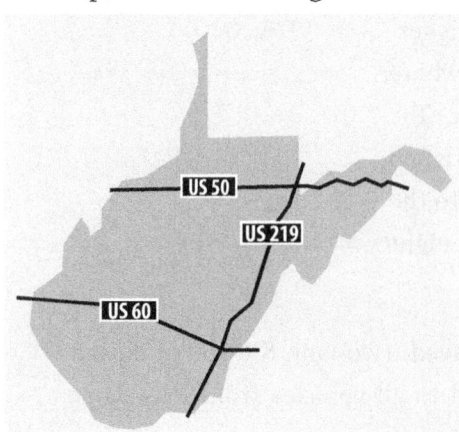

battlefields, farm lands, rock formations, waterfalls, wetlands and sinkholes, coal camps and power plants, and repeated breathtaking vistas of the New River Gorge. Named a national scenic byway, the Midland Trail has been obsessively signed every mile.

US 50 begins near Romney in the east and ends its West Virginia passage in Parkersburg at the Ohio River. It was the primary game, tribal and pioneer trail from the Valley of Virginia to the Ohio. George Washington proposed a wagon road west along the approximate route in 1784. Development was eventually turned over to French engineering genius Claude Crozet who surveyed and blazed the Northwestern Turnpike along the wilderness route in the 1830s. Farms, deserted roadside motels, a virgin forest, switchbacks, grand vistas, and giant log and coal trucks all add to the fun for contemporary drivers.

US 219 is 150 miles of rhododendron-lined, dip and squiggle road along the western edge of the Eastern Continental Divide, from the Virginia line in Monroe County north to the Maryland border near Cathedral Forest. It was originally known as the famous Seneca Trail, a major artery through the rich hunting lands of West Virginia for various native tribes. High points include breathtaking views, the charming art towns of Lewisburg and Elkins, Pearl Buck's museum home, Beartown State Park, Lost World Caverns, Kumbrabow State Forest and the Fairfax Stone Monument. Much of US 219 in West Virginia weaves in and out of the vast Monongahela National Forest.

Light At The End Of The Tunnel

Setting aside harrowing mid-blizzard drives along US 50 or I-68, my wildest adventure drive was the **Dingess Tunnel** in Mingo County. Dug with picks and shovels for the Norfolk and Western in 1892 and upgraded in 1914 as a mile-long railroad tunnel, it is now a paved, one-lane road, used daily.

It was a sunny day as I turned off SR 65 in Lenore onto CR 3/5. Suddenly, this narrow, high arched tube of pitch black appeared in front of me. I stopped and pondered whether the tiny pinpoint of light I saw in the darkness was moving or whether it was the proverbial light at the end of the tunnel. Cars began stopping behind me. Pressure built. I had to make the fateful decision to lead a line of cars into the blackness and hope a huge coal truck wasn't behind that point of light. Discerning no change in the light, I took a deep breath

and led my parade into the darkness. Even with the interior painted white, it was DARK, especially coming from the bright sun. Relief washed over me as I emerged on the other side, noticing with dismay another line of vehicles, including a school bus, waiting their turn.

How can folks stand the stress of doing this daily? What happens when there's fog and you can't see what's coming? And once you're through, it's not over. Further along the road there's another, shorter one-lane tunnel and a one-lane bridge. Fortunately for the trust I placed in oncoming traffic, I did not discover until months later that trucks loaded with marijuana often use that route. Another nerve-wracking rumor later heard is that ghosts of those killed in tunnel train wrecks haunt the place. My advice: hang a right onto Old Mose Fork Road as soon as you emerge from the tunnel. It's an easier way back to civilization. One thing is certain: you do not want to go back the way you came.

Another former Virginia Railway tunnel is used for one-way auto traffic to **Guyandotte Campground** north of SR 97 on the upper waters of R.D. Bailey Lake.

Other Notable Driving Oddities

★ Once it was a heavily trafficked railroad town. Today, to reach the town of **Thurmond** by car from US 19 north of Beckley, it takes six curving miles of narrow CR 25, crossing and re-crossing river and rail. There are seven one-lane bridges and countless rock overhangs. The final approach to the restored Thurmond Station is over a single lane, block-long, open-decked structure that has been "grafted" onto the railroad bridge. *See* "Things That Used To Be There" for more on Thurmond.

★ The directions are correct, believe it or not. From US 50, vehicles enter downtown **Clarksburg** through the parking garage at the Second Street exit. There's no fee for passing through.

- **US 250** follows a ridge-skimming path for twelve to fifteen miles south of Moundsville. As other ridges gambol alongside like puppies, the road reveals million-dollar views at every turn.

- As bad as the traffic is in Morgantown, the real city of weird driving has to be **Williamson**. First there is Goodman Street and others of its ilk winding up the mountain at an amazing incline, barely one lane wide with both slapdash and solid houses perched on its edge. Parking the wrong way on city streets is endemic. Many of the downtown traffic lights are no longer working although they remain in place with STOP signs by their sides. Downtown streets come into each other at all angles, changing from one-way to two. Roads go both over and under the railroad tracks which are everywhere in this major Norfolk and Southern rail center where trains, loaded with coal, run almost continuously.

> **Calhoun County** *has no stoplight but a flashing red light in Grantsville; folks in* **Monroe County** *are quick to point out that they have neither.*

- **Coffindaffer cross clusters** are two short blue crosses flanking a taller yellow one. They were planted around the world by the late Craigsville businessman, Bernard Coffindaffer. He used his millions from his coal-cleaning plant to hire workers to plant the crosses in response to a vision that told him to erect cross clusters throughout West Virginia "for the glory of Jesus Christ." One count has 249 of the clusters set in varying West Virginia landscapes including on a rock in the Gauley River at Gauley Bridge. Response to Coffindaffer's visionary inspiration was, and is, often controversial.

- Beware of McMechen and the short stretch of open road between Wheeling and Moundsville. It is a **notorious speed trap**, as is Summersville further south. In fact, many of the small towns see speeding and parking tickets as budget balancers.

Mountain Biking—Ride Like The Devil

At least a half-dozen full-service outfitters are busy with bike rentals and guided tours in the Mountain State. World-class mountain bike races are routine events. Some mountain biking pros are relocating here because, reportedly, West Virginia riding is very Euro.

The **North Bend Trail** runs through 13 tunnels and over more than 45 bridges and trestles on its 72-mile route from Parkersburg to Wolf Summit. One tunnel, the 1,376-foot Silver Run, is reputed to be haunted by a beautiful woman with raven hair and a white dress. Another two tunnels lie next to the trail and are available for exploration. Part of the coast-to-coast American Discovery Trail, North Bend is a West Virginia state park. Like the B&O Railroad that it replaced, the North Bend Rail Trail, goes through the middle of Cairo. Once a booming oil town, today tiny Cairo is a perfect trail stop with shops, services and restaurants.

The **Greenbrier River Trail** is seventy-eight miles of beautiful vistas and historic relics running along a mostly level former C&O rail bed from Caldwell north to Cass. Designated a Millennium Legacy Trail, it parallels US 219 and the Greenbrier River, the longest free-flowing river in the East. It is the second longest rail trail in the United States.

The Greenbrier River Trail is the second longest rail trail in the United States.

The trail is part of the West Virginia state park system. The tracks are gone and the trail consists of hard packed dirt, limestone chips or railroad ballast along the entire route. The Greenbrier River Trail has two tunnels, thirty-five bridges, an antique bank safe and the bizarre remains of a grease reservoir along the way. Other remnants from its past life as a railroad are a 1923 water tank and turntable. The Droop Mountain Tunnel, about thirty miles north of the trail's southern terminus, is 402 feet long. Sharps' Tunnel is 571 feet with a 229-foot bridge.

The "Other" Biking—Motorcycles Rule

Twisting mountain roads and minimal traffic make the state one of the best for motorcyclists. Ask U.S. Senator Joe Manchin about it. He's a devoted Harley man and often on the road. There are Harleys to rent, rafting/biking packages, mapped rides on area websites, and thousands of bikes showing up annually at events in Morgantown and Martinsburg. In Berkeley Springs, **Ridersville Cycle** is the largest dealer in the world for several different bike types.

Fly The Empty Skies Of West Virginia

West Virginia is paradise for general aviation. The mountains are the right altitude for single engine planes, air traffic is low, and controlled airspace is limited. Snaking rivers, surreal rock formations, mountains worn by time or chewed up by mining, and farms in hollows and on hillsides all guarantee the scenery is never boring. Abundant forests filled with hardwoods make fall a paisley of brilliant colors. Thirty-eight public use airports are spread across the state, and most are close enough to walk to attractions and towns, although it's easy to hitch a ride from friendly airport folks. There are more than a hundred private strips, at least half unlisted on any maps.

My pilot husband and I have flown to Bridge Day, enjoyed homemade pie at Fairmont, and walked down to the marina at Summersville Lake and hung out with hospitable air traffic controllers in their tower at Clarksburg. Government pork brought an oversized airport to Elkins and the secret government bunker at The Greenbrier did the same for Greenbrier County. *See* "Truly Incredible"

The geography of the Allegheny Front creates strong west winds that plunge over the plateau edge and are deflected upward by ridges to the east. In Grant County, this natural reality is called the Petersburg Wave, a rising column of air that is so strong in March that it attracts glider-plane pilots from around the world.

The airport in Charleston was built on three leveled-off mountain tops in 1947 then leveled off more for a recent expansion. Only the building of the Panama Canal moved more earth. It was rededicated in 1985 as **Yeager Airport** to honor West Virginia's aviation hero, Brigadier General Chuck Yeager, the first man to fly faster than the speed of sound.

Aviation history is also represented. The airstrip in **Petersburg** was once an emergency field when commercial transcontinental flights were young. Both **Wheeling Airport** and **Cumberland Airport** in Mineral County showcase flying history in their terminal museums. The last known operating beacon of the "highway in the sky" light system that guided airmail pilots stood proudly on **Rich Mountain**. Originally lit by gas, the beacons were placed at ten to fifteen mile intervals across the country.

Wild Rides In The Southern Tier!

As one of sixteen designated as a National Millennium Trail, the award-winning **Hatfield and McCoy Trail** brings ATV riders, mountain bikers, hikers and horseback riders to the southern tier coal counties, careening along more than 600 miles of twisting timber and coal roads at their varying speeds. Trailhead centers are open near Logan, Man, Julian, Pineville, North Fork, Bramwell, Matewan and Williamson, offering access to these historically notable communities in the region. Even more important to often-scorned ATV riders, the towns welcome them on their streets. Outfitters, restaurants, campgrounds, B&Bs and vehicle service centers are repopulating the business profile of the area.

Named for the world famous feud based in the area, the Hatfield and McCoy Trail is rain forest lush and teeming with game—in radical contrast to dry western trails. It is the largest multi-use trail system in the east and the only trail of its kind entirely on private lands. Tens of thousands of ATV riders have bought and used trail passes on seven trail systems.

A five-day trail fest in October offers everything from poker runs and mud pits to a huge ATV parade in Gilbert.

CHAPTER TWO

Amazing Architecture

Wealth in West Virginia tended to be transitory, never staying long enough or within the state's boundaries to fund grand and lasting metropoli. It did trickle down to create workingman towns and small cities. The state's relative isolation during the development-crazed years of the past generation or two has allowed working artifacts to flourish, not yet eliminated by the bland sameness of national franchises. There are nearly 150 historic districts in the state and most are intact retaining both the architecture and the social fabric of the original communities. In some towns, a few provocative new buildings are scattered among the antiques.

Must-see Historic Districts

- ★ **Victorian Wheeling** is a treasure trove of six historic districts and more than 900 townhouses built between 1837 and 1891. Every decade of Victorian style is represented. Stained glass, brick, stone, tile, wood, chandeliers and even the nails were crafted in Wheeling. Many of the buildings have the pressed, stamped metal ceilings for which the city was famous, known appropriately as "Wheeling Ceilings."

★ Tiny **Union** in Monroe County has twenty-nine antebellum structures on two main streets within its six-block downtown area.

★ Lived-in armory houses of the 1830s and '40s dot Washington Street in **Harpers Ferry**. Forty-four steps climbing to St. Peter's Church and the upper town were hand carved by townspeople in the 1830s, in the virgin rock formation of the hillside known as Harpers shale. Cliffs were blasted out for houses and shops. For more on this tiny town that is 100% historic district with 1920s model street lamps and a neighboring National Historic Park, *see* "Historic Oddities."

★ **New Martinsville** could be a Main Street theme park. First the railroad then the highway limited the town's growth to a ten-block area along the Ohio River. A ballpark, courthouse, community college, churches, residences and a three block commercial area with a post office and bank represent a full range of 19th and early 20th architectural styles and convey the bygone feeling of small town life.

★ The 18th century town of **Martinsburg** is the state's fastest growing city in the early 21st century. Its historic buildings offer an almost unbelievable array of architectural styles and periods from colonial to early 20th century arranged in livable, walkable blocks as the town expanded.

★ **Bluefield** was booming in the 1920s and 30s and the merchant princes designated Parisian-trained architect Alex Mahood as their architect of choice. A driving tour showcases more than a dozen Neoclassical Colonial Revival homes. Downtown has the integrated look of a city that was built within a short time span.

Parkersburg's jewel is the **Julia-Ann Square Historic District**, *(above) dominated by the state's most concentrated grouping of Italianate Second Empire and Queen Anne mansions, all along brick streets. Still splendidly lived in today, the district is an easy morning walk from the historic Blennerhassett Hotel.*

★ Shepherdstown's **German Street** thrives with blocks of working artifacts—18th and 19th century commercial and residential buildings now housing contemporary businesses from organic groceries and coffee houses to successful dotcoms. The tiny **Shepherdstown Library** was built in 1800 as a Market House. Since the town owned no land except the streets and alleys, the powers that were plopped the library in the middle of a street in the middle of town. Navigating traffic around it is more challenging than at the four-way stop down the street. With plans for a new library underway, the next identity for this building remains unknown.

★ A walking tour of **Charleston's historic East End** ranges from the sublime to the ridiculous. St. Paul's is a distinctive cruciform Gothic church resplendent with stone parapets. The Stephenson-Toovey House is an ornate pink and purple Queen Anne style Victorian. The non-descript first floor brick structure that houses the Empty Glass Cafe is topped by a four-square two-story house that was moved there to make room for the State Theater in 1939. Three parallel city blocks in this neighborhood are each half a mile long, making them among the country's longest.

Industrial Strength Beauty

Martinsburg is a railroad town and the sixteen-sided **B&O Roundhouse** is its defining characteristic. Sandwiched between the railroad tracks and Tuscarora Creek on East Martin Street, the 25,000 square foot west roundhouse was a pioneer in the use of cast-iron skeletons and is the only one of its kind remaining. Inside, an enormous clear space expands under an umbrella design of concentric beams, spoke-like rafters and slanted columns anchored to the floor. Trestles were built in the roundhouse machine shop, loaded on

flatbed cars and taken to other parts of the rail line. Turntable mechanisms for the trains remain in the center of the floor. A ring of clerestory windows separating two roof levels makes fanciful patterns of illumination.

The adjacent frog and switch shop, built in 1867, used wood trusses and metal tension rods to span a 100-foot roof with no columns. Sections of the floor are still paved with unusual wooden bricks. Switches built in that shop are present in a relocated switching tower on the property, one of five remaining in the country.

The ten-acre complex of three buildings and a ruin is crammed with fine workmanship and detailing in the buildings, bridges and aqueducts. It is an ongoing restoration project. Special events bring visitors across the tracks on a substantial pedestrian walkway and into contact with early industrial style.

There's dramatic social as well as industrial history embedded in the roundhouse complex. The first national railroad labor strike in the United States was initiated there in 1877 when 1,200 brakemen and firemen seized the Martinsburg depot, stopping all freight. The upheaval in turn led to one of the first uses of federal troops in a labor strike. The original roundhouse (1854) on the site was destroyed by Stonewall Jackson in 1862 and rebuilt in 1866.

Twin Splendor

Henry Davis and his son-in-law Stephen Elkins were an industrious pair. Both made their fortunes by bringing the railroad to Elkins and then taking the coal and timber out. Both served as U.S. Senator from West Virginia. And both built mansions on the bluff overlooking the town. Today, **Halliehurst** and **Graceland** are architectural gems restored to original Victorian perfection and open to the public on the campus of Davis & Elkins College.

In 1890, Senator Stephen Elkins built Halliehurst and named it for his wife, Hallie Davis. The 56-room Rhineland castle was designed by New York architect Charles Mott. There are towers and turrets, floor to ceiling sash windows opening onto rambling wrap-around porches, hipped slate roofs, and a spectacular view of the town below. Massive fireplaces with marble and wood mantles include one in the library with hand-carved signs of the zodiac.

Named Secretary of War in 1890, Elkins soon filled his new home with visiting presidents, cardinals, and millionaires. Today, the building houses college administration and public rooms. During Augusta Heritage workshops in the summers, knots of musicians gather for porch music. Spread out along the porches' splendid expanse, they are protected from hearing each other by a quirk of Victorian architecture.

The huge third floor ballroom was once used as a gym for high school basketball games.

Halliehurst's Ice House still stands. Each winter from 1890 to 1923, ice was cut from a pond on the estate and stored in the cylindrical stone structure to be used during the summer. Circular floors with an open core allowed the ice to be cut downwards from the top level. In 1969, the college renovated the structure. It's been used as a coffee house and pub since.

The witch hat towers and leaded glass windows of Halliehurst's Gate House now stand guard at the entrance to campus.

See Graceland in "Unusual Places to Stay," Augusta Heritage in "Art Wonders."

Building With Coal

Two of the USA's only three coal buildings are in West Virginia.

The oldest and largest coal building, the **Williamson Coal House**, is the location of the Tug Valley Chamber of Commerce. Built in 1933 from donated materials, labor and cash, it used 65 tons of locally mined coal and was designed by H.T. Hicks, who also designed prominent public buildings in the town of Welch. It is the only building constructed entirely of coal and has walls that are two feet thick. A fire in 2010 gutted the interior and destroyed photographs and artifacts; the coal block exterior was untouched. The interior was rebuilt.

A colorful, life-size statue of Chief Logan dominates the plaza in front of the building.

A former gift shop and residence stand side-by-side in White Sulphur Springs just down the road from the Greenbrier. The shop was built from 30 tons of Clay County cannel coal in 1959; the house was built two years later using 100 tons.

To build these structures, cannel coal is cut into blocks and shaped with a hatchet. Cannel is the only type that can be shaped without fracturing. Mortar is colored with lamp black and the finished structure is coated with clear shellac. To answer the most burning question, it is not—a fire hazard that is.

Most Traveled Public Building

John Brown's brief insurrection of 1859 ended when he and his small band of men were besieged and captured in the armory fire engine house along the Shenandoah and Potomac rivers in Harpers Ferry. It was the only building of the complex left standing when the armory burned during the Civil War. Renamed **John Brown's Fort,** the building traveled to the 1893 World Exposition in Chicago. Sold after the Exposition, it was ransomed by African-Americans and returned to a site on Murphy's Farm near the edge of Harpers Ferry. In 1910, it was relocated to Storer College on the hill. Eventually moved to its current location, it is open to the public.

Old Jails, New Uses

Pence Springs Hotel was an elegant, 1920s resort later turned into a women's prison then back to a hotel and now is a private school.

Blue Ridge Bank (now City National Bank) in Martinsburg was once the Berkeley County Jail. Where the concern was originally to keep criminals in the structure, today the concern is keeping them out. Victorian brownstone trim looks like nailed boards, an architectural fancy that works for past and present purposes.

As befits one of the world's preeminent hotels, **the Greenbrier** once served as its most elite prison. For 201 days in 1941 and 1942, more than 1,600 diplomats from Axis nations were detained at the Greenbrier with their families while awaiting repatriation. These satisfied inmates left more than $65,000 in gratuities for the excellent service of the Greenbrier's staff. They depleted the Greenbrier shops, spending the American dollars they were not allowed to take home. There also was a spate of foreign babies named Virginia. Unfortunately, security concerns prevented them from enjoying the renowned golf links. For more on the Greenbrier *see* "Truly Incredible."

Inmates were removed and a popular tour including the Dungeon of Horrors developed in the shell of **Moundsville Penitentiary.** *See* "Tours and Trips Not to Miss" for the gory details.

Bell Tower Judge

The **Jefferson County bell tower** has an impressive town clock. It overlooks the historic town, up a narrowing five flights of stairs into a tiny room. The clock was manufactured by E. Howard & Co. of Boston and installed in the more than 80-foot tower in about 1885. Hand wound until the 1950s when electricity took over, the brass gears turn four 6-foot shafts that attach to the four-foot diameter clock faces. The bell tower space is shared with a 4,000-pound bell made in Troy, NY in 1872. Today the clapper is unattached; once the bell tolled for fire alarms or special occasions.

Eccentricities and Anomalies: More Architectural Nuggets

★ The brooding Gothic presence of **Trans-Allegheny Lunatic Asylum** with its fanciful roof lines, white clock tower and sweeping lawns dominates more than a square block along the West Fork River in downtown Weston. The river is wider along the quarter-mile in front of the building because the native blue sandstone was cut from its banks. Alleged to be the largest hand-cut blue sandstone building in America with nine acres of floor space, the Asylum was designed by Baltimore architect, R. Snowden Andrews. Advice from noted mental health reformer Dorothea Dix to locate the building elsewhere was ignored although curative powers were designed into the structure.

The first financial transaction of the newly created state of West Virginia was the borrowing of $60,000 to complete construction begun before the Civil War by Virginia. The loan was repaid.

★ Built in 1930 when Weston was flush, **Citizens Bank** still dazzles depositors with its art deco decor and 45-foot metal ceiling with the state seal inlaid in gold leaf. It is said to be the tallest one-story building in the country. Walnut paneling, mirror laminate, traditional tellers cages, ornamental ironwork and 30-foot arched windows are simply a prelude to the vault nestled under an arch and guarded by an ornate wrought iron gate. The 25-ton vault door is so well balanced it can be moved with one hand. Only the Persian carpets are gone.

★ **Camp Washington Carver,** the first African-American 4-H camp, boasts the largest chestnut log structure in the United States. The Great Chestnut

Lodge is 110 feet long and built with 534 logs—corpses harvested from the chestnut blight. Built by the WPA from 1939-42, it is irreplaceable. Those giant chestnuts are gone forever.

★ **Woodburn Hall** is the traditional symbol of West Virginia University. An archetypal college structure, it has a domed clock tower where students once led a cow. Since cows won't go down steps, it had to be lowered by an improvised derrick.

★ The 1835 **Pioneer Farm** at Twin Falls State Park was rebuilt around the remains of the original four log walls in spite of bureaucratic opinion that

the best course of action was for the ruins to be hit by lightning. Legendary park superintendent Smokey Harsh dealt with the plans for his reconstructed farmhouse drawn up in Charleston by chinking them into the walls and reporting honestly that, "your plans have been incorporated." There's a waiting list of folks willing to live in and maintain the picturesque facility.

★ **The Pocahontas Opera House** in Marlinton opened in 1910, and is one of the oldest reinforced concrete structures in the country. Meticulously renovated, it presents music and other productions year 'round.

★ **The Round Barn** of Mannington was built as dairy barn by Amos Hamilton in 1912 for $1,900 and today is a prize-winning restoration project and

*The **Quaker State Windmill** was driven by a car engine and its sole purpose was as an attention getter for the service station. Now serving food as a family restaurant, the windmill still catches the eye in downtown Parkersburg.*

museum operated by the West Augusta Historical Society. The barn was built with a spring fed watering system that the cows could turn on and off. Natural gas deposits on the farm are still used to heat the barn. A Shaker invention, first built in 1826, round barns purportedly kept the devil from hiding in the corner. More prosaic, the extra large loft allowed for hay storage.

★ **Natural gravity railyards.** Coal flowed downhill from the rich Pocahontas fields to naturally stop at the weigh station along the railroad in downtown Bluefield.

★ **McDowell County Courthouse** in Welch sits atop granite steps leading up the hill. The impressive four-story, ivy covered granite Romanesque Gothic building also boasts a hand cut stone wall, a tower and a bell that rings each day at noon.

★ **West Virginia Wesleyan** in Buckhannon is a movie-set college campus. Built in 1890, the twenty-three modified Georgian brick buildings occupy an eighty-acre square with Wesley Chapel, the largest in the state, at its center.

★ Additions and studios at the **Huntington Museum of Art** are the last designs by Walter Gropius, founder of the Bauhaus School. His famous clerestory windows bathe the rooms in natural light.

★ The Queen Anne style **Cooper House** on Main Street in Bramwell has the first copper roof in America, as well as a doghouse built into the outside chimney. The house, with one of the first indoor swimming pools in the

Star House. *A star cutout in the gable of a gingerbread Victorian on Union Street in Hinton was a symbol for the hobo community during the Depression—anyone needing a meal could come here to get one.*

There are bigger and more splendid structures in West Virginia, but the collection of stone towers and battlements overlooking the historic spa town of Berkeley Springs earns the title of castle. Constructed of stone and visions of England in 1885, **Berkeley Castle** *was built as a summer cottage and tribute to love.*

state, was built in 1910 of orange brick imported from England.

★ **Ramsey School**, the oldest in the city of Bluefield, is built on the side of a hill. Its seven entrances on seven levels earned the school a mention in *Ripley's Believe It or Not*.

★ A patented **semi-circular swimming pool** was built for the first time anywhere in Cameron as a Public Works Administration project in 1939. The Cameron City Pool's underwater lifeguard station makes it difficult to recruit lifeguards with the necessary breath control.

★ Known as the **Crazy House**, this rough stone residence overlooking the Potomac River in Harpers Ferry has bottles, keys, plates, jugs, coins, spoons and war relics of all sorts embedded in its walks, columns and plaster walls. Slogans are printed on pavements, porch floors and steps and chains are stretched between the columns.

★ Huntington's **Memorial Arch** is a smaller stylized version of the Arc de Triomphe in Paris. More than 40 feet high, it bears the name of 91 men who died in World War I.

Old & Odd Churches

★ For those who consider geometry divine, tiny **Alberts Chapel** is a find. Built in 1903, it is the only octagonal church in the state. The bell tower is also octagonal and carrying out the theme of odd geometry, windows are triangular-headed.

★ **Our Lady of the Pines** always has its door

open. Claiming to be the smallest church in 48 states, (reportedly the builder knew of smaller ones in two of the 50 states) the tiny sandstone building can seat twelve. All of its fixtures are handmade. Part of the memorial park includes the smallest mailing office, another contested claim.

★ **Ruble Church** in Wirt County is one of the oldest in the state still attended. Built from massive hewn logs in 1835 by Aaron Ruble (*right*), it is heated by a pot-bellied stove and lit by kerosene. Antebellum graves are in the churchyard. The church stated, "All are welcome here except those of Northern Principles."

★ The **Weston Episcopal Church** is a blue sandstone wonder with twin towers that are not quite twin. One is shorter than the other because the parish ran out of money in 1896. They must have spent it all on the splendid stained glass windows.

★ Wheeling is a city of massive churches including the state's only Catholic cathedral, **St. Joseph's** (*right*). A co-cathedral was later designated in Charleston. The Romanesque structure was designed by noted architect Edward Weber of Pittsburgh and constructed in 1926 on the site of the original church built in 1847. It stands 148 feet to the top of the dome.

For other frontier churches *see* "Superlatives" and "Things That Used to Be There."

Bridge fans rejoice

Technically, rivers are geologically trapped water, and West Virginia has an

*Reuschlein's Jewelers stands on broad 4th Avenue in downtown Huntington. Today, its ornate, four-faced, 20-foot **Seth Thomas clock**, over 100 years old, presides over the entrance to the building in spite of its being knocked over by a truck during the 1970s.*

abundance of them. Their relentless path through the mountains has led to the building of remarkable bridges. Some resemble old erector sets; others are sleek and new concrete. Some are stone covered, double barrel culvert bridges spanning tiny creeks while others carry superhighways across major rivers.

★ The **East Huntington Bridge** looks like a giant harp resting on its side as it spans the Ohio River. It was the first cable-stayed bridge in the country to use triple strength concrete.

★ Built to carry Warm Springs Road across Opequon Creek (*below*) outside Martinsburg in 1832, the three native limestone arches of **Vanmetre Ford Bridge** support the oldest intact bridge in use in West Virginia. Hurry if you want to drive over it though; preservationists have succeeded in persuading the state to build a new working bridge adjacent to the historic one.

★ A favorite on-foot adventure in Wheeling is walking across the Ohio River on the historic **Wheeling Suspension Bridge** (*right*) from the city proper to Wheeling Island, although the best views of the Marsh Stogie sign and the renovated waterfront come with the west to east stroll. During the 4th of July Sternwheel Festival, the entire roadbed of the bridge is the staging area for a spectacular fireworks display.

Built between 1847 and 1849, it was the first bridge over the Ohio. The designer, Charles Ellet Jr., also built the Brooklyn Bridge. He tested out several engineering innovations on the Wheeling span, which was the country's first long-span, wire-cable suspension bridge. For many years it was the longest in the world. Originally a toll bridge on the National Road, it had tumultuous periods. Pittsburgh boat operators complained that it sat too low to the water and obstructed river traffic. A court case in 1850 and subsequent Act of Congress in 1852 were required to declare the bridge lawful. Four years later, high winds set the bridge in motion destroying its deck. Rebuilt and reopened for traffic in 1856, it is the most significant remaining pre-Civil War bridge in the United States, the oldest long span bridge in the world, and a National Civil Engineering Landmark.

The bridge came perilously close to demolition in the 1970s after a parallel span across the Ohio was built as part of I-70. Driven by local sentiment, a major restoration was completed in time for its 150th anniversary. Vehicles join foot traffic on the 1010-foot long red, white and blue painted structure but watch out for the drop as you first get on headed west.

★ Its 53 stone piers made it the longest bridge of its type in the world when constructed in 1869-71 to elevate the railroad through downtown Parkersburg. The masonry work on the **Sixth Street Railroad Bridge** (*right*) remains unchanged today.

★ At more than 3,000 feet long and 876 feet high, the **New River Bridge** on US 19 in Fayette County (*below*) is the Western Hemisphere's longest single arch steel bridge and the highest bridge east of Mississippi. Designed with computer-aided methods, the steelwork was so accurate that when the arch halves were joined no metal shims had to be used. Daily tours on the two-foot-wide, steel-grate catwalk under the bridge offer a close-up look at the engineering.

Covered Bridges

A Central European design used to protect hard-to-replace wooden bridge timbers allowed hundreds of covered bridges to become an invaluable part of West Virginia's nineteenth century turnpike system before railroads and automobiles made them virtually extinct. That brief span of time when a traveler is protected from prying eyes led to covered bridges being nicknamed "kissing bridges." Today, seventeen such bridges remain. Here's a complete list of historic covered bridges in the state.

Barrackville crosses Buffalo Creek on US 250/CR 32 at Barrackville in Marion County. A fine example of the Burr truss, the structure was built in 1853 by Lemuel Chenowith. Originally constructed as an open bridge, it was covered in 1867 and restored in 1999. It has the longest clear span of the seventeen remaining bridges, and allows no vehicular traffic. 145' long.

Carrollton over the Buckhannon River, built in 1855 and still in use, has an inside sidewalk. Drive CR 36 through it, one mile from US 119 south of Philippi. 140' long.

Center Point crosses McElroy Creek on SR 23 twelve miles north of US 50 in Doddridge County. Built in 1888, the bridge was restored and is owned by the Historical Society. 42' long.

Dents Run. Built in 1889 and restored in 1984 it is open but not used by traffic. Just off US 19 and CR 43 near Morgantown, it is the last one standing in Monongalia County. 40' long.

Fish Creek east of Hundred in Wetzel County is still used by traffic on CR 13 off US 250. It was built in the early 1880s. 36' long.

Fletcher. Built in 1891 in Harrison County, it is still in use over Ten Mile Creek near Wolf Summit on CR 5/29 north of US 50. 58' long.

Herns Mill. Located west of Lewisburg, it is still in use on Muddy Creek Mountain Rd. over Milligan Creek. It was built in 1884. 53' long.

Hokes Mill crosses Second Creek on CR 62 off US 219 south of Ronceverte in Greenbrier County. 81' long.

Indian Creek. The bridge sits off US 219 six miles south of Union, just beyond Salt Sulphur Springs in Monroe County. Walk the old road down and through the bridge. Built in 1898 by teenage brothers, Oscar and Ray Weikel, it was restored in 2000. 50' long.

Laurel Creek was built in 1910, and is still in use on Lilydale Rd. north of Union and Salt Sulphur Springs in Monroe County. At 24', it is the smallest in the state.

Locust Creek has a rare double intersection truss design. Located just off US 219 on CR 31 south of Hillsboro near the entrance of Calvin Price State Forest, the bridge was built in 1888. Today, only foot traffic is permitted. 113' long.

Mud River has a rare wooden arch feature between wooden X trusses added for strength in 1893. The bridge was originally built in 1875-6. Reassembled in Pumpkin Festival Park in Milton, only foot traffic is permitted. 112' long.

Philippi. This rare two-lane bridge crosses the Tygart River on US 250 in Barbour County. 285' long.

Sarvis Fork. Originally built in 1889 over Big Mill Creek west of Ripley, it was dismantled and moved in 1924 to its present location over the Left Fork of Big Sandy Creek about 1.2 miles north of Sandyville on CR 21. Located in Jackson County, the bridge is still in use. 101' long.

Simpson Creek. Preserved in a small park, this bridge is still in use on CR 24/2 near Bridgeport. Take exit 121 off I-79 in Harrison County. 75' long.

Staats Mill is an outstanding example of a pure, long-truss covered bridge of notable length. It was constructed over Tug Fork of Mill Creek in 1887 and moved three miles to Cedar Lakes Conference Center complex in 1983 as part of a flood control project. Located in Jackson County just off SR 33 west of Ripley, only pedestrian traffic is allowed through the bridge. 97' long.

Walkersville. This bridge traverses the right fork of West Fork River. Still in use, it is just off US 19, one mile south of Walkersville in Lewis County. 39' long.

Lemuel Chenoweth was the state's most creative covered bridge builder; two of his unique designs are still standing. A mathematical whiz, he adapted and improved the basic Burr Arch Truss principle.

The two-lane **Philippi Bridge,** built over the Tygart River in 1852, was Lemuel Chenoweth's masterpiece. He beat out several engineers to get the contract

by standing on his bridge model to prove its strength. During the Civil War battle of Philippi, victorious Union troops used the bridge as a barracks. Made of yellow poplar, the 286-foot Philippi Bridge was burned in a freak accident in 1989. Local preservationists using Chenoweth's plans under the direction of West Virginia University rebuilt the bridge as close to its original condition as possible. The Philippi Bridge is the only two-lane covered bridge currently in use on a federal highway.

Covered bridge building is not all in the past. Among more than a dozen private covered bridges that span ditches and streams is Benny Aronhalt's 68-foot covered bridge in Mineral County. Naming it **Rock-n-Wood Heaven,** Aronhalt also uses the 1995 bridge for storage. He enclosed two small "troll houses" beneath the bridge as playrooms for his kids. Eat your heart out Chenoweth!

Tunnels

The best way around many West Virginia mountains is through them. Tunnels abound for automobile, train and canal. Most were engineering marvels at the time of their construction.

Tunnelton's pair of hand-dug 4,100-foot railroad tunnels were the longest in the world when completed in 1853. Walking up the tracks can earn a glimpse of the dual entrance.

The **Paw Paw Tunnel** is the largest man-made structure on the C&O Canal, the latter now a National Park. It took fourteen years of labor unrest, epidemics and bankruptcy to hand carve the mountain tunnel which was dubbed one of the wonders of the world when it was completed in 1850. The 3,118 foot long, 24-foot high tunnel was built to avoid six miles of Potomac River bends. Lined with six million bricks, the dry, intact structure is open year 'round for walkers and bikers along a well-maintained towpath.

A free standing stone railroad tunnel cut through solid rock in 1906 stands to the west of SR 54, north of Mullens in Wyoming County. It is featured in a train mural in the town. For more on the Mullins murals *see* "Art Wonders."

Just Plain Weird

Chapmanville Towers is a residential unit in Logan County that hates to lose a tenant. The front yard is a cemetery.

In **Williamson** town fathers have really punished the Tug Fork River for its rampages. Not only is there a flood berm with a floodwall and walkway, but the wall extends above the walk at least another six feet so you can barely catch a glimpse of the usually placid river nearly 70 feet below.

CHAPTER THREE

Art Wonders

Based on standard head counts, West Virginia is rated 100% rural. In spite of this, or perhaps because of it, the state is a natural magnet for artists. Museums and galleries are well established and share the artistic landscape with artists' home studios tucked away in hollows and along streams. There are long lists of West Virginia authors and music is an integral part of the warp and woof of the state's fabric.

The art may be quirky—one of the state's two symphonies was conducted by the tiny, all-in-black-clad ex-wife of a former governor; or it can be traditional—pickin', quilting and flat foot dancing. Most unexpectedly, it may be sophisticated with internationally recognized contemporary artists whose work is at home in European galleries, Japanese shops and on New York stages.

Passion on the Potomac

The setting for the **Contemporary American Theater Festival (CATF)** is all wrong. Gritty plays that reflect "ear-to-the-ground" trends of modern society belong in cities, not in a bucolic hamlet along the Potomac. A resident troupe of equity actors spending eight summer weeks in taking the risks that new plays involve seems a little out of place at Shepherd College, which has an academic theater program younger than CATF.

The price is wrong too. Tickets for the full repertoire—all five plays plus other art events—cost less than a single ticket to a Broadway show. The seats are better in Shepherdstown, the play is often a world premier, and an after-show drink almost certainly brings you face-to-face with some of the cast.

Then there's the passionate imp who founded CATF in 1991 so that he could influence the future of American theater by producing and commissioning new plays. As long as it's new and provocative, Ed Herendeen loves it. He is awash in passion for new American plays and recognizes contemporary truth everywhere. American literary icon, Joyce Carol Oates, spent three summers in Shepherdstown, working on her cutting-edge plays before taking them public. Her unique vision of Marilyn Monroe—*Miss Golden Dreams*—had its kinks worked out at CATF.

Herendeen's brainchild is unique in other ways as well. For eight weeks in June and July, CATF creates a casual and unpretentious summer camp for theater folks from techies and publicists to playwrights and actors. They live together in two residential apartment buildings on campus, work together, hang out in the town's pubs, play darts with folks and bump into each other all over town. The family-like setting of the intensive season influences casting choices. Not only must the actors demonstrate on-stage talent but they must also be people who can live with and contribute to the camaraderie of the group.

It is an odd and wonderful twist that turned the oldest town in West Virginia into a crib for the newest theater works in America—and a theater success story.

At the Feet of a Heritage Master

Augusta Heritage Festival should have a warning label: "Beware, addictive!" You'll keep coming back for more. Back for more companions, friends, high moments of creation with hands, feet, voice or musical instrument. "This has changed my life," is a routine comment.

Augusta is the biggest and oldest traditional heritage workshop series in the world. Dancers adore it. For traditional and blues musicians it's a chance to work with a legend for a week in small classes, then jam through the night. Hands-on folks do everything from make instruments and build stone walls to hunt and cook herbs. Lots of teens come with their parents and legends include the 12-year-piper who entranced the 25th anniversary session.

Augusta Heritage Arts workshops began on the campus of Davis and Elkins College in 1973 with an earnest dedication to the conservation and teaching of traditional arts. A cluster of little old ladies were concerned that the traditional mountain crafts they practiced would die out. They lured one hundred people to Elkins from all over the country for the first five-week summer session.

In 1981, one-time volunteer Margo Blevin was hired. She broadened the scope of the program, made it self-sufficient and propelled Augusta onto its path of internationally revered cultural icon collecting awards along the way. Margo noticed that the folks there for the crafts wanted something to do at night, so music offerings were expanded and evening concerts and dances were born. Blues mini-classes turned into nightly jams then became Blues Week. She departed from the Appalachian emphasis to add Irish Week, Cajun Week and Swing Dance Week. The resulting unique pattern that blends music, dance, crafts and folklore is well illustrated by the recent Augusta catalog listing more than two hundred different classes.

Clustered in five week-long intensive workshops, classes are small and very structured. The classes last all morning. Afternoons offer more classroom work or gatherings of the whole group with guest artists, cultural presentations, or special workshops. Evenings are filled with concerts, jam sessions, craft showcases and dances in the outdoor pavilion. A public dance concludes each weeklong session.

More than 2,600 students, instructors and musicians pass through the summer-long program. Master artists come from all over the world to teach, and students range from beginner to expert. Scholarships are given to talented West Virginia youth and within various ethnic communities to help keep the traditions alive.

People connecting at Augusta is made easy by traditional dancing and playing which includes everyone, and by dorm housing centered around the class and performance spaces. Folks come to learn. When they leave with a fulfilled yearning for cultural connection and the joy of creating, they come back. A few turn pro and another generation is well established.

The Augusta Festival concludes the summer session in mid-August with an open-to-the public three-day celebration of music, dance, poetry, crafts and food in Elkins City Park. Spin-offs from the summer workshops include Spring Dulcimer week in April and the Old Time Fiddlers Reunion in October.

The impact of Augusta on the arts has been recognized repeatedly with a variety of awards, the latest from the Folk Alliance International for lifetime achievement.

Handcrafted Heaven

No other state in America has attempted what West Virginia has by jamming all the state's handcrafted art under one very unique roof. Both the roof and the assemblage of art at **Tamarack** are truly incredible.

The cultural center's most prominent external feature is its roof featuring 20 red-shingled glass-front peaks rising from a huge circular core, exploding above the Beckley exit on I-77. According to Tamarack's architect, it was inspired by traditional quilting patterns and the surrounding mountain peaks.

The surreal roofline not only provides abundant daylight for the interior but also creates waterfalls when it rains. The center of the building is an open courtyard ideal for displaying large sculpture pieces.

Once inside, there is no escaping the art of Tamarack. The "retail avenue" is a circle under the pointy roof moving the shopper around and around through 60,000 square feet of art before they may recognize a piece of what they've seen before. The rule for wise shopping becomes buy it when you see it. There is so much to see, you may never find your way back.

Filled with literally tens of thousands of art objects all created by more than 2,600 West Virginia artists from all fifty-five counties, among Tamarack's biggest sellers are the noted West Virginia marbles ranging in price from 5-25¢. What a deal for art! There are also one-of-a-kind pieces with four-figure price tags displayed both in living pods that blend objects in real-life room displays, as well as in gallery spaces. Everywhere else are sections filled with wood, glass, pottery, jewelry, fabric, books, music and other art forms too many to name. My favorite Tamarack art buy was acquired on my first visit soon after the place opened. *Those Shoes* with their psychedelic colors and painted star design screamed my name. I wore them to a wedding soon after. A guest observed that she had shoes like mine but only wore them when she was working as a clown. "How unfortunate for you," I replied. "I get to wear them all the time."

Part of the attraction of handcrafted art is the personal connection with the artist through their work. The name and address of any artist producing a piece is available from the section clerk who prints it out on a register slip.

Food is another art practiced at Tamarack. It offers more than a thousand food items produced in the state. Apple butter is the most popular item on a list that includes jams, wines, sauces, chocolate, honey, syrup and vinegars.

It's not all shopping at Tamarack. The theater offers entertainment from all over the state. A gallery hangs ever-changing art exhibitions and studios house resident artists and demonstrations.

Although Tamarack was named for an obscure West Virginia tree, its impact since opening in 1996 has been enormous, and not simply for the artists whose work is being sold. It also has raised the perception of West Virginia handcrafts to a new level. Hundreds of cars with license plates from all over the United States and Canada often fill the parking lot, advertising Tamarack's appeal as a must-see stop on the road south, or back. And now, throughout the state, there are shops advertising themselves as offering Tamarack-like sections and buying from the Tamarack distribution system. "The Best of West Virginia" is selling well.

For dining at Tamarack *see* "Local Food."

Another Carnegie Hall

Performers perk up their ears when they receive a call from **Carnegie Hall.** Everyone wants it on their resume. Built for the Lewisburg Female Institute in 1902 as a gift from philanthropist, Andrew Carnegie, "the other" Carnegie Hall is the center of artistic and cultural life in Lewisburg. The Greek Revival building, the first one in Lewisburg to be lit by electricity, is one of four remaining Carnegie Halls in the world. Brilliantly renovated, it hosts an annual program of more than two hundred events including classes, gallery shows, concerts, dance, theater and film.

Art Conglomerate

No benefactor in the world gets more for their donation than those who support **Oglebay Institute.** This cultural empire includes theater, art films, fine art, historic buildings and the noted **Glass Museum**. If Charleston is West Virginia's Washington, then Wheeling must be New York. Oglebay Institute makes that easy to believe.

In the early 1900s, wealthy industrialist Earl Oglebay transformed an antebellum farmhouse into a palatial center for his summer estate. His progressive-method Waddington Farms was noted for research in soil culture, crop rotation and Guernsey cattle. The neo-classical structure has been Oglebay's Mansion Museum since 1930, and was the first accredited museum in the state. Its seven tall case clocks are a prominent feature as are the surrounding Waddington Gardens with breathtaking flower, water and lighting displays in every season. Lecture tours are regularly available.

The **Stifel Fine Arts Center** occupies another historic home, and is surrounded by formal gardens and manicured lawns. Built in 1910 and donated to Oglebay by the Stifel family in 1976, the stained glass windows, grand central staircase, original Oriental carpet and large rooms make an ideal setting for fine art gallery exhibits that change monthly. The Stifel fortune came from a world-famous calico manufactured in Wheeling for more than a century, and trademarked with a boot. Thanks to Stifel's insistence that the house be fireproof, there is no structural wood in it—only concrete, steel and brick hidden from view by hardwood paneling, marble and fine plaster.

Other Oglebay Institute art wonders include the restored Towngate Theater downtown with both live performances and art films. The extremely popular Artists' Market draws 80,000 to Oglebayfest in early October.

For more on Oglebay's Glass Museum and the Sweeney Punch Bowl *see* "Remarkable Collections" and "Superlatives."

Readin' & Writin'

While the commonplace image of the state may be poor illiterates, there is a rich literary history including several "firsts." **Anne Newport Royall** of Monroe County was the first woman newspaper reporter in America. The scoop that made her famous, or infamous, was her interview with President John Quincy Adams that she obtained by sitting on his clothes. Adams was well known for skinny-dipping in the Potomac every morning.

Pearl Buck, whose homeplace is a shrine in Pocahontas County, (*see* "Remarkable Collections") was the first woman to win both the Pulitzer and Nobel prizes for literature. The first winner of the nation's O. Henry Award for the short story was West Virginian **Margaret Prescott Montague**. Another innovator in the short story arena was **Melville Davisson Post** who wrote the first detective stories where criminals escaped punishment. **Martin Delany**, who is honored with a plaque on the Masonic Temple in Charles Town, was the first Black novelist published in the United States. Delany was also a physician, the first Black major in the Civil War and a noted journalist. Contemporary literary stars include National Book Award winner, **Mary Lee**

Settle and American Book Award winner, **Denise Giardina**. While **Linda Goodman** may not be rated "literary," her books have probably sold more copies than any other state writer. A noted astrologer, **Goodman** began her career as a journalist in her home town of Parkersburg. Were a complete Literary Map ever to be printed it would be covered with hundreds of dots identifying sites written about or connected with noted authors.

Big Screen / Small Screen

In the pre-YouTube days, award-winning funky videos were most often the product of WNPB-public television in Morgantown, and are now classics. Filmmaker Jacob Young became a cult favorite with ***Dancing Outlaw***, a video featuring Jesco White, a Boone County flat dancer and Elvis impersonator. A couple decades later, *The Whites of West Virginia* was a reality television series. Young followed the bizarre Jesco video with *Holy Cow! Swami!*, a three-hour documentary on the Hari Krishna community near Moundsville, which was beset by allegations of murder and racketeering. Young's remarkable film includes rare footage of the founding of the Hare Krishnas as well as interviews with various devotees, public officials and the swami himself. For more on Moundsville's Palace of Gold, *see* "Truly Incredible."

Homer Hickam's childhood memoirs of **Coalwood** became a best-selling book and a hit movie entitled ***October Sky.*** This popularity made the coal camp and slag pile where a teenage Homer designed and launched his prize-winning rocket a tourist attraction, complete with a new municipal park built around a NASA rocket. Although a small coal company still operates in the town, the company store and white columned Clubhouse where bachelor miners lived are closed. A sign identifies Homer's white, two-story corner house.

West Virginia's film industry woke up in the 21st century with several hot titles including *Super Size Me* and *Win a Date With Tad Hamilton*. *Super 8* is the blockbuster hit that took over Weirton for a couple months including torching a residential block. Most West Virginians rank *We Are Marshall* as the most important film made in the state. Telling the true story of the tragic plane crash on November 14, 1970 that killed most of the Marshall football team, the movie filmed at 18 locations in and around Huntington and had an A-list cast including Matthew McConaughey and director McG.

There are several noted movie stars who hail from the state. Like most West Virginians, they are proud of their homeplace. Heading that list are Jennifer Garner, John Corbett, Chris Sarandon and Morgan Spurlock along with the late greats Don Knotts and Bob Denver. Country music fans cheer Brad Paisley and magazines love to point out Lady Gaga's connection through her West Virginia grandmother.

Theater Marvels

According to theater historians, the **Robey Theater** in Spencer is the longest continually operating movie theater in America although its early years are murky. From its founding in 1907 to 1912 it had four different downtown locations and changed names but kept the same owner and never missed a show. Today's Robey opens daily at 6:30pm. It has a balcony, wooden seats and a popcorn stand that opens onto the street as well as into the theater lobby. The antique ticket grinder still used by the usher to crimp your ticket co-exists with new 3D equipment.

Typical of the neighborhood movie houses that once thrived, the **Star Theater** in Berkeley Springs is one of the few remaining. Comfy, overstuffed couches replacing several rows of seats are often reserved weeks in advance. The 1949 seven-foot, glowing-red Manley popcorn machine reputedly makes the best popcorn in four states. Committed to keeping their working artifact current, Star owners went digital in 2013. Another neighborhood theater—the **Ritz** in Hinton—was renovated and reopened for weekend films in 2001.

The opulent **Keith Albee Theater** in Huntington opened in 1928 with 3,000 seats making it the second largest in the country at the time. Designed by architect Thomas Lamb, its intricate detail, baroque ornamentation and Moorish design pushed the eventual cost nearly ten times over budget. The Ladies Suite on the lower level has four rooms and more space than most modern multiplexes. The once grand auditorium and balcony area has been divided into four screen areas but the majestic lobby remains. In 2006, *We Are Marshall* premiered there complete with Hollywood pomp and a "green" carpet gala. Today it is home for the Marshall Artists Series.

Several other historic theaters have been reactivated. Built in 1913 as a plush movie house, the **Apollo Theater** in Martinsburg is the oldest continuously operating theater in West Virginia. Today it presents only live entertainment. In 1909, one of the country's first movie theaters was opened in Shepherdstown. It later was the first theater in the state with sound. After years of being closed, it reopened in 1992 as the **Shepherdstown Opera House** showing art and foreign films then evolved under new ownership to a live theater venue showing occasional films. You'll need a pillow for the individual, one-of-a-kind chairs. The **Capitol Theater** in Charleston was built for vaudeville in 1912 and became a movie theater in the late 1920s. Currently it houses the theater projects of West Virginia State College. Built in 1926 as a vaudeville and movie house, the **Smoot Theater** in Parkersburg was rescued in 1989 and remains open for a variety of entertainment. The noted **Logan Theater** showed movies at its current location from 1938 through 1995. After two years "dark" the 1,300-seat theater reopened as the **Coalfield Jamboree Theater**, a local version of Grand Old Opry. In Buckhannon, the **Lascaux Micro-Theater** not only shows underground films but is literally underground.

The **Metropolitan Theater** in Morgantown was billed as "West Virginia's most beautiful playhouse" when built in 1924. Renovated, it's now back featuring live performances. You'll know it by the star on the sidewalk honoring Morgantown's favorite hometown actor, Don Knotts.

The **West Virginia Historic Theater Trail** gathers 22 operating structures into a single brochure.

Once there were as many as 76 drive-ins; today it's four and these face an uncertain future with the mandated and expensive shift to digital technology. These are the **drive-in theaters** remaining at print time. The Grafton Drive-in still provides audio exclusively by pole speakers.

Cinematic adventure is still available at the rare drive-in. Here's a list:

* **Hilltop Drive-In:** Chester, Hancock County; 304-387-1611.
* **Meadow Bridge Drive-In:** Meadow Bridge, Fayette County; 304-484-7878.
* **Pipestem Drive-In:** Athens, Summers County; 304-384-7382 (at Speedway).
* **Sunset Drive-In:** Shinnston, Harrison County; 304-592-0405.

Show Your Cowbell

Started in 1933 on the stage of the Capitol Theater and broadcast on famous WWVA radio, Wheeling's **Jamboree** has been tops in the arena of live country music literally forever. Only the Grand Old Opry has been around longer. When the world famous stars yell for sold-out audiences to: "show your cowbell and they'll know you've been to Jamboree," they respond by ringing the signature cowbell given to each one. The practice originated with farmers who would travel to Jamboree and signal their loved ones at home with the distinctive ring of their cowbell.

Capitol Theater where Jamboree originated is a wonder on its own. Built in 1928, for years it housed eight broadcasting radio stations and a shop full of country music gifts. The 2,500 seat main hall retained its original 75-foot walls and ornate ceiling, and had state-of-the-art sound, lighting and projection screens. Jamboree shared the stage with the Wheeling Symphony. Threatened with extinction in 2007, the Capitol was saved by its convention bureau, renovated and re-opened but without Jamboree which spent a few years as a gypsy moving its 80-year show to the historic **Strand Theater** just next door in Moundsville, to Wheeling's **Victoria Theater** and currently to **Wheeling Island Casino**. Wheeling Symphony was able to stay at the Capitol.

They'll Know Us By Our Songs

Mountain Stage has taken West Virginia's music scene national with a vengeance. The two-hour Sunday evening show, featuring nationally and internationally known musicians, is popular on 130 stations of National Public Radio. Originated in Charleston by Andy Ridenour in 1983, and co-produced by singer-songwriter Larry Groce, the show went national in 1986. It is now the longest running live music program on national radio and has broadcast nearly 2,000 artists. After 38 years as host, Groce turned the reins over to beloved native songwriter Kathy Mattea in 2021.

The shows are recorded before a live audience at the Cultural Center. Taped and edited into one-hour shows, Mountain Stage is a musical picture postcard of West Virginia mailed out to the planet.

Two universally known songs were written by WV native "Jack" Rollins in 1949 and 50: Frosty, the Snowman *and* Here Comes Peter Cottontail. *Rollins was inducted into the* **WV Music Hall of Fame** *with more than 500 songs to his credit.*

West Virginians may be able to sing or at least name the state song, but the anthem the world knows best is the popular *Country Roads*, written in 1970 by Bill Danoff who had never been to the state. John Denver helped finish the song then released it to great acclaim. In the decades since it's been sung by everyone from Ray Charles to a Hawaiian singer and shown up in soundtracks of several television shows. In recent years, Danoff has performed in West Virginia, most memorably at the clothing-optional Avalonfest.

Michael Lipton turned his decades of covering state music through his publication *Graffiti* and accumulated stacks of recordings into the **West Virginia Music Hall of Fame.** It has annual inductees and a traveling exhibit that features an interactive map of all 55 counties. Touch a county and a few of its musicians show up. A permanent exhibit is at Tamarack. The **West Virginia Country Music Hall of Fame**, with shrines to Patsy Cline and Ernest Tubbs, is housed in the **Troubadour Lounge** out along a ridge in Berkeley Springs. Owner Joltin' Jim McCoy played with Cline. McCoy was inducted into the National Traditional Country Music Hall of Fame. **Country Store Opry** may have started in Pansy nearly half a century ago but today their classic country music show performs around the Potomac Highlands.

In 2011 Landau-mania swept the state as a young singer went from detailing cars in Logan and "doing the Sinatra" for charity events to winning *America's Got Talent* and selling out concert halls. Eugene Landau Murphy Jr. was named WV Artist of the Year in 2012 in 2012 and still performs to rave reviews.

Outdoor Ads Invented

Mail Pouch barn paintings were an advertising gimmick originated about 1908 by Aaron and Samuel Bloch, the Wheeling manufacturers who invented chewing tobacco in 1879. They named it West Virginia Mail Pouch two decades later with the slogan "The Real Man's Choice." In 1925, the company began putting ads on barns. Harley Warrick was the legendary painter who did 16 to 18,000 barns in his 35 years with Mail Pouch occasionally misspelling to see if anyone noticed. The tobacco is still manufactured in the same  building by current owners and the signs are federally protected landmarks. Traditionally, the company paid for the paint and the work and farmers got their barns painted. Today, the barns are vanishing and the signs are often maintained by local artists. More than 100 barns remain in 34 West Virginia counties.

Get Your Tickets Now

The **Clay Center** dominates the arts and science cultural scene and the Charleston skyline. The planetarium doubles as a large format movie theater. Its dome has a 10,000 star ball and defines the ten-story profile of the building. The grand concert hall has no bad seats, a mechanized ceiling space over the stage to store scenery for three complete shows and a sprung floor for dance. A wireless hotspot makes the whole building a classroom. Scores of interactive science exhibits like the laser harp turn the Avampato Discovery

Museum into a child's delight. Cost for all this splendor in the state's capital? 43 cents per pound—half what you would pay for a bag of onions.

Lawn Art Rules

From silhouetted farmers with corncob pipes to the ubiquitous holiday-specific inflatables, West Virginians love decorating their property. I visited two of the most unique arrays in one memorable week. An anonymous phone call sent me to Arthurdale to see the fantastic gardens of Vicki Cummings whose main goal was to be included in this book. Her yard art areas are sorted by category: bathroom area where flowers overflow from a commode, clawfoot tub and wringer washing machine; bedroom area where vines crawl over a bedstead; kitchen with a cook stove held together with rocks and bricks and filled with plants.

Centerpiece of her nearly one-acre spread is a 1950 Dodge Ram pick up that sports at least two dozen different areas of blooming plants. "I found it in a nearby field," said Cummings. "It has one headlight missing so I call it my one-eyed rambling rose." Cummings is looking for a big rock to announce the name of her domain: Vicki's Part of Heaven.

Just over the mountain from my homeplace is a 25-foot **Midas Muffler Man** in the yard of Pam and George Farnham. George knows all the stats on his lawn art, a 50th birthday gift from his wife. "There are only about 400 left in the country," he said. "They were done about 1950 and all the molds were broken. This one is even rarer because he's holding a muffler. Very few actually had mufflers." George passed up the chance to own a Midas Muffler Man holding a hot dog.

Like eating potato chips, Farnham could not be satisfied with just one. The collection continues to grow. Among the new arrivals is a bare-chested young man holding a coke that dwarfs Muffler Man. Inspired by the attention the figures draw, Farhnam applied the principal of lawn art to a political protest. He mobilized scores of Morgan County residents to create artistic outhouses as a means of opposing development.

Art Gems

★ Stained glass windows in the century-old former church building are duplicated in the tile countertop of the **Cathedral Cafe** in Fayetteville. Hand-painted tabletops are all unique.

★ **Pickin' in the Park** is a free acoustic jam session featuring old time and bluegrass music staged in Elkins City Park every Wednesday, and on Davis & Elkins campus in winter. Bring your spoons and washtubs. Not far away in Webster County, the **Jerry Run Summer Theater** showcases regional acoustic bands especially bluegrass on Saturday nights. Audience and musicians take a tiny footbridge over the creek to the handcrafted music hall. In Shepherdstown, eclectic and old timey music are featured at **O'Hurley's General Store** in a Thursday night open jam that's been going on forever.

★ **Artsbridge** of Parkersburg is one of only two successful bi-state arts organizations operating in the United States. It supports a full program of arts events on both sides of the Ohio River.

★ **Concord United Methodist Church** in Athens glows with 18 priceless stained glass windows by a mystery artist. Two windows feature the image of a huge eye.

★ The 1,000-pound bell hanging at **St. Patrick's Church** in Hinton continues a century-old daily tradition of tolling out the *Angelus*. Daily mini-concerts fill the mountains around **Concord College** with the varying tones of the noted 48-bell **Marsh Carillon**.

★ Jude Binder has been inspiring children and adults in Calhoun County with her remarkable **Heartwood in the Hills** school for the arts since 1982. A dancer and mask maker, much of Jude's work focuses on nature and issues of social justice.

★ The unique **Peace Totem** adorns the outdoor yard of the **Youth Museum in Beckley**. Assembled as a community project, it is the only painted work by master sculptor, Mark Blumenstein. Stained glass artist and former Marine in Vietnam, **ragtime**, is creating **1000 Points of Peace** as his effort to follow the path of lighting a candle rather than cursing the darkness.

★ The giant **Red Cross** in front of the organization's Huntington headquarters dominates the riverfront. It was dedicated in 1978 at an event where DJs stayed on top of the cross until they collected a certain amount of blood from willing donors. Another Huntington icon is the **Frostop** mug still spinning on the roof of its namesake drive-in. The mug was recently repainted to keep its foam looking incredibly lifelike. Huntington painter Allen Storm Pattie snagged the coveted job.

★ N.C. Wyeth, patriarch of the notable painting family, created **Christmas in Old Berkeley** as a promotion for a textile factory in 1928. Today, the 5x12-foot original oil painting hangs in the **Martinsburg Public Library.**

★ Painted quilt blocks from designs chosen by the public are hung on 38 barns along various back roads as the Monroe County Quilt Trail. Other barn-based quilt trails are in Mason and Roane counties while Old Central City in Huntington displays its quilt blocks on buildings. In Berkeley Springs, May is Quilt Month. More than 40 yard square quilts hang in windows downtown for six weeks before being auctioned and the annual quilt show fills the Ice House.

★ Since 2005, Charleston turns itself over to art for ten days in June. More than 100 events at the award-winning **Festivall** showcase everything from theater performances and concerts to a street long art fair. Inspired by former Mayor Danny Jones, the event accomplished the near impossible by bringing together dozens of arts groups to play nice together. As part of Festivall, ten selected artists each year paint ten of the piers holding up Interstate 64 through the heart of town. It takes a couple months and a lot of art to cover a pier ten feet tall and 13 feet around.

★ **Gary Bowling's House of Art** makes the whole experience art as well as the items he and other local artists create. On the top floor of the former City Hall, the expansive space is filled with two and three-dimensional art as well as a stage and tables for special events. Oh yes—it also has a cellblock, remnants of its history as the Bluefield Jail.

Murals

There are enough spectacular murals that a statewide contest would be quite competitive.

Point Pleasant has turned their **Ohio River Walk** into a combination art gallery and history lesson through 13 murals covering more than 600 feet of floodwall. Scene after scene shows authentic details of Native American and frontier life including the murder of Cornstalk. Noted mural artist, Robert Dafford with various student helpers, painted them over five years.

Mullens has murals inside and out. The Virginia Mural is a 20 by 90 foot depiction of an old Virginia Railway steam engine and cars passing through a nearby freestanding tunnel. The 120-foot building that serves as the "canvas" for the train mural was built in 1924 and now houses the Mullens Family

Clinic. A little further on Howard Street is a three-panel fire truck mural on the fire hall. Sarge McGhee was the artist during the late 1980s and early 90s. He would sketch out the details and platoons of volunteers would spend hundreds of hours painting them. Most recently, McGhee

did a series of indoor murals in the Veterans Memorial Building depicting scenes from ten different wars involving the United States. Two major murals cover the back of City Hall. Queen Becky and her continent-crossing Art Car reported another wonder in Mullens: a stonewall boasting a map of the US with each state an individual stone. The walls are common, supporting houses cut into hillsides.

There's another railroad mural in **Chicory Square Park**, Bluefield. Fire engines in motion decorate the **Hurricane Fire Hall** on Main Street. Morgantown has a missing block of its past painted on a brick wall of its present and Richwood's murals highlight state history. Welch chose to highlight its own rich history in three murals, one on a water tower.

CHAPTER FOUR

Far-Out Festivals and Other Happenings

The oddities tour outlined in this book grew from a seed planted at two West Virginia events absolutely unique in the world—**Bridge Day** and the **Berkeley Springs International Water Tasting.** Together they rank #1 and #2 as generators of worldwide publicity for the state.

Annual festivals and events are one-of-a-kind by their very nature. There's always the weather, or the crowd, or some peculiar occurrence that stamps the event as singular even when activities remain the same.

More than 200 major festivals happen each year in virtually every county. Some of the most original are featured here, both those that draw from heritage and others that embrace the present with fervor. Sort through the collection, pick, choose and trust that whether it's sipping water, celebrating dandelions, calling hogs or jumping hundreds of feet into the rapids, nothing is more fun than a fabulous festival.

I Tasted Kirk Douglas' Water

After years of worker bee status at the **Berkeley Springs International**

Water Tasting, I was eventually promoted to be a judge at the largest water tasting ever held on the planet. Trained by watermaster Arthur von Wiesenberger in the intricacies and subtleties of discriminating among samples of a liquid that is tasteless at its best, I was ready for the task. It had to be easier than hiding in a back closet defending the top-secret list that matched municipal water name with its anonymous number. And, I was able to dress in sequins.

A buzz swept the clutch of judges as we sat on risers, staring into the room crowded with spectators. Zip code 90210 was represented, reported the judge to my right. Von Wiesenberger nodded. It was true. Somewhere among the twenty-five municipal waters set in glasses before me and the dozen other judges was celebrity water from Beverly Hills. A note verified that it had been drawn from the tap in actor Kirk Douglas' bathroom by his son, Peter. Celebrity water! It was a first for the Berkeley Springs competition.

Since the judges taste blind—meaning we know nothing about a water but its assigned number—I had no idea which of the identical looking fluids was the one Kirk used to brush his teeth every morning. I searched for a clue. None of them seemed to have even the slightest hint of a cleft chin, piercing eyes, or the square-jawed look of *Spartacus*.

I performed the tasting ritual judges are taught each year. Glass by glass I looked for brilliance, sniffed for unwanted aromas, and rolled a sip of each water around my mouth. "The tongue has more than 100,000 taste buds," von Wiesenberger told us. "You need to wake them up, get them all involved." After the fifteenth glass, my taste buds were in a coma.

Taste is rated in three categories: flavor, mouth feel, and aftertaste. Von Wiesenberger's manual of water tasting terminology was the guidebook we used. Did water #24 have the finesse required by a movie star's palate, I wondered? Was it a balanced water with harmonious minerals? Or did it have the "sucking on a wet band-aid" taste we all dreaded to find in our unsuspecting mouths? Maybe Kirk's was #16, which seemed to have the breeding—the elegance and thirst-quenching capacity—one would expect to find in Beverly Hills. Surely it wasn't #19, assaulting my nose with a wave of chlorine odor. My face scrunched in sympathetic dismay with my harassed taste buds.

Tasting and rating water was more difficult than I imagined. I couldn't distinguish celebrity water from tap water drawn in Nowheresville.

Tabulators worked to add up ratings from all the judges. Emcee J.W. Rone collected the scores and dramatically announced the top five municipals, beginning with the fifth place water. If Kirk's water won, would he attend next year's competition? Would a host of celebrity waters enter in future years?

Finally, the winner was on the tip of Rone's tongue. Would Kirk Douglas' bathroom tap provide the world's best tap water? Would Beverly Hills replace defending champion, Atlantic City, or two-time winner, Charleston?

No! Number one was not Beverly Hills, it was Kent, Ohio. Ohio. Home of... of...Ohioans. I was crushed. Not only had Kirk's water not placed in the top five, but neither had any West Virginia water.

After we tasted our way through still and sparkling bottled waters, I searched out the list that matched name with number. Kirk's water was #20 and placed seventh! I checked my rating sheet to see if I had noticed a special sparkle, a certain greatness to #20. Nope—only a mediocre 32. My eyes raced down the column to check for comments. I froze. Flabby! I had rated Kirk's water as flabby! Lacking vitality. How embarrassing.

No one was watching as I slipped the offending sheet into my pocket. Kirk Douglas never needed to know that I thought the water of *Spartacus* was flabby.

Note: In 1994, it was a Mountaineer sweep with the top three waters in the world all hailing from West Virginia sources. In 1998, Kirk's water did indeed win, submitted by his provider, the Metropolitan Water District of Southern California. After more than two decades, 45 countries had entered the contest and all but four states in the USA. What's wrong with Rhode Island, Oklahoma, Nevada and South Dakota?

Jump Boys, Jump

It was a gorgeous Saturday in mid-October, and the New River Gorge was ablaze in fall colors as we flew along its jagged path into a private airport almost within walking distance of the bridge. We were in Fayette County for **Bridge Day.**

One incredible sight after another paraded before our eyes. The northbound lanes of US 19 on both sides of the New River Bridge were closed to traffic and served as miles of parking. The closed north side of the world's second longest single arch span bridge—3,030 feet long—was open to legal foot traffic for the only day of the year. Thousands of denim-clad human butts lined up along the edge of the bridge watching more than 450 jumpers hurl themselves off an aluminum diving board. Jumpers were aiming at a circle of stones on the river's sand beach, but often landed in the rapid-strewn river nearly a thousand feet below. Colorful nylon chutes filled the air.

The overwhelmingly male BASE (bridge, antenna, spans and earth) jumpers, rappellers, and rafters in the river are the one-day show of Bridge Day. They come from all over the world to jump from the only major vehicle bridge in the world that allows it on the one day it is permissible. More than 250,000 people—and global television—are the audience for what is the world's largest extreme sport event. There's also a sideshow of 250 vendors stretched on the bridge roadway offering everything from roadkill cookbooks to Italian sausage sandwiches and sweet potato French fries. Religious groups of all persuasions are out in force. Chanting Hare Krishnas are cheek to jowl with Fundamentalist Christians peddling Bibles.

The first year, 1980, saw five jumpers. In 1997, a dozen people set the world record for simultaneous jumps. That same year a five-man Elvis team jumped, dressed all in white. Many jump in costumes, others with lit cigars. In 2003, the aluminum diving board was introduced allowing for multiple flips and twists from the aerialists. There have been only three fatal leaps since the event began; the most recent was in 1987. In 2001, a controversial decision by the Bridge Day committee canceled that year's event because of concerns over security from terrorist attacks; hysteria was canceled the next year and Bridge Day resumed.

Electrified in Wheeling

Driving through the arched tunnel of dancing snowflakes was magical, and it was just the entrance. More than a million lights in nearly 60 animated displays are the shining center of **Oglebay's Festival of Lights.** The city of Wheeling joins in with nearly 300 giant snowflakes and 200 twinkling trees. Started in 1985 and now the nation's largest light show (not counting the daily lighting of Las Vegas,) the Festival of Lights draws more than 3,000 buses and a million visitors. Folks are welcome to drive themselves or take a trolley around six miles and 300 acres of hillsides, golf courses and a lake to see the well-designed collection of beautifully-lit folk icons.

Cinderella's coach races towards the castle, while mice frolic around a pumpkin in a display that took two years to make. There are toy soldiers that march and salute, and a boy who waters the ground where flowers then grow and bloom. The Funny Fisherman perpetually catches and loses fish in Schenk Lake, and dinosaurs roam over a football field-sized dell. The poinsettia wreath and candle display is the tallest light sculpture, reaching 60 feet. The Gardens of Light have baskets of lights and thousands of lighted flowers and trees choreographed for animation.

New displays are added each year and others are retired. They are all fabricated by industrial arts students at Wheeling Park High, who have worked with the designers since the beginning. From November through early January, the million or so lights are on from dusk to 11:30pm. But don't be concerned about environmental impact—all the light displays are LED energy efficient.

Oglebay's Good Zoo joins in the fun with a choreographed light and music display and holiday laser light shows at its theater.

Biggest and Oldest

A legend since 1930 and a mecca for every politician including four U.S.

Presidents, the Mountain State Forest Festival in Elkins draws the most people, has the most princesses (40 at last count, plus a queen) and lasts more than a week every end of September into October. The events are diverse including a parade of children, muzzleloader competition, stagecoach to an elegant ball, chainsaw carving and a precision motorcycle exhibition as well as forest related ones like wood chopping, tree felling and axe-throwing. It also has all the usual festival stuff—food, music, crafts and exhibits.

Weird and Unusual Doings for Every Season

★ At midday on January 1, nearly an hour of weird floats and zany folks parade through downtown Lewisburg. There's a grown man in a diaper and a $2 bill for everyone. Otherwise, reports of the annual **Shanghai Parade** are vague and content is spontaneous, making it the most inexplicable of West Virginia celebrations.

We do know that it has been a Lewisburg custom for most of the past 120 years to parade along Washington Street on New Years Day. Whether it represents the ultimate "day after" event or a tribute to the new beginning is all in your point of view. Post-Christmas caperers and dudes dressed-to-kill both figure in speculation about the origin of the custom, and newspaper reports from the nineteenth century always used the plural—Shanghais. Today, as in the past, there is no need to sign up in advance. Paraders are self-invited and simply fall-in for the march. A popular repeat entrant is a flatbed truckload of Witch Women with wands and elaborate designer hats. Events like this helped earn Lewisburg the honor of being Coolest Small Town in America 2011.

★ West Virginia has long been a major manufacturing center for marbles (right). Three manufacturers remain today: Marble King in Paden City, Champion Agate in Pennsboro, and Mid-Atlantic Glass in Ellenboro. Millions of marbles a week are made and sold all over the world. There are even dueling marble festivals with Cairo's in May and Sistersville in September. The **West Virginia Marble Festival** in Cairo features trading, a shooting contest and contemporary marble artists. This history may rub off. In 2000, a Doddridge County youth, earned second place in the National Marbles Tournament. No word on whether he won with West Virginia "aggies."

★ **Luminaria.** On the last Sunday before Christmas, 2,500 candles in paper bags line a mountain road north of Bruceton Mills going to old time Salem Church. Lit by parishioners at 4 p.m., the illumination lasts most of the night.

★ Through its annual mountain music competitions, the **Vandalia Festival** provides the premier stage for what may be the state's greatest contribution to the art world. It is the place to see a barely teenage *wunderkind* debut by beating an octogenarian fiddler. While music rates as the main attraction, the most unique competition is the **Liars Contest** in which scores of folks compete for the Golden Shovel award. The tallest tale may feature anything from a favorite hound dog to magical trains and talking fish.

★ Each year, a Saturday in mid-October finds more than a hundred living history volunteers reenacting the tumultuous **Presidential Election of 1860** on the streets of Harpers Ferry National Historic Park. Local electors dressed in top hats and facial hair make speeches and stump for their candidates up until the balloting at day's end. Temperance ladies urge their cause on passers-by, set up in a tent next to an Election Day tavern. The militia marches up and down the street in formation. Anyone may cast a ballot. A

> **Fasnatch** *is a Swiss pre-Lenten Mardi Gras bash and ritual where hundreds of folks don scary masks and Ol' Man Winter is burned in effigy at midnight in Helvetia. The Hutte Restaurant and friends cook Swiss treats for days. After parading through the tiny town with lanterns costumed merrymakers end up in Star Band Hall for music, dance and yodeling.*

Victory Parade follows the announced results late in the afternoon. In case you've forgotten what really happened in 1860, Abe Lincoln won, but not in West Virginia, the area he made a state three years later.

★ The **Irish Spring Festival** spans the days between St. Patrick's Day and Spring Equinox with events ranging from harp concerts and mulligan stew cooking to limerick and fried potato contests. Logically located in the town of Ireland, the festival also celebrates the astonishingly long life of original settler Andrew Wilson who reportedly enjoyed 114 springs.

★ The "other" residents of Eire claim descendants in the Scots and Celtic tradition and celebrate the culture in May at the annual **Scottish Festival and Celtic Gathering** in Bridgeport Park with a schedule that includes Bagpipe Contest, Highland dances, hand bell ringers and food galore.

★ Seventy descendants of the Osborne family—a band of Cherokees that settled in Clay County—relive their heritage each year during the local Golden Delicious Festival on the third weekend in September. They stage a two-hour drama entitled **Solomon's Secret** which traces the original band's trail of tears from North Carolina with a bit of Christianity thrown in as well. It began as a 15-minute play at a family reunion and now includes an authentic Cherokee wedding ceremony and several original songs.

Distinctions

★ Arden Cogar Sr. is a worldwide celebrity thanks to ESPN, which broadcasts the **Webster Springs Woodchopping Festival** every Memorial Day weekend. He deserves the honor, having won the festival's Southeastern U.S. World Championship of woodchopping dozens of times! Competing since 1956, Cogar has won nearly 50 championship titles in the United States and Australia. The Webster Springs event is one of three world champion competitions. As if that's not enough, the turkey calling contest and Firemen's Rodeo—both for state championships—are also staged during the weeklong wood chopping fest.

★ It's the ultimate insiders event. Join Robertson Associates' private cavers group just once and you can attend the **Old Timers Reunion** forever. As many as 3,000 attendees from all over North America and beyond stake out a big field on the Tygart River near Dailey every Labor Day weekend for the world's largest cavers convention. Bare breasts decorated with day-glo are a favorite spontaneous exhibit for folks who spend their spare time in dark caves.

★ Another public reunion festival is probably the only one in the world celebrating a family feud. Each year in early June, Hatfield and McCoy kin and wannabes gather from around the world for **The Hatfield and McCoy Reunion Festival and Marathon**—four days of races, tours, movie viewings, entertainment and general partying in Williamson and Matewan.

★ The **State Fair of West Virginia** has the usual display of prize-winning sheep and carnival rides. In addition it offers the only opportunity to watch harness racing in West Virginia. As unusual as the giant vegetables are the parking arrangements. Guaranteed by a land grant that stipulated parking will always be free, the 1,000-acre fairground hosts a temporary city of nearly 1,500 camper units averaging four people each. It's a captive audience for the nine-day event.

★ **Mountain State Art and Craft Fair** is rated the best traditional fair in the nation. Spread over a hundred acres at Cedar Lakes near Ripley, works by more than 250 juried craftspeople and artisans make for great shopping. There are craft demonstrations, traditional entertainment and mountain food. For half a century, the fair has been held for several days during the July 4th holiday.

★ What makes an octogenarian West Virginian sing and dance? The old time square dances and over-50 fiddle and banjo contests at the **West Virginia State Folk Festival.** Held in Glenville every mid-June since 1950, this is the best place for young traditionalists to jam with un-amplified, "uncontaminated" musicians from the hills and hollers while everyone else gets to listen in.

★ Highlights of the annual **Charleston Boulevard Rod Run and Doo Wop** include river cruises (for boats not cars), machine shop tours, boat parade and concerts. The car show spreads more than 1,000 antique and rare vehicles of all sorts along the river. It's a stretch to believe these vehicles belong to the same species as your ride.

Funky Food Festivals

★ The weirdest native food of all is celebrated at the **Feast of the Ramson**—a tribute to ramps, the pungent, early spring wild leek, member of the lily family. Proclaiming itself "Ramp Capital of the World," Richwood has hosted the granddaddy ramp dinner feast since 1937.

Community ramp dinners are also held in Helvetia, Clay, Pickens and assorted spots around the state. Attendees at ramp feeds are not hard to locate. The distinctive pungent odor lasts for about 72 hours after eating.

★ In 1968, Edeline Wood of Parkersburg had a wild food party using recipes from Euell Gibbons and invited him to attend and speak. He did and returned annually for years until his death in 1975. Gibbons considered West Virginia the wild food garden spot of the world. Ms. Wood created and still runs the National Wild Food Association in his honor.

Natural Wonder Wild Food Weekend at North Bend State Park in mid-September is the outgrowth of Ms. Wood's party and now the longest-running wild food event in North America. People come and forage under a botanist guide, help with the cooking and eat the truly wild entrees in the event's cooking contest and feast. The list of foods demonstrates how foraging can be spun into epicurean. There could be chocolate-covered ground cherries and wild greens quiche competing with rattlesnake salad and squirrel. Venison mincemeat muffins, turtle stew, milkweed bud casserole, barbecued groundhog, quail supreme, bear casserole, and sumac lemonade have all been on the menu.

★ For more than seven decades thousands of folks have descended on Kingwood to celebrate the area's former chief crop—humble buckwheat. In the process, they eat 16,129 (the standing record) sour buckwheat pancakes and six tons of home-ground whole hog sausage, all served with syrup and applesauce. It's the ultimate in all-you-can-eat. All the ingredients are produced locally including the buckwheat, still ground in season at Hazleton Mill. Related to the rhubarb not the cereal family, buckwheat can be eaten by those with wheat allergies.

The **Buckwheat Festival** also has a lamb dressing competition. Entrants are not dressed to be eaten; they are dressed-to-kill with fashionable bonnets, capes and other attire set to annual themes ranging from movie stars to presidents and first ladies. It may sound tame but it's not. The four-person team has to catch a barnyard lamb and dress it in less than ten minutes. There's even a real-life buckwheat fairy tale. The first Buckwheat Queen and King, meeting at their coronation in 1938, fell in love, married and lived in wedded bliss for nearly fifty years.

★ Pancake feeds vie with a ham and bean buffet for culinary treats at the **Maple Syrup Festival** in Pickens. The real reason to go in mid-March is to visit the authentic maple syrup camp, collect sap, and watch it boiled in the sugar house. Or, maybe it's the muzzleloading contest.

★ West Virginia legislators with too much time on their hands spent weeks debating a bill that allowed folks to take their roadkill home and eat it. Next they'll be requiring expiration date tags for roadkill left behind. No one in Marlinton cared. Their annual **Roadkill Cook-off**, with regular entries ranging from barbecue bear and rabbit sausage to porcupine stew, makes special allowance for entries that come from roadkill acquired on the way to the event.

The rules of disposing with roadkill became a hot political issue in 1998.

★ On Columbus Day weekend, eaters flock to Baker Island in Webster Springs for the **International Burgoo Cook-off**. Anyone can enter their "burgoo" which is defined as a highly seasoned stew made of just about anything and cooked in a large pot outdoors.

A Roman Holiday

Rated one of the best heritage events in the United States, the **Italian Heritage Festival** in Clarksburg is West Virginia's most extravagant, three-day street party. Organizers scour the state for young beauties of Italian heritage and make them princesses for a week. There are pepperoni rolls galore, a pasta cook-off, beer and wine in the streets, and continuous free entertainment from two stages featuring famous Italian-American performers and opera. Street dancing on Saturday night continues until midnight and hundreds assemble at the church in the center of the action for Mass on Sunday. As the state's most notable enclave of Italian-Americans the array of Italian food delicacies is astonishing and authentic.

Hot Dog Heaven

Huntington and vicinity inexplicably make-up the center of the region's hot dog universe with both producers like **Heiner's Bakery** and eating spots including **Hillbilly Hot Dog** and **Stewarts**. Since 2005, the **WV Hot Dog Festival** takes over Pullman Square on the last Saturday in July. Along with dogs you can eat, live dogs are also featured in everything from wiener dog races to a pooch parade.

Beards

He's a huge hit every year at **The Honey Festival** in Parkersburg and year 'round at his honey-producing **Thistledew Farm**. Steve Conlon is the man with the most exotic beard imaginable—bees! Steve lures the bees by strapping their queen in a tiny basket to his sturdy chin; the rest follow. He reports fewer stings from the beard demonstration than from his general work around his 700 hive bee farm. Perhaps it's his affinity with the real honey producers that catapulted him to the honor of serving as chair of the National Honey Board.

Photo courtesy Steve Conlon

Babes judging beards always draw a crowd and dozens of contestants at the annual **Apple Butter Festival** in Berkeley Springs. The facial hair contest (*below, right*) renders such notoriety that

contestants have been known to work from one year to the next to win. One local park bum wore his blue ribbon around for two weeks. This is genetic politics at its best.

It's a Haunt at Halloween

Halloween brings unique hauntings all over the state from a coal mine and theater in Beckley to a ski trail in Snowshoe, a hotel in Bluefield, and a cave in Lewisburg. There are Halloween train rides from Huntington and Kingwood. Ghosts come and go, so check with visitors centers in these areas to find out times and locations of seasonal **hauntings.**

Halloween also brings **pumpkins** and nowhere more of them than in Kenova where for more than 20 years upwards of 3,000 of them, carved and lit, take up residence in and around a Victorian home. Come quick, they last no more than a week.

The big two sites for Halloween are the haunted prison tour at **Moundsville Penitentiary** and a series of scary tours and a huge costume ball at the **Trans-Allegheny Lunatic Asylum** in Weston. *See* "Tours and Trips."

Cornfield Labyrinth

Each fall, Kim Cooper has his six-acre bottomland cornfield with 13-foot corn stalks carved by an expert into the **Milton Maize Maze**. Hundreds of visitors spend an hour or more twisting and turning through the labyrinth occasionally needing Cooper to rescue them. Come in at night, and you'll be given a glow stick to light the way.

CHAPTER FIVE

Fast Living

The commonplace image of West Virginia tempo is relaxed, if not downright slow. The fastest movement that comes to mind is the banjo picker's fingers or the clogger's feet. In real life, there's more speed than that in the mountains and along the rivers. There's bona fide fast living—and even some unusual nightlife that gives lie to the notion that it's lights out after dark. One contributor to Wild and Wonderful's fast living is the ratio of three strip clubs for every 100,000 residents, highest in the USA.

A PhD in Speed

Sounds of squealing tires and roaring engines accelerating through the multiple gears of twenty Ferraris ricochet around the two and a half mile, ten-turn **Summit Point Raceway** in Jefferson County.

Three days later, the two-lane asphalt highway track in the woods is the site of Accident Avoidance School. The following week, Advanced Driver Training addresses students wanting to drive safely at high speeds and under threatening circumstances. The training programs emphasize realistic techniques and provide ample opportunity for students to practice under controlled conditions and the watchful eyes of top-notch trainers who ride along. During the standard day of school, five and a half hours are spent driving the car. Various intelligence and law enforcement agencies train their workers in the courses to protect them in high-speed chases and terrorist attacks.

Summit Point has developed into an industrial park devoted to Homeland Security and anti-terrorism training activities including a built-to-order tactical training center. Its advanced driver training has become a hot item and its trainers often find themselves on temporary assignment driving for the likes of top American diplomats in the Middle East. There are new elements added including how to commandeer a car which means knowing what type car can be easily stolen when you are in a hurry to escape from pursuing bad guys.

Brandishing a Yale PhD and a championship racing career, Bill Scott is Summit Point's energetic center of speed and action. His anti-terrorist training includes role playing in nearby towns while consumer courses encourage owners to bring their own cars—like the ever-popular Camaro—and learn to drive at top road speed, spin-out safely and make the always handy J-turn at 60 mph.

The day I visited, Scott drove me around his track at a speed we often fly our plane, slowing to under 100 mph so he could casually demonstrate a 180-degree turn. "This was the technique that helped a defense attaché save himself from a rock throwing mob in Peru," he explained as I relaxed my death grip on the door handle.

Although Summit Point is more a participatory than a spectator track, it does host an array of open-to-the-public races including vintage motorcycles, go-karts and formula cars.

The Summit Point Raceway garage houses the motorized symbols of Scott's diverse interests—a rare pair of gleaming red Porsche diesel tractors.

Mother Nature's Rush

White water rafting is a top echelon adrenalin sport, and West Virginia has the best white water in the east. A quarter of a million river runners a year can't be wrong about that. Ten rivers and several mountain streams provide 200 miles of whitewater. Commercial rafters have at their disposal a full range of all six levels of rapids during the white water seasons of spring, summer and fall. The New and the Gauley rivers are paramount among those with tossing waters, matchless scenery and history. Both are part of the largest federally protected watershed in the eastern United States. In recognition of this pre-eminence, the first time the world whitewater rafting championships were held in North America was on the New and Gauley. World whitewater rafting champs were made in West Virginia that year, and so were the custom rafts each team used.

The huge New River watershed provides enormous water volume that squeezes through the narrow canyon creating big, roller coaster waves as the river falls 750 feet in fifty miles. The Gauley River is second in difficulty among the nation's rivers with 100 rapids, fifty major ones, in a 26-mile stretch that drops nearly 700 feet.

With gargantuan boulders and rapids named "Pure Screaming Hell" and "Heaven Help Us", the Gauley lives up to its reputation. The upper Gauley has such turbulent chutes and rocky routes that the minimum age to run this section of the river is 16. The 12-mile stretch of the lower Gauley is a watery roller coaster with an age limit of 12.

The ultimate of the ultimate is the **Gauley Season**: 22 days of Friday through Monday weekends beginning in mid-September when the Army Corps of Engineers stages its annual drawdown of water backed-up by the huge Summersville Dam. One million gallons of lake water gushing through the Summersville Dam tunnels each minute create an irresistible, three-week wave of turbulence across the river rapids. White water enthusiasts flock to ride rafts and kayaks, sometimes twice a day, on the nearly inaccessible Gauley River. It's strictly for the experienced.

Many experienced rafters rate the Gauley River as the best two-day white water trip in the world.

Since the high water rafting releases prevent fishing on the Gauley during that season, white water outfitters compensate the fishermen by stocking the river with an additional 1,000 pounds of trout. During November, the West Virginia Film Office can arrange "River on Demand," a calm or raging river for motion picture or television productions as a complimentary service of the Army Corps of Engineers through their drawdown of the lake.

White water is a multi-sensory experience with roaring sounds, drenching wetness and heart-pounding anticipation. There are stretches of placid drifting surrounded by scenic wilderness and coal camp remnants. The wild Cheat River has holes called hydraulics, breeders of whirlpools that capsize rafts. At its best during April, May and June, the Cheat has 38 rapids in 11 miles.

In spite of amenities including gourmet lunches and luxury cabins, white water rafting is not for creampuffs. All the rivers offer hidden waterfalls, churning rapids, and rock-strewn channels, so be prepared for white water sports. The rapids require real paddling and dunks in the drink are commonplace.

Inflatable kayaks, known as duckies, are sufficient for the mild rapids and quiet pools of the Upper New, and provide an easy way to see the gorge close-up.

Inaugurated in 1968, today's white water industry in West Virginia has more than 20 commercial outfitters offering everything from kayaking clinics to rafting trips for the handicapped. Guides are an indelible part of the white water experience. They are expert pilots, often well versed on the history and ecology of the river, and generally eccentric with abundant rafter jokes. Since adrenalin junkies are seldom satisfied with a single, life-stretching experience, most of the rafting companies also provide rock climbing, rappelling and ziplines.

Summersville Lake, created by the dam, is a hotbed of water sports unexpected in a state known for its mountains and boasting only one tiny natural lake. Avid divers seek out the 3,000-acre man-made lake for its crystal clear water with visibility up to 60 feet, rocky cliffs, underwater boulders and water caves. A dive shop and jet skis round out the water sports menu.

There is additional scuba diving at **Mt. Storm** in Grant County where the power plant creates water temperatures comparable to your bath regardless of the season. Plan to throw the invisibility cloak over breathing apparatus and wet suits since the power company currently has a prohibition on any diving in the 1,200 acre lake.

For more about the New River—possibly the oldest in the world—*see* "Mother Nature's Wonders."

More Speed

★ White water companies are merging then branching out, adding death-defying ziplines and creating adrenalin-soaked adventure theme parks. Two of them exploit their location on the **New River Gorge** adding an unmatched level of excitement to the standard tree canopy menu of obstacles, bridges, swings and tree platforms.

ACE Adventure had the first zips in the state. Their 1,500 acre park marks ACE as North America's largest adventure resort and they hold the Guinness world record for the most zippers in a single hour: 180! **Adventures on the Gorge** features one of the longest ziplines in the US at 3,100 feet where two zippers can race against each other at up to 60 mph.

In Harpers Ferry, **River Riders** uses trees for its aerial adventure park with bridges, platforms and rock climbing. A tower-strung zip line along the Potomac River has a bonus feature of the breathtaking view that captivated Thomas Jefferson.

Nelson Rocks Outdoor Center has spectacular views of the double-fin Tuscarora quartzite Nelson Rocks, a canopy tour and miles of breathtaking, awe-inspiring hiking trails.

Moundsville's **Grand Vue Park** has dual zips with suspension bridges offering scenic views of the valley.

★ **Jet Boats at Hawks Nest.** Fast living at **Hawks Nest State Park** begins with walking down into the dizzying view of the New River Gorge from the outer deck of the lodge. A two-minute aerial tram ride takes adventurers further down to the dock where the 21-foot jetboat—the Miss M. Rocks—floats on the river, waiting to take off under a railroad/walking bridge. For 35 minutes, water-sprayed passengers speed upstream along the rocky cliffs of the gorge pockmarked with beehive ovens where local coal was coked.

Rick, the gravelly-voiced boatman on my trip, narrated colorful tales of the river and pointed out wooden boxes posing as fishing camps all along the barest edge of shoreline. Dragonflies pace the boat as it slows to turn at Fayette Station rapids under the world-famous New River Gorge Bridge. Soaking up passengers' awestruck glances, the second highest bridge in the United States arches gracefully against the sky above the river.

★ **Summerfest** brings high-powered craft from all over the country into Huntington in July or August to race along the Ohio River for the national speedboat title. The National Power Boat Association stages its national championships odd-numbered years at Bluestone Lake in Hinton during the **State Water Festival** in mid-summer. More than 500 drivers in modified stock speedboats and hydroplanes scream over the lake at speeds in excess of 90 mph.

★ Dirt track car racing enthusiasts go to **West Virginia Motor Speedway**. Getting to this Mineral Wells NASCAR track is a driving adventure in itself requiring transit through a narrow culvert tunnel under I-77. For fantasy lovers, radio-controlled cars have a dirt track of their own at **Pipestem State Park**. It's partnered with a NASCAR concrete oval.

★ Volunteer instructors, unique techniques and equipment like monoskis, outrigger poles and sit skis guarantee winter adventure for those with handicaps as part of **Snowshoe Mountain's** Adaptive Skiing program. Challenged Athletes of West Virginia is an irreplaceable partner in the operation.

★ **Canaan Valley Resort** decided skiing was not speedy enough for that winter rush so they were the first in the region to add snow bodyboarding. Using traditional mountainside ski slopes, there is nothing between you and high-speed travel down the mountain but an inflatable sled known as an Airboard. The truly crazed can risk the slope with jumps and berms. Slightly less life threatening is the snow tubing park with the longest run in the region.

Las Vegas Goes Hollywood

You step from blinding sunlight through the vaguely Mission-style entryway of the 65-year-old Charles Town Races into—Las Vegas, or more accurately, **Hollywood Casino**. It's all there, albeit in miniature. No natural light, star splashed walls, eye-catching video ribbons with dozens of screens including one 90-feet long and rows and rows of 3,500 colorful slots each with a flashing red light on top. Even on weekdays, the two floors of well laid-out gaming are humming and at least one of two poker rooms is full.

The expansion to table games had a dramatic beginning. At midnight on July 1, 2010 a check for $1.5 million was handed over to state officials for the new license. Literally one minute later, a fleet of trucks loaded with equipment headed across the Potomac into West Virginia. Within 36 hours, folks were playing and continue to do so 24 hours a day, every day of the year.

Traditional aspects of the Charles Town Races have not disappeared. Horses, for example. The nags are everywhere—nearly 1,200 of them during the more than 200 days of live racing and substantial purses including more than $1 million for the **West Virginia Breeders' Classic** alone. The horse races are free. No admission or seating charge for the sport of kings. A simulcast center shows races of thoroughbreds, harness or dogs winking out on more than 300 screens of all sizes. Also strewn around for the gaming cogniscenti are computer terminals—self-service betting machines—and private cubicles in the VIP room with your own video screen.

The Hollywood Casino has more than gaming. It invested in first rate dining including a noodle bar in its food court and a high-end Hong Kong cuisine restaurant for its substantial Asian clientele. Menus for both come in Chinese and English. No chain eateries here.

In case you think gambling parks like Charles Town have no heart, think again. The Thoroughbred Retirement Foundation was established to save over-the-hill race horses from being turned into dog food. The track and the state Horsemens Benevolent and Protective Association partnered to make it so.

The Northern Panhandle has two gambling opportunities. Perched in the middle of the Ohio River, **Wheeling Island** has a greyhound racetrack set to the accompaniment of the slots and table games including a 24/7 Poker Room. As an entertainment bonus, the casino stage is current home of the world famous country music **Wheeling Jamboree**, adding an entertainmment bonus to the gambling fun. **The Mountaineer Racetrack** in Chester blends slots with horse races on both turf and dirt.

The classiest setting for gaming is at the **Greenbrier Casino Club** built underground under the main entrance area. Exclusive to resort guests and with a dress code, the casino is understated with noiseless slots and table games.

Just in case you think fast living doesn't pay off for citizens, the state keeps more than half of all casino revenues to the tune of a half-billion (yep, that's a "b") dollars each year.

Guns

What's a wild state without weapons? There are more than 30 public shooting ranges and dozens of privately owned commercial or club shooting facilities. Defensive firearm training is available at the **Summit Point Raceway.** A combo cycle and shoot package can be found in Lewisburg with a day of biking on the Greenbrier Trail and a day of shooting on the move and from a vehicle at the **Savannah Lane Shooting Association's** Defensive Handgun Course.

The really big guns are outside Keyser where the 1,640 acre Allegany Ballistics

Lab makes parts for rockets—real rockets used by the U.S. military—in 250 state of the art buildings staffed by a vast array of robots, and hundreds of people. Their parts go on everything from ammunition to shoulder launch anti-tank weapons to Sidewinder air-to-air missiles.

The east coast's largest shooting sports complex, **Peacemaker National**, is one of three that sprang up in Berkeley County when the state limited the public range at Sleepy Creek to shotguns.

Pool Parlor Memories

With the demise of The Strand in Charleston, **The Met** in Morgantown may be the last great outpost of pool hall splendor operated by crusty old owners in the state. The pool hall occupies the same basement area in the Metropolitan Theater that was built for it in 1924, with the same dozen tables—one billiard, eleven pool. Longtime owner, Bill Bonfili, tells poignant stories of old, nearly blind West Virginia University alums clambering down the steep stairs on their walkers, opening the door and saying, with relief: "Nothing's changed since I wasted my youth here." Open from 11am to 3am, the Met begins to get busy around 9:30. Beer and pool are its only products. WVU students and faculty are its primary denizens.

Nightlife With Tractors and Couches

Steve Brown's tractor dealership in Mt. Nebo—a dot along US 19—failed in 1998. He stalled the bank guys who came in their fancy Lincoln to board him up. It started as a joke but three years later, the **Mt. Nebo Tractor Bar** was a huge hit. The showroom and work area of the former dealership are now a bar room with pool tables and a great dance hall with live music every weekend. So that no one forgets the roots, the bar stools are tractor seats and a steel-wheel tractor is painted up as a centerpiece.

When we arrived just before 5pm, the place was locked. Two guys in a pick-up arrived and let us in. "Are you the owners?" I asked. They chuckled. "We're just good customers," they replied as they slipped behind the bar to grab a beer. That beats just knowing your name.

Moose Heads

Thomas is a two street town—one stacked atop the other—in the middle of a lot of empty space. It has art and music and an aura of hipness that transcends its obscure location. Every weekend the **Purple Fiddle** brings musicians and audiences from all over and seats them cozily around a platform stage in worn couches. Oh yes, they claim to have West Virginia's largest beer selection. The front doorway is marked with a moose head.

CHAPTER SIX

Great Plumbing

Mother Nature sets the pace with natural plumbing wonders, especially the network of thermal and mineral springs along the eastern spine of America in West Virginia. The springs bring up source water and nearly a score of rivers on both sides of the Eastern Continental Divide hustle it out to sea. Rivers or creeks run under and past most cities and towns.

Numerous springs inspired man-made plumbing marvels that include historic and contemporary spa towns and resorts.

The Pursuit of Bathing

The presence of the only monument to presidential bathing gives a hint. The official name of the town around the warm mineral waters of **Berkeley Springs** clinches it. George Washington and his cronies named the town Bath when they founded it in 1776 to serve as America's first spa. The town remains Bath today, though the world knows it by the post office name of Berkeley Springs. Real place or state-of-mind, the purpose remains unchanged through history and pre-history: to bathe in and drink the waters.

The water George Washington came to drink and soak in is unchanged—warm, clear and lightly mineralized. It serves as the drinking water for Berkeley Springs, is bottled commercially and available, as the colonial Virginia legislature prescribed, free to the public from a fountain under a 19th century springhouse in **Berkeley Springs State Park.** Thousands of people come regularly from near and far to take the waters home with them. Plastic jugs are a profitable sideline for the Park Foundation.

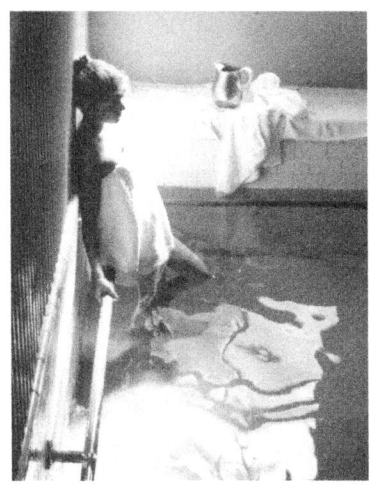

The variety of bathing options and treatments available today would stagger old George, who made do with large hollows scooped from the sand, lined with stone and screened from view by woven brush. His bathtub monument along the west ridge of the park replicates this historic fact, minus the woven brush screens.

Washington could have bathed in two bathhouses. One was a private one built by his mentor, Lord Fairfax in 1768; a wooden one for the public was built in 1784. Today, thousands of people a year re-enact history when they slip into four-foot deep tubs filled with the slightly buoyant, warm mineral waters heated to 104 degrees. All this indulgence takes place in the nine private bathing rooms of the **Roman Bath House,** built in 1815 on the same spot as the original bathhouse. Interested in recouping the costs of a modest renovation of the Roman Baths, the state park encourages bringing a friend—or even two.

The Bathing in Bath Doesn't End in Historic Chambers…

Across the park, there are soak tubs and more Roman Baths in the **Main Bathhouse** built in 1929 and fabulously renovated in 2011. The west ridge of the park between the two bathhouses is lined with wild versions of the baths presenting the largest open display of thermal waters in the Blue Ridge. The wild versions are open 24/7. There's a long channel with tiny waterfalls, where kids love to wade during summer concerts and big pools including one with sinking sands where the springs bubble free.

Trace the waters under streets and bridges throughout Berkeley Springs and other exotic plumbing is revealed. Luxurious pink baths at **The Country Inn's** spa offer a panoramic view of the town. Other private spas and inns have whirlpool baths filled with the same healing springs water. The often-controversial town seal, created in the 1870s, features a barely clad lady sitting at a spring. There's even a Madonna in a bathtub-based grotto at the Catholic Church across from the springs.

The 19th century park bath keeper, old John Davis, believed that the chief end of man was to bathe. While soaking in the waters is still the most direct way to experience Berkeley Springs, there are new pleasures that John Davis never imagined. The historic spa town now boasts three times as many massage therapists as lawyers. Bodywork treatments are provided by trained practitioners, ranging from Reiki masters and a Chinese physician and acupuncturist to the exotic Chinese-Malaysian owner of **Atasia Spa**. The latter has given more than 15,000 massages in the Thai technique he learned from a personal master in the noted Wat Po Buddhist Temple in Bangkok. Mud wraps, aromatherapy, European facials, sugar scrubs and hot stone treatments round out the exotic menu at Berkeley Springs' year 'round spa feast. I am proud to report that I have tried them all and take old John Davis' philosophy one step further by proposing that woman's highest purpose is to pamper her body.

Fire Hoses and an Opulent Pool

It's the incomparable light that makes the first impression. Gold and white and exhilarating, light streams through the billowing white fabric covering the glass dome over the pool and ricochets off topaz mosaics and tile floors. The brightly decorated lounge filled with white rattan, tropical prints and exotic vegetation loves the light.

When built at **The Greenbrier** in 1911, the Roman-inspired indoor pool with its arches and pillars was one of largest in the world. The 100x42 foot pool remains the dominant feature of the **Mineral Baths and Spa** building and the entryway to the recreational spa. Designed as a luxurious "European Cure in America" just in time for World War I, the spa retained the continental flavor of an exclusive clinic. With the turn of the 21st century, the Greenbrier expanded the spa and evolved cutting edge treatments including seasonal scrubs like watermelon, pumpkin and cranberry as well as sea mud packs, paraffin wraps and aromatherapy while keeping traditional favorites.

My spa experience was under the old regime. It began with a white-clad attendant scrubbing me down with seaweed and a loofah mitt. Then I was guided to the Swiss shower and Scotch spray area where I was battered by multiple showerheads and hosed down by another attendant in white. In the next area I was rubbed with moisturizing cream, wrapped in hot towels and left to marinate in preparation for a traditional Swedish massage.

The Greenbrier's sulfur water is available for drinking outside at the distinctive dome built over the spring in 1830 and inside the hotel in the spring room— not that many people drink it these days. Since 1913, drinking water for the hotel has been piped in from Alvon Springs 12 miles away. Both waters are available for baths in the spa.

The Greenbrier began with a miracle cure for rheumatism in 1778. Today there's a unique **Greenbrier Diagnostic Clinic** that includes up to eight hours of face time with your assigned physician — a plethora of preventive care for if you can afford it.

For more on the Greenbrier *see* "Truly Incredible."

Plumbing Wonders of Shepherdstown

Shepherdstown is a shining star of eccentric plumbing. Some of its plumbing marvels are natural, like Town Run, which is fed by 27 springs and surges less than two miles under town buildings and along the main street over drops sufficient to drive the founder's 18th century grist mill. The mill is still standing today and claims to have the largest and oldest overshot waterwheel in the world.

Other marvels are man-made. Each of **The Bavarian Inn's** extensive collection of private whirlpool baths can easily accommodate two. There are piles of large eggshell-white towels and a toiletry basket with body cream, appreciated after a long soak. If the municipality would decrease the chlorine in town water, the Bavarian baths would be perfect.

The European-born owners of the Bavarian provided bidets in nearly all the rooms. This continental indulgence with a strong hygienic argument was a mystery to me. Without instructions, I was forced to follow logic and found it worked. After repeated usage in a brief overnight stay, I added bidets to my list of treatments, like massage, that feel good and are good for you.

Wonder of the World

Known to colonial travelers as Fort Lick for the herds of game that were attracted to its salt springs, Webster Springs' water proved to be the basis of fame and fortune in the 19th and early 20th centuries. The 300-room hotel, owned by CSX railroad and centerpiece of the health resort, burned in 1926. Today, only the foundation of the original springhouse remains.

Webster Springs is one of those towns, like Berkeley Springs, that is known by its postal name. It must be a springs thing. The official name of the municipality is Addison.

★ At 3,860 feet, the outhouse at the raptor lookout on **Peter's Mountain** (*left*) offers the best view in the state.

★ Water is available from the original antique fountains in the halls (*right*) at the **General Lewis Inn.** For more on the Inn, see "Unusual Places to Stay."

★ Sulphurated and void of bacteria, **Pence Springs'** water can sit on a shelf for a year

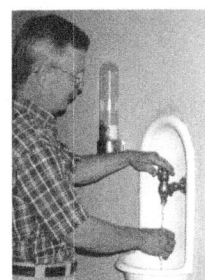

without treatment (left). The springs' former owner, Ashby Berkeley, proclaims it the "best water in the world."

Long favored by wandering animal herds, the springs were first tapped in 1872 when Andrew Pence sank a 30-foot gum log, attached a spigot and began selling bottled water. By the time Pence added a hotel in 1897, the spring area was tiled and he was selling a couple hundred cases of his water each week. In 1904, the water won a silver medal at the St. Louis Worlds Fair, and was sold nationally in ginger ale and root beer through the '20s. Historically, the water has been noted for assisting poor digestion.

★ The 65 degree water of **Capon Springs** was long known to native tribes, and was discovered by colonial settlers in the mid 1760s. While its origin may be a mystery, the mineral content of the water is well known. Calcium bicarbonate predominates, with a rare touch of lithia. It is an alkaloid spring similar to Vichy, France or Carlsbad, Germany.

In a familiar pattern, a town—complete with a small boarding house and cabins—sprang up soon after the founder of Capon Springs brought his wife to be cured. The fame of the water spread and Capon Springs evolved into one of the most fashionable of the 19th century spa resorts along the Virginia/West Virginia border. In mid-century there was a large bath colonnade with forty bathing rooms and hot and cold plunge baths. Water fountains scattered around the green walkways still deliver the famous spring water directly to guests' lips.

To celebrate the 75th anniversary of the current family operation, Capon Springs brought back the baths, missing for nearly a century. A spa building has a bathing wing with large tiled tubs complete with jets for each private room. Family time is set aside in the evenings. The other wing offers massage and reflexology, the latter a third generation experience like much of the rest of the resort.

For more on Pence Springs *see* "Things That Used to Be There"; for Capon Springs, *see* "Unusual Places to Stay."

The Ultimate In Bathing Pleasure

Many West Virginia lodgings are rustic and take advantage of the rugged outdoor beauty of the state. But there are sybaritic pleasures to be found, especially those of the bath.

More than a hundred lodging spaces in every corner of the state offer in-room Jacuzzis or whirlpools for those intimate moments with no bathing suits, no time limits and no sharing with strangers. Here are some favorites.

★ **Highlawn Inn** of Berkeley Springs takes its cue from the world famous warm mineral waters in the park down the hill. This Victorian empire—run by the queen of West Virginia B&Bs, Sandra Kauffman—boasts two rooms with whirlpool baths, a house with a whirlpool room bigger than most bedrooms, and the most elaborate bathroom in the state.

Nothing is more luxurious than a whirlpool bath in the room.

Highlawn's secluded Carriage House has a pink whirlpool bath framed in dark green tin panels from the ceiling of a turn-of-the-century building downtown. Molded with armrests, there's no struggling to stay upright in this tub. A wall of windows and a pair of French doors set on the oblique separate the tub from the bedroom. Adjacent to the tub is a pedestal sink and marble-topped long English washstand with tiled backdrop. The enclosed toilet area flaunts a whimsical triangle window, cut like those on an outhouse door.

★ Three honeymoon cabins at **Smoke Hole Cabins** along the river go all the way with heart-shaped Jacuzzis in front of a roaring fire and satin sheets on the beds. **Black Bear Resort** near Canaan Valley has pedestal homes with two-person whirlpools and luxury cottages with separate spa rooms.

★ Five of the mini-suites at the elegantly restored **Hotel Morgan** have whirlpool tubs. The hotel provides cordless phones in each room allowing for luxurious conversations while bathing—as long as you can out yell the gushing jets. Drop the phone and it becomes more than a whispered endearment that gives you a jolt.

★ Choosing a Jacuzzi with the best view takes you to the palatial Presidential and Royal Suites on the top floor of an Alpine chalet at the **Bavarian Inn** overlooking the majestic Potomac River. The Bavarian also offers river views and whirlpools in more than 30 other rooms.

★ The two-person whirlpool tub at **Country Inns and Suites** is conveniently located next to the bed and within view of the television.

★ An opulent array of restored historic structures comprise the Purple Iris at Hartwood Mansion. The **Carriage House** has been restored and converted into a boutique hotel with three guest rooms each featuring a double whirlpool tub. The Neo-Georgian mansion includes the **Purple Iris** restaurant as well as event rooms all surrounded by landscaped lawns.

★ Six rooms in the contemporary log **North Fork Mountain Inn** have private Jacuzzis. Vacation cottages at **Creekside** have Jacuzzis and a view of Indian Creek. There's also a kidney-shaped pool and a hot tub illuminated at night by fireflies. Harman's **North Fork Cottages** have Jacuzzis and rock fireplaces.

Private Tubs in the Great Outdoors

The luxurious, owner-built **Mill Creek Cabins** heat five whirlpool tubs with two wood burning stoves. Other cabins or chalets with private, outdoor hot tubs abound in the New River Gorge area including **Country Road Cabins** and **Ace Adventure Center's** A-frame chalets.

Heated pools and whirlpool tubs are indoor/outdoor at **Stonewall Jackson Resort** so rain won't ruin your last night soak.

Riverside log, fieldstone and redwood cottages at **Cheat River Lodge** *have seven-foot outdoor hot tubs where soakers can fish from the river.*

For more on springs and bathing, *see* "Things That Used To Be There."

CHAPTER SEVEN

Historic Oddities

For more than 10,000 years, humans have lived within the boundaries of today's West Virginia. Quirks of history have linked U.S. presidents, revolutionaries, rebel spies and labor leaders with the state which itself is a historic oddity—the only one formed at gunpoint from the lands of another state.

The Ancients

Giant skeletons, enormous burial mounds and mystery carvings are found at nearly a hundred primitive sites in West Virginia, remnants of civilizations that reigned long before the pyramids were built in Egypt. With few exceptions, early settlers disregarded these ancient wonders. Since 1990, state law protects all burial remains.

The larger of these burial mounds evidently had sufficient sacred juice to keep the invading white man at bay long enough for the mounds' worth to be appreciated. Farmers and town builders, however, leveled countless smaller ones. A century ago the Smithsonian Institution documented 50 Indian burial mounds in the Mountain State. It was one of the largest groups in America. The mounds were built between 2,000 and 3,000 years ago. Today only a few remain, including the largest conical earthen mound of its kind, **Grave Creek** in Moundsville.

Grave Creek is big and impressive, being 295 feet in diameter and 69 feet high. It is composed of 60,000 tons of earth; all moved by hand more than two millennia ago by a people known to the Indians as "the old ones." Today archeologists call them Adena. Originally a moat, 36 feet wide and four feet deep, surrounded the mound. Although 18th century natives never mentioned the old ones' size, archeologists postulate that they were smaller than modern man. However, evidence of seven-foot-tall giants was found both among mound skeletons as well as etched in stone.

Excavations conducted at Grave Creek twice during the 19th century turned up a crematory, complete with burials ranging from full and partial cremations to the burial of bones or disarticulated flesh. Only a few whole skeletons were found, along with the shell jewelry, weapons, tools, robes, tobacco pipes and food containers buried with them. Also uncovered was a mysterious sandstone tablet etched with runic figures, undeciphered to this day.

Between excavations, local residents treated the mound as a geographic feature worthy of no more respect than the mountains some chewed up for coal. In 1858, a county fair and racetrack operated at the base of the mound. The top was leveled off for a saloon. Soon after, like a macabre joke, the brooding hulk of Moundsville Penitentiary was built within spitting distance. For decades, the warden and his inmates maintained the mound.

Today, there is a museum housing artifacts and telling the story of the mound builders as we know it. Visitors can climb stone steps that spiral up the mound to the stone obelisk and low stonewall at the top. Down on the flatland, I found Marshall's Dairy Bar where an old man, a daily denizen of the place, told me he had been up the mound once as a child.

Cresap Mound, an Adena site with petroglyphs, is about six miles down the Ohio River from Grave Creek. Dated to about 2 B.C., Cresap was excavated in 1958 and found to contain 54 human burials. The mound is 15 feet high and about 70 feet in diameter.

At 35 feet high and 175 feet in diameter, the **South Charleston Mound** is second in size to Grave Creek. It has a similar recent history including horse races held at its base in the 1840s. Built near the Kanawha River, it was first identified in 1803, and excavated by the Smithsonian Institution 80 years later. A giant skeleton surrounded by a dozen others was found along with the requisite artifacts.

The South Charleston Mound is now a small park marked by *Burial Attendants*, a modern sculpture by Cubert Smith. Stone steps spiral up the mound to a circle of stone at the top, where you can look down on a decidedly non-sacred scene of major industrial plants. Other burial mounds are found nearby in Sunset Memorial Cemetery in Spring Hill, Shawnee Golf Course in Institute, and South Charleston High School campus.

Continuing the tradition of mound as entertainment, present-day **Camden Park**, the amusement park outside Huntington, is home to the third largest mound in the state. A 20-foot high conical Indian burial mound lies alongside the vintage roller coaster and bumper cars. It has never been excavated, although at one time the top was flattened and it was used in the early 1900s as a concert bandstand for the park.

The **Romney Mound** remains true to its original purpose and is the center of the Indian Mound Cemetery at the western edge of town. Reportedly the largest Hopewell Indian burial mound east of the Ohio River, the seven-foot mound was never excavated. Based on other excavations, tribal populations in the South Branch date back to at least 6000 B.C.

Oak Mound in Harrison County is twelve feet high and was never excavated. Other mounds are nearby in West Milford.

Other archaic sites include **Ben's Run** in Tyler County, one of the most extensive Indian fortifications remaining in the United States. Two parallel walls of stone and earth are three miles in length and enclose an area of more than 400 acres.

Nearly 9,000 years ago, Ice Age hunters valued **Blennerhassett Island**. The site of the reconstructed mansion was formerly occupied by one of the earliest sedentary villages in the region dating to about 1000 A.D. Later villages grew as large as 1,000 inhabitants who existed on a simple agricultural way of life supplemented with deer and fish. For more on the extensive collection of ancient artifacts housed at the Blennerhassett Museum, *see* "Remarkable Collections."

Petroglyphs are identified at twenty-seven recorded sites in sixteen West Virginia counties. Some of the most significant in the eastern United States have been found along the Guyandotte River in the small town of Salt Rock, Cabell County. Indian Cave petroglyphs are easily accessible in the small Harrison County town of Goodhope. Wildcat petroglyphs showing birds and a beaver are found on a large rock near the banks of a creek leading to the Big Sandy River in Wayne County. Symbols or figures rubbed or pecked into sandstone with flint, petroglyphs are used like runes by shamans to embody information and magical technique. Images found in West Virginia range from birds and serpents to suns, bear tracks and abstract symbols.

A short path from the railroad tracks near **Lilydale** brings you face to face with another set of possibly apocryphal etchings, chalked by contemporary

archeologists as a means of making them more visible for study. The story goes that a group of Irish monks came across the Atlantic centuries before Columbus and made their way to the remote area that is today's Wyoming County. After examination, a controversial linguist claimed the scratchings were Ogam, an ancient Irish alphabet that is composed not of letters but of lines. Allegedly, the carvings translate into an observation by monks that once a year on Christmas the sun shines through a notch in the mountains at that point. Skeptics say the scratchings are more likely the result of Indians sharpening tools on the sandstone. They also point out that an overhang was once blocking the sun on Winter Solstice, and every other day.

One of the most controversial of the petroglyphs is the seven-foot **Maiden of the Rock**. Found on the roof of a natural stone shelter overlooking a small valley in Putnam County, the huge slab has been removed to a mini-park in downtown Hurricane. Although authentic points, stones and tools were found at the site, and the figure matches ones found in other locations, some claim that three Putnam County teens etched—or at least embellished—the figure in 1925.

It's not surprising that monks enterprising enough to work their way from the northern coast to Wyoming County should also make their way a little further west to Mingo County. Another set of controversial petroglyphs described as Irish writing dating from 1200-1400 is enshrined on two huge boulders sitting in state at **Laurel Lake Wildlife Management Area.** The inscribed stones were moved from a future strip mine site near Dingess where they were found in 1987.

Cornstalk's Monument and His Curse

Colonial settlers poured along the rivers and over the mountains into the western wilderness of Virginia, grabbing land wherever they moved. The Shawnee resisted. They laid claim to the lands that are now West Virginia as their ancestral home and hunting grounds. Standing tall and majestic, **Cornstalk** (Keightughqua) was one of the great Shawnee chiefs and leader of the Northwestern Confederacy of native tribes.

The geopolitics of the time made Shawnee and English allies against Americans who were moving west. After an early career as a warrior, Cornstalk saw the merit in compromise and worked to avoid fighting until 1774 when marauding settlers near Wheeling murdered the family of Logan, a friendly Mingo chief.

Reluctantly, Cornstalk began listening to the English who were stirring up trouble on the frontier and abandoned his peace attempts. He led nearly 1,000 Shawnee and other warriors to engage an equal number of Virginia militia. They met on October 10, 1774 in a fierce daylong battle on a thumb of land between the juncture of the Ohio and Kanawha rivers. Hundreds of Indians and Virginians were slaughtered in the hand-to-hand combat. It was the biggest Indian battle to take place on West Virginia soil and one that Cornstalk knew would be the most important the Shawnee would ever fight.

Though Cornstalk led his men away undefeated and met with the Virginians to establish a peace treaty, he would not live to fight again. Three years later, Cornstalk went to warn Americans of an Indian alliance with the British. He was taken hostage along with his son and brutally murdered. The Shawnee retreated west and the Battle of Point Pleasant turned out to be the end of the Indian wars in West Virginia and the Ohio Valley.

Legend has Cornstalk cursing Point Pleasant with his dying words. Twentieth century activities linked to the curse include reported UFO activity and the collapse of the Silver Bridge in 1967 when 46 people died within sight of the historic battlefield.

Today, the four-acre **Tu-Endie-Wei State Park** is dominated by an 86-foot granite obelisk honoring the fallen Virginians and dedicated in 1909. Almost as an afterthought nearly a decade later, a smaller monument was erected to Cornstalk and eventually moved to the park from the Courthouse. His bones are in a metal box at the base of the monument. Later the state park placed rest rooms nearby, hardly a way to relieve the curse.

Cornstalk's daughter, **Aracoma**, comes alive in an outdoor drama bearing her name and performed every summer in **Chief Logan State Park.** Aracoma married Bolling Baker, who shed his white identity and became a Shawnee chief. Both are buried in Logan County.

Geography guaranteed Point Pleasant would always be noticed. Along the river side of the battlefield is a plaque planted in 1749 by French explorer Joseph Celeron de Blainville recording that he had been sent to "re-establish tranquility in some Indian villages." Blainville's exercise planting lead plates at forks of various rivers with the Ohio was part of a French effort to establish sovereignty in the region while the British dilly-dallied. Twenty years later, Ben Franklin proposed the 14th colony of Vandalia west of the mountains, with its capital at Point Pleasant.

Tecumseh

Like Cornstalk, **Tecumseh** was a great Shawnee warrior chief with ties to West Virginia. According to some, he identified a village along Hacker's Creek as his birthplace. Legend has it that in 1806, on a spot overlooking Tenshwatawa Falls at **Holly River State Park**, Tecumseh provided information about an impending solar eclipse which he had gained from a white friend so that Tecumseh's medicine man brother could demonstrate his power.

First Citizen

George Washington was America's premier land developer, and modern-day West Virginia was his favorite piece of 18th century real estate. His footsteps criss-cross the state from the Potomac to the Ohio Rivers. He eventually acquired 30,000 acres in "West Augusta," a common colonial designation for the trans-Allegheny area now known as West Virginia. Some of the land was granted for his service in the French and Indian War, the rest was purchased from other veterans.

America's best-prepared teenager, George began his career at sixteen, surveying the western lands of his native Virginia. Two years later he used his salary as a surveyor to purchase 550 acres along Bullskin Run in Jefferson County. It was 1750 and the beginning of George's lifelong investment in the land that would become West Virginia. He spent a month in 1770 traveling in a canoe from Pittsburgh to Point Pleasant scouting land along both the Kanawha and Little Kanawha rivers. He described this stretch of the river as "the Ohio River crowded with islands." One of the places he stopped along the Ohio is today's Point Park, site of Parkersburg's early settlement and docking point for the boat trip to Blennerhassett Island.

Many farms still follow the boundaries Washington set while surveying the Lost River and Capon Valley area from 1748-52. In Wayne County, he named a creek Twelve Pole because it was twelve poles or rods wide. He surveyed land above the Ohio River at Parkersburg for the **Henderson Hall** land grant signed by Patrick Henry, then governor of Virginia. The telescope he used for surveying the Kanawha Valley is on display in the **State Museum.** Other artifacts are housed in the **Washington Western Lands Museum** at the Great Bend of the Ohio near Ravenswood where Washington owned 6,700 acres in two tracts.

Washington patented a tract of 587 acres in Round Bottom in 1784 that today is the site of the Washington Lands Elementary School. He patented nearly 5,000 acres that embraced the sites of today's towns of St. Albans and Dunbar. In 1775, he patented 125 acres on the Kanawha River upstream from Malden that contained a bituminous spring (oil and gas) making George a pioneer in West Virginia's 19th century mining industry. Washington described the spring in his will. "It burns as freely as spirits and is as difficult to extinguish."

From the beginning, Washington focused on filling the western wilderness with prosperous industry and communities. He supported early iron smelting and hired inventor James Rumsey to design locks for navigating the Potomac River. He foreshadowed the Morgantown Chamber of Commerce when he met with Morgan Morgan's son at John Pierpont's home in 1784 to discuss the feasibility of a trade route through the area to the Ohio River. Rating Harpers Ferry as the "most eligible spot on the river" (Potomac) for one of two federal gun factories, Washington lobbied hard for his district and the famous armory was built there.

As a young officer in the French and Indian War, Washington marched his militia through Hampshire County and ordered a string of forts built along the South Branch of the Potomac in 1755 to protect the frontier. The area returned the favor and provided beef to feed Washington's soldiers during both the French and Indian War and later at Valley Forge. Only one of these frontier forts remains: **Fort Ashby** in Mineral County. Washington used this frontier fort again in 1791 when he mustered soldiers of the region here to aid in suppressing the Whiskey Rebellion.

George Washington could even rank as West Virginia's first white water rafter having run the rapids of the Potomac near Harpers Ferry.

Although most of the land he owned was west of the mountains, it was today's Eastern Panhandle that captured his heart leading the area to establish the **Washington Heritage Trail**, a national scenic byway. During an early buying spree, Washington and his brother Lawrence acquired tens of thousands of

acres in Jefferson County. The area elected him to his first political office in the Virginia House of Burgesses. Brother Charles inherited much of the acreage and established **Charles Town** in 1786 with streets named for family members. Today, Washington-related sites are everywhere including a half dozen family homes open for occasional tours and a cave marked with his signature. His first purchase—Rock Hall Tract—is now the location of **Hillbrook Inn**, a European-style country house hotel with rooms on eight levels of limestone ridge. It's noted for its seven course dinners. Almost 80 Washington family members are buried in the **Zion Episcopal Church Cemetery** (1852) in the center of Charles Town, including at least three George Washington namesakes. The **Jefferson County Museum** has one of the last letters ever written by Washington, as well as one of only three copies of the first printing of his will.

Washington raised numerous troops from the Eastern Panhandle and a historic rumor claims that he once considered Shepherdstown for the nation's capital. In 1775 when the Continental Congress issued the first call for troops, The Berkeley Riflemen marched from Morgan's Springs, near Shepherdstown, in two groups, starting July 15 and July 17. Moving quickly on a **"bee-line"**, they reached Boston on August 10. Among the first soldiers from outside New England, no company rendered more faithful service during the Revolutionary War. In recognition of this, when it looked as if the newly established country might be losing, Washington said "Give me but a banner to plant upon the mountains of West Augusta and I will gather around me the men who will lift our bleeding country from the dust and set her free." Mountain hearts truly do breathe free.

His bathtub monument in the state park highlights the intimate relationship Washington sustained with **Berkeley Springs**. According to his journals, "ye fam'd warm springs" was the first West Virginia stop on his initial surveying trip into Lord Fairfax's wilderness in 1748. He returned to the rough spa town with his family several times over the next two decades, and prized his large tract of land west of town along the Potomac. He would ride daily to Prospect Rock and use the panoramic view to fuel his dreams of a way west. When Lord Fairfax's domain was "liberated" in 1776, Washington's family and friends established the town of Bath around the springs and George bought two prime lots. After the Revolutionary War, he resumed his pre-war habit of "taking the waters" at Bath and contracted with James Rumsey to build him a summer house there. Two wooden shacks resulted, hyped during the 20th century into "the first summer white house."

Gat Caperton reenacts George Washington's first visit to "ye fam'd warm springs" in 1748.

Another Famous Washington

Booker T. Washington was a freed slave who migrated from Virginia after the Civil War, with his mother and siblings, to the saltworks known as the Kanawha Salines. He walked back to Virginia to attend college at Hampton Institute and then returned to Malden where he married a local girl and began his career as one of America's most notable educators. At the age of 25, he was selected as the first president of the vocational college that evolved into Alabama's Tuskegee University. Historic sites connected to Washington are preserved in Malden's Walking Tour including the African Zion Baptist Church where he learned to read. Behind the church is a reconstruction of Washington's boyhood cabin. The charming Women's Park surrounds the site of his sister Amanda's brick home

Cleopatra of the South

Told at age ten that she was too young to attend a party her father was throwing, **Belle Boyd** countered by riding her pony into the ballroom of the 27-room house in Martinsburg that serves today as her museum. Belle's willful and impulsive nature earned her a prominent place during the Civil War, one of the few women to grace the history of that period.

When Union forces captured Martinsburg in 1861, a blue-clad soldier manhandled Belle's mother as she tried to defend her Confederate flags. The 18-year-old Belle promptly shot the man, thus beginning a career that would find her in and out of jail, condemned and lauded as a Rebel spy.

Repeatedly, Belle used her considerable charms to wheedle information from Union soldiers, which she then turned over to the Confederacy, once saving Stonewall Jackson from a Yankee attack. Sent on a mission to London, Belle was captured at sea. She wooed the U.S. Navy officer who was her captor, promising to marry him if he defected with a book of information. He agreed and the pair had a big wedding in London. After another round of arrests and releases, former Captain Harding and his wife Belle took to the London stage, a career that Belle continued even after their divorce. She eventually performed in America with her third husband, an actor half her age.

Belle contributed to her own legend publishing her book, *Belle Boyd in Camp and Prison* in 1865. Though the portrait that hangs over the museum's mantle shows a fierce looking brunette with a prominent nose, a recently discovered period letter described her as a "black-eyed vixen...courted and flattered by every lieutenant and captain in the service," because of her "smart pertness, quickness of retort and utter abandon of manner and bearing...". Belle's lifetime of exploits attests to a seductive power the popular press captured when it labeled her "Cleopatra of the South."

Unusual Places With Notable History

★ In 1855, Thomas Friend carved three huge wine cellars with two foot thick walls from a stone mountain near Dunbar, reportedly once owned by George Washington. For six years they served as the site of a thriving wine making industry. After that they were never used again, possibly because the true purpose was to serve as way stations on the Underground Railroad.

Restored in 1981 as the centerpiece of a 316-acre city park, **Dutch Hollow Wine Cellars** are one of only two such cellars east of the Mississippi. The heavy wooden doors on the cellars are locked at night and re-opened early each morning, ostensibly to avoid nighttime boarders.

★ Discovered in 1704, Thomas Jefferson found the bones of a three-toed sloth in his 1791 visit to **Organ Cave.** He sent its eight-inch long toenails to the Institute of Science in 1797 while the jawbones were displayed at Monticello. Mined since 1812  for the saltpeter needed to make gunpowder, it was a prime source of the material for the South. Thirty-seven of Robert E. Lee's saltpeter hoppers remain in the cave—the largest intact collection in America. Ranked as one of the largest caves in the United States, it was large enough to shelter a thousand Confederate soldiers one winter, and is filled with their Civil War graffiti. The cave is named for the 40-foot calcite column that once emitted beautiful music when struck with a hammer. Damaged by souvenir hunters over the years, the column is now silent.

For more on touring Organ Cave *see* "Tours and Trips."

★ Untouched for more than 135 years, **Fort Mill Ridge Trenches** are among the best-preserved Civil War earthworks in existence. The huge fortification is perched atop Mill Creek Mountain, just west of Romney. The panoramic view of Mechanicsburg Gap demonstrates why Union forces selected this location and invested three months in 1863 digging an outer circle of nearly a mile of three to four foot deep trenches connected to an inner circle that protects an earthen walled fort. A hard-packed trail guides visitors to the site. Signs provide abundant information to interpret the story that the trenches and earth forms tell.

Romney was a hotbed of guerilla activity during the Civil War changing hands 56 times, a record of activity second only to Winchester, Virginia. In 1862 Stonewall Jackson penned his resignation at a still-standing Romney house only to reconsider and continue the fight. McNeil's Rangers were active in the region.

The heart of the region was clearly with the South. In 1867, the Daughters of Old Hampshire made their sympathies known by constructing the first monument in the country to Confederate soldiers. The ten-foot white marble pillar topped by an urn and bearing the names of dozens of soldiers, was erected cheek to jowl with the cemetery's Indian Mound. It is dedicated to "her heroic sons who fell in defense of southern rights." This followed the nation's first decoration of Confederate graves that took place there the previous year.

★ Lord Fairfax considered the western limit of his land to be the headspring of the North Branch of the Potomac River. In 1746, one of the oldest markers in the United States was set at that spot on Backbone Mountain. That marker, the **Fairfax Stone,** was used to establish the state boundaries of Maryland, Virginia and Pennsylvania as part of the Mason-Dixon surveying mission. In 1767, the western terminus of that famous line was set on Browns Hill, northwest of Morgantown. It was the first scientifically accurate boundary in the then-American colonies. Determined by the secant method using star positions it delineated the joint boundaries of Pennsylvania, Maryland, Delaware and Virginia and evolved into the de facto division between north and south more than a century later.

Daniel Boone, founder of Kentucky, left that state because of land title disputes. He ended up in Charleston and was elected to represent Kanawha County in the Virginia Assembly in 1791.

The current stone—a six-ton natural boulder with a bronze tablet—is the fifth to be used as the marker. Souvenir hunters chipped all the previous stones away. The original was reportedly a sandstone pyramid with the letters FX engraved. The second was destroyed by vandals in 1884 and a similar stone was created and placed by a local coal company. A pyramid-shaped concrete marker was set by the Joint Boundary Commission in 1910. West Virginia replaced that version in 1957 when the state acquired the landmark and made it part of the park system.

HISTORIC ODDITIES

Another historic geographic starting point is found just north of Chester. A monument marks the place where Thomas Hutchins, first geographer of the United States, began the **Line of the Seven Ranges** in 1785.

More Weird Historical Flashes

★ Robert E. Lee's horse, Traveller, came from a farm in Greenbrier County. Lee first saw the horse near his camp during the Sewell Mountain campaign in 1861, and bought him from Major Thomas Brown of Charleston for $200.

★ Two municipalities in what would become the state of West Virginia were incorporated on the same day in 1762. Both **Shepherdstown** and **Romney** lay claim to being the oldest town in West Virginia. Purists would award the title to Romney since Shepherdstown was incorporated originally as Mecklenburg.

★ Anticipating continued growth, in 1901 town fathers of Union placed the 20-foot **Monroe County Confederate Monument** in an empty field south of town (*above*). Today it is still an almost empty field. The Italian marble statue carved in Hinton remains on its native blue limestone base in the middle of nowhere, surrounded by grazing cows. Union has always had an attachment to the military having earned its name from the union of militia units that mustered in the Royal Oak Field each spring and fall from the 1790s through the Civil War.

★ The small town of **Alderson,** split by the Greenbrier River and CSX railroad, has population in three counties: Greenbrier, Monroe and Summers. Memorial Bridge links the two sides of town and was built in 1914. Today, the bridge is open only to foot traffic. At 453 feet, it is the longest earth-filled reinforced concrete arch bridge in the state. Tiny **Montgomery** owes allegiance to only two counties- Fayette and Kanawha.

★ **John W. Davis** of Clarksburg is the only West Virginian to run for U.S. President, so far. A prominent attorney who ranked with Daniel Webster in arguing the most cases before the Supreme Court, Davis was nominated by Democrats on the 103rd ballot. He ran in 1924 against Calvin Coolidge. He lost the election, West Virginia and his home county of Harrison.

Davis was noted for his independence, refusing to give up his New York law practice to make himself more acceptable as a Democratic nominee. The speech he broadcast from his front yard in 1924 was the first political speech ever broadcast over the radio in the U.S.

★ **Charleston** was finally selected as West Virginia's capital through both the oratory of 21-year-old Booker T. Washington and the generosity of John Lowlow the clown, who allowed a pair of Charleston leaders to travel with the circus and speak for their position.

In 1921, major explosions from truckloads of guns and ammunition seized during mine wars and stored in the **State Capitol** *attic caused the building to burn down.*

★ Widely known through folk tunes, the steel-driving **John Henry** was memorialized in 1972 by a larger-than-life bronze statue—2.5 tons and eight feet tall, to be precise—in a small park above Big Bend Tunnel in Talcott. John Henry allegedly challenged the track-building machine a century earlier. Eyewitnesses claim the competition was fact and that ex-slave John Henry collapsed after beating the machine, never to work again. The 6,500-foot tunnel was carved through the mountain from 1870-72 for the C&O railroad; a twin tunnel was added in 1932. Rail traffic through Big Bend Tunnel ceased in 1974.

★ In 1995, famous television and movie actress Mary Tyler Moore purchased a red brick home built by her great-great-great-grandfather, Conrad Schindler, Jr. on German Street in Shepherdstown. She turned it over to Shepherd College for use as a scholarly research center on the Civil War and named it the **George Tyler Moore Center** after her father.

★ Lydia Boggs Shepherd Cruger reportedly had "a way with a man." According to local legend, she was able to persuade Henry Clay in 1819 to reroute the **National Road** right past her home, making Wheeling rather than Wellsburg the road's western end. In return, the Shepherds erected a stone monument to Clay on the property. The Georgian stone mansion was built in 1798 by her husband, Moses Shepherd, and hosted such notables as Lafayette, Andrew Jackson, James Polk and the memorialized Clay. Today, Lydia's stone house is the headquarters of the Osiris Masonic Temple.

★ In 1780, Mike Fink—legendary mountain man and fighter—and Adam O'Brien were hunting at Low Gap in today's Calhoun County when they were fired on by a pair of Indians. Fink killed one; the other killed him. **Mike Fink's Grave** is a roadside shrine.

★ Two iron doors, an odd key and an unusual bolt draw lock mechanism attest to the former life of a contemporary law office in Weston. Once the Exchange

Bank of Virginia, the safe room held $28,000 in gold, captured when Virginia seceded. It became seed money for the new West Virginia treasury.

★ A 20th century bluegrass tune speculates on the story of a 19th century grave meticulously chiseled from a boulder near the Ohio River. It is rumored that wealthy homesteader Benjamin Willard liked his drink so much he wanted the stone grave to be filled with fine whiskey, his body to be placed in it and the entire cocktail covered with glass. It never happened. Nearly seven feet long, three feet deep and three feet wide, the **grave in the rock** remains a local wonder.

In A Class By Itself

The only town with its own national historic park, **Harpers Ferry** has a long and notable pedigree, beginning with Mother Nature's attributes. Located at a break in the Blue Ridge, where the Shenandoah and Potomac rivers meet, Harpers Ferry has always been an important stop on the way west, by either boat or train.

George Washington gave Harpers Ferry's destiny a boost when he built a Federal armory there in 1794. Eventually a complex of twenty buildings, the armory was the site of important industrial firsts. The first U.S. military rifle was built there, as well as the first percussion rifle. John Hall was first to perfect the use of machine-produced interchangeable parts on an industrial scale at the armory rifle works on Virginius Island. In 1803, Meriwether Lewis came to the armory to get guns and the unique metal boat frame he took to explore the Louisiana Territory with William Clark.

On the eve of the Civil War, Harpers Ferry was booming. The armory drew the railroad and both made Harpers Ferry the most valuable property along the emerging north/south border. When a radical Ohioan who dreamed of establishing a black republic in the hills of Maryland seized the arsenal in 1859, he wanted the 100,000 rifles stored there. **John Brown** initiated the spirit of the Civil War with his failed insurrection and Harpers Ferry was ultimately destroyed in the process. In one of those odd quirks of history, Brown was captured by U.S. Marines led by Robert E. Lee and J.E.B. Stuart. Luke Quinn was the only soldier killed in Brown's raid. A U.S. Marine, Quinn is buried in a cemetery along the highway. A Marine flag flies daily over his grave.

Two years later, Lee and Stuart were on the other side of the Civil War and the armory had been burned and dismantled by both sides along with bridges, railroads and much of the town. The largest surrender of U.S. forces until 1942 took place in 1862 when Stonewall Jackson took Harpers Ferry and 12,693 Union troops.

The 1870 flood finished the area as an industrial power when it washed away Virginius Island where a third of the town and much of its industrial infrastructure had been located. Today only the ruins of a pulp mill remain on the island.

The National Park Service restored a dozen buildings, as well as the third of the town along the riverfront, to their respective condition in 1859, which was Harpers Ferry's height of fame and fortune. Today, many of the municipality's 300 residents live in more than 125 historic houses. The town also boasts a charming row of shops, tightly climbing the cobblestoned hill up from the riverfront; the latter being the lowest point in West Virginia. **Harper Cemetery** offers both ancient gravesites and a spectacular view of the Shenandoah River. Summertime tours and living reenactments are replaced in winter by stark views and the solitude to explore museums, exhibits and trails on your own.

Storer College was established in four abandoned government mansions on Harpers Ferry's Camp Hill in 1867 as one of the earliest institutions for educating former slaves. At its peak, Storer had 100 students and 20 buildings. W.E.B. DuBois held the first meeting of the Niagara Movement on U.S. soil in

1906 in the town, drawn by Storer and the legacy of John Brown's raid. The meeting prompted establishment of the NAACP to take aggressive civil rights action.

Closed in 1955, historic Storer College now houses the Mather Training Center of the National Park Service. Its grounds are open and an informative display is housed in one of the park buildings in town. For more on Harpers Ferry *see* "Things That Used To Be There" and "Amazing Architecture."

Treason!

Jefferson County Courthouse was constructed in 1836 on land donated by Charles Washington. Its fame derives not from its Greek Revival architecture or its Washington heritage, but from a historic roll of the dice that made the courthouse the setting for two of America's three pre-World War II treason trials.

Within two months of his capture in 1859, John Brown was tried there for his Harpers Ferry insurrection. He was jailed in the building now used for the Charles Town Post Office. Crowds of onlookers watched from a farmhouse as he was hung in a nearby field. Today the farmhouse is the Iron Rail Inn and the hanging site is a private residence at 515 Samuel Street. Future presidential assassin, John Wilkes Booth, came to town for the trial and gave dramatic readings from Shakespeare in the Episcopal Reading Room.

In 1922, four union leaders and more than 700 miners were indicted for various crimes—including treason against the state—as part of the **Battle of Blair Mountain,** a rebellion of 10,000 miners against coal company officials in Logan County. The only trials that ever occurred were the few staged in Jefferson County, including that of William Blizzard. Leader of the uprising, Blizzard was later acquitted of treason.

Forgotten Inventor

History books credit Robert Fulton with the first successful steamboat, but Eastern Panhandle devotees of **James Rumsey** claim the honor for their guy. Working in Berkeley Springs and Shepherdstown more than twenty years before Fulton, Rumsey was an inventive character who left behind a trail of mill buildings and steam engine trials. He won the support of George Washington for his new method of boat propulsion, and his efforts to protect his inventions led directly to the patent system in the U.S. Constitution.

In December 1787, Rumsey and eight Shepherdstown ladies successfully tested his steamboat on the Potomac River, a short distance from the ford of the river where townspeople watched. From Shepherdstown, Rumsey went to England with the support of Benjamin Franklin who established the Rumseian Society. Rumsey died in London in 1792, literally on the eve of success.

A sleek Ionic column of granite topped with a globe was erected to honor Rumsey in 1914. A half-scale working version of Rumsey's steamboat, displacing 5,000 pounds, was built in the 1980s by Shepherdstown aficionados who float it about once a year. On weekends during the summer season, the boat can be seen at the Rumsey boathouse behind the Entler Hotel. Another Rumsey exhibit, featuring more than twenty of his patents, is housed in the **Museum of the Berkeley Springs**.

America's Most Famous Feud

Long, complicated and still debated, the feud between the **Hatfield and McCoy** families was the original example of what tabloid media exploitation can do to fact. The feud spanned nearly 60 years and was entangled in war, politics and labor battles, in Matewan and across the river in Kentucky. It began when two families found themselves on opposite sides in the Civil War, then continued with lawsuits over ownership of a pig and a Hatfield/McCoy forbidden romance and abandonment. These disputes resulted in 13 killings in both families during the 1880s. The governors of Kentucky and West Virginia called up the National Guard in each state but thankfully faced off in court instead of on a battlefield. Tabloid news coverage of the feud by a *New York World* reporter was turned into a book. Published in 1889, it introduced the hillbilly image to the world. The Greek tragedy allure of the feud was turned into a *History Channel* television mini-series in 2012 that resulted in the highest ratings ever for commercial cable.

"Peace in the Valley" was finally declared in 1978 when the feud was officially ended during the dedication of a McCoy family monument in Kentucky.

In 1920, Sid Hatfield was Chief of Police in Matewan. He sided with the miners and locals in a battle against the coal company and their Baldwin-Felts detectives. The **Old Matewan National Bank** building in the center of town has bullet holes in brick walls and second floor windows from the deadliest gunfight in American history. A self-guided audiotape explaining the battle is mounted on the outside wall. This May 19 conflict continued through that summer with strikes, blown up railroad cars and beaten miners. The National Guard and State Police attempted to keep order. On August 1, 1921, Hatfield was gunned down by retaliating detectives on the McDowell County Courthouse steps in Welch. Later in the month, miners staged a violent uprising at Blair Mountain. John Sayles captured this bloody chapter in his film *Matewan*.

For more on Matewan *see* "Truly Incredible."

Labor History

Federal troops were used for the first time during a labor strike in 1877 at the **B&O Roundhouse** in Martinsburg.

More than 40 years later, labor unrest unleashed another military first. Bomber squadrons commanded by General Billy Mitchell were ordered to the Blair Mountain uprising, the only time that military aircraft were used by the United States against its own people. Six bombers were wrecked by accidents in the mountains. The five-day battle of Blair Mountain along a 17-mile front in August 1921 pitted 3,000 deputies and mine guards against 10,000 armed coal miners led by William Blizzard in the largest armed insurrection in the United States since the Civil War. The battle and subsequent treason trials prevented the United Mine Workers from organizing in the state for more than a decade. Many artifacts of the battle remain and supporters are fighting to keep **Blair Mountain** from being mined.

In 1907, 361 miners died at **Monongah** in Marion County in the worst coal mine disaster in the United States. Two large coal mines were wrecked by a series of explosions and fires. Four men escaped through air holes; all but one died a few days later.

Completed in 1932, the construction of the **Hawks Nest Diversion Tunnel** was the worst industrial disaster in the United States. Of the 2,000 miners who worked cutting a 40-foot square, 3.2-mile long tunnel through the almost pure silica rock of Gauley Mountain, few escaped having their lungs shredded by glass-like dust. Their deaths triggered a Congressional investigation four years later and eventually led to recognition of acute silicosis as an occupational disease. The tunnel served to redirect the New River through the mountain to Union Carbide's power plant on the other side. Today, the tunnel mouth lies hidden behind huge green doors visible from **Hawks Nest State Park** overlook.

Rumor has it that Jimmy Hoffa may be buried at the **Pullman Plaza Hotel** in Huntington. The last project he was known to be working on was this Teamster-built hotel. There is a storage room with a poured concrete floor that no one can explain.

Never Surrender

Known as the Alsace Lorraine of the United States

*The Hatfield clan patriarch, **Devil Anse Hatfield**, is captured in an impressive, life-sized Italian marble statue in the family cemetery near Sarah Ann. He was immortalized for millions as portrayed by Kevin Costner in the Hatfield and McCoy mini-series. Another notable Hatfield was the outlaw Belle Starr's mother.*

for its politics not its minerals, Jefferson County continued to think of itself as a nation in exile—part of Virginia—until World War II. The mother state agreed and twice sued for the return of its three counties—Jefferson, Berkeley and Morgan. It was 1871 before the local Jefferson County newspaper accepted the inevitable and placed West Virginia on its masthead.

Wheeling and National History

★ At **Wheeling Airport's** terminal museum, you can sit in the leather chairs that once supported the bottoms of John and Jacqueline Kennedy while they waited for delays in ground transportation to Wheeling during the 1960 presidential campaign.

★ On September 24, 1952, candidate Dwight D. Eisenhower met at Wheeling Airport with the man who shared his ticket—Richard Nixon. At that meeting, the first since Nixon's controversial "Checkers" speech, Ike made the decision to keep Dick on the ticket. And, as the saying goes, the rest is history.

★ An obscure Wisconsin politician, Joe McCarthy, got his start on Lincoln's Birthday in 1950 when he addressed a Wheeling Republican Women's Club on February 9 and waved a piece of paper claiming to be a list of Communists in key positions throughout the government.

A Pair of Statues in the Woods

Chief Logan of the Mingo tribe is commemorated in various sectors of the state. Deep in Monongahela National Forest on WV 51 at Mingo in Randolph County there is a large statue of him. A little further along the same road is another historic statue. This one is a young Robert E. Lee, rare for being clean-shaven.

CHAPTER EIGHT

Local Food Specialties and Memorable Eateries

Locals in certain parts of West Virginia will often tell visitors: "There's a place in _____ but it's always closed *'cause nobody eats there."* Ignore the stereotypes. People are not starving and living off road kill in West Virginia no matter what impression comes from state legislation removing the criminal status of picking up roadkill for the pantry. There are unique food treats and world class dining to be found in the Mountain State.

The State Food Of West Virginia

It's the food that Mountaineers have shipped around the globe, that brings them back again and again no matter where they roam. "It's a valued commodity in my world, traded regularly for housing," said one devotee. Generally available for a dollar, it's a primary food group for struggling artists and students, and the only food I found worthy of a quest. Everyone I interviewed agreed with my choice—**pepperoni rolls** are the ultimate state food of West Virginia.

Giuseppe Agiro invented the taste treat in 1927 as a one-hand, one-bite lunch treat for Fairmont coal miners. His son "Cheech" continued the tradition at the family's **Country Club Bakery** making about 4,000 of the famous rolls a day for area stores until his death in 2002. The baking continues under the ownership of the Pallotta family.

From its Fairmont birthplace, pepperoni rolls have spread to dominate a quadrant of the state from Morgantown to Weston. When I asked a 16-year-old in Elkins where I could search out a pepperoni roll, she looked at me as if wondering where my home planet was. "In any gas station," she said.

The concentrated geography made my quest for the perfect pepperoni roll logistically easy, balancing the impossibility of identifying culinary champs. Even the knock-off versions located near the cappuccino station at every convenience store in the pepperoni district are edible.

Here are my observations from extensive and ongoing tasting sprees.

The traditional pepperoni roll is the six-inch torpedo still made today by **Country Club**—cholesterol-free plain yeast dough rolled around two thick sticks of spicy pepperoni. The bread bakes into twin tunnels around the pepperoni sticks that, in turn, soak the fluffy white bread with their oil, making the inner core the ultimate taste sensation. A packaged dozen pepperoni rolls bought at the bakery are an incredible bargain.

Most supermarkets in the pepperoni district make their own rolls, as well as stocking one or two boutique brands like Mama Leona's of Dailey. Several convenience store clerks assured me that people do have their favorites. Supermarket and convenience store knock-offs generally use sliced pepperoni, a step down in taste intensity. Sliced pepperoni also lacks the bite quality a stick provides. Cheese can often be found as a component of the core. Not always a tasty addition, the cheese can be a problem when eating the pepperoni roll cold. Agiro, the inventor's son, avoids using cheese because "good cheese melts out."

The bread is generally improved with heating, although I've found using a microwave degrades the pepperoni sticks. However, to serve as quality road or trail food, pepperoni rolls have to be acceptable at body temperature.

All the bread is basic white and usually undistinguished. Exceptions include the originals from Country Club and the large, almost-glazed bun with abundant sliced pepperoni and cheese homemade at **Tony's Butcher Block** in Berkeley Springs. Tony and I starred in a serendipitous video for **American Food Roots** magazine discussing the merits of pepperoni rolls as a root food.

My favorite pepperoni roll breakfast—a bag of three-inch long fingers with stick pepperoni—came from **Tomaro's**, a family bakery in Clarksburg. It's important to note that this northern tier city with a strong Italian population base also claims to be the pepperoni roll homeplace. **D'Annunzio's Health Bread Company** touts the product made at their 80-year-old Italian bakery as the "crème de la crème" of pepperoni rolls.

I had the ultimate pepperoni roll experience with a modified version that would disqualify it from consideration by purists. I turned off US 33 onto SR 20 heading into Buckhannon. On the left a sign caught my eye. *DONUTS* read the top line; *Pepperoni Rolls* read the next. Obviously, this was not a chain. I ordered a 99¢ pepperoni roll, not quite certain what I was getting. I jumped in the car and drove off, taking a bite, then another. Incredible! Ground pepperoni, sautéed and put in a large square white bun and layered with spicy cheese. "It's not a pepperoni roll unless the meat is baked in the bread," said one expert with disdain. Whatever it was, I turned the car around and went back for a second one. Later, a certified insider nodded his agreement. "That's the **Donut Shop**, where everyone goes for breakfast," he said about my Buckhannon find.

The pepperoni is chunked in **Colasessano's** overstuffed version, served in a large, crispy roll with homemade tomato sauce, melted cheese and peppers. A family business in Fairmont for 80 years, Colasessano's evolved from a crammed neighborhood beer joint and political center to a still tiny carry-out and bakery, providing frozen pizzas to stores around town. The traditional footrest and bar countertop remain, handy for waiting while the roll is prepared. It's a busy place and their pepperoni rolls are bought in multiples.

It's not all smooth sailing and thick sticks in the world of pepperoni rolls. The federal government tried to impose meat shop rules on West Virginia bakeries making pepperoni rolls but after a major battle, the state legislature prevailed and ruled that pepperoni rolls do not require a meat handlers license.

To take your own pepperoni roll tour, stop at every convenience store and grocery chain along I-79 with gourmet stops in Clarksburg, Fairmont, and Buckhannon. The tour gets tricky when you reach the Eastern Panhandle. In 2007, the Harrison County Rogers and Mazza Italian Bakery started delivering their traditional pepperoni rolls to nearly a dozen convenience stores in Martinsburg. **Shepherdstown Sweet Shop Bakery** makes their own version of the treat while **King's Pizza** in Martinsburg offers a delicious but heretical New York version where a diaper of pizza dough enfolds pepperoni slices and cheese accompanied by a tiny dipping container of marinara sauce.

As the birthplace of the famous treat, Fairmont has the right to celebrate with the world's first (and probably only) pepperoni roll world eating championship annually at the **Three Rivers Festival.** This follows professional and amateur pepperoni roll bake-offs. I'm still waiting to be invited as a judge.

King Hot Dog

Pepperoni rolls may be the state food, but hot dogs have more iconic locations. How to accessorize your dog is the source of a longstanding conflict: sauerkraut or cole slaw?

If someone offers you a taste of **West Virginia cole slaw** and you are not sitting at a lunch counter somewhere, turn it down unless you are a fan of Mail Pouch chewing tobacco. For more on Mail Pouch, *see* "Art Wonders."

Mail order chili has **The Custard Stand** producing more than a thousand pounds a day of the sweet, meat-rich topping for hot dogs invented by the

current owners' grandfather in the 1920s. What doesn't get shipped out goes to some of the 50,000 hot dogs sold at their four locations there all year. To eat it at the source, drive up to the original family-owned rustic eatery in Webster Springs.

We were over-impressed dining at **Hillbilly Hot Dogs** (*left*) especially when a young couple from Los Angeles explained they'd driven 100 miles out of their way just to experience the place. They sang the *We Got the*

Weenies theme song from HHD's website explaining that it was a favorite in their office at Disney. The girls in the kitchen regularly sing the song after clanging the dinner bell to announce: *Your dog is ready, come get it!* The dining room is a pair of renovated school buses with stools and a decor that includes a stuffed vampire. Hot dog choices range from junkyard dog to hound dog and include the 15-inch home wrecker.

Carhops have been the mainstay of **Stewarts Original Hot Dogs** in Huntington since 1932. Once a job only for boys, today's curb service is provided by girls as well. Not much else has changed. It's the same location, same family and same secret chili sauce on the hot dogs. Stewarts supports other Huntington businesses using Logan hot dogs and Heiner's buns. *See* "Tours Not to Miss" for Heiner's.

Another longtime carhop serviced hot dog stand is on SR 10 in Stollings, Logan County. **Morrison's Drive-In** (*right*) features crispy homemade onion rings, a secret hot dog sauce and legions of fans branding their dogs best in the state.

Fairmont's jewel is the shack that lies at the downtown end of the big bridge. Most days around lunchtime people in suits and overalls walk in and out of the shack carrying paper bags and school-size cartons of milk. Inside the shack is a phenomenon most would only assume takes place in bigger cities. **Yann's Hot Dogs** is the home to amazing chili dogs that natives swear by. Mr. Yann, the owner, makes a predetermined number of hot dogs a day and when he sells out he closes shop.

Coleman's Fish Sandwich

I heard it from everyone in Wheeling: "Wait until you have a **Coleman's fish sandwich.**" I scoffed. I had childhood memories of Friday night fish fries that would be hard to beat, but I went to Centre Market, stood in a lunchtime line and ordered a fish sandwich at a bustling stall offering fresh fish as well. Lots of sweet fish, dipped in a secret coating, fried perfectly crisp in canola oil—even wrapped in white bread, Coleman's fish sandwich matched my memories of the best. *Gourmet Magazine* agreed, naming it America's best fish sandwich in 2001. In case you cannot make it downtown to Centre Market where nearly half a million fish sandwiches a year are sold, a drive north of Wheeling along SR 2 will offer a variety of clubs that advertise Coleman's Fish Fry on Fridays.

Farm to Table Movement

Whatever the title, the state is experiencing a tsunami of local foods in fine dining restaurants around the state, young boutique farmers, regularly scheduled farmers markets and organizations like former chef Dale Hawkins' **Fishhawk Acres Farm** and Center for New Appalachian Agriculture.

A former star chef, Hawkins turned in his toque for a farmer's overalls growing ingredients for restaurants and staging monthly locavore parties. His West Virginia brand was enhanced by an appearance on the Travel Channel demonstrating the fine art of preserving groundhog meat.

Since 2005, the **Cast-Iron Cook-Off** *has been the throw-down of regional foodie chefs and their teams.*

Both **Lot 12 Public House** and **Panorama at the Peak** in Berkeley Springs have been active in building the statewide movement. Both have been honored for their dedication to local foods with the Snail of Approval from the Slow Foods folks in Washngton, D.C.

The two-day, open-to-the-public **Cast-Iron Cook-Off** includes a symposium as well as competition. It moves locations around the state. As an event devoted to showcasing the emerging 21st century Appalachian culinary cuisine, it is fitting that all competitive entries are cooked in traditional cast-iron and use mostly local ingredients. To keep the adrenalin flowing, the competition is against the clock as well as other teams.

LOCAL FOOD SPECIALTIES

Both **Lot 12 Public House** and **Panorama at the Peak** in Berkeley Springs have been active in building the statewide movement. Both have been honored for their dedication to local foods with the Snail of Approval from the Slow Foods folks in Washington, DC.

Swiss Specialties

When we visited Eleanor Mailloux's **Hutte Restaurant** in Helvetia in the late 1990s, her daughter Kathy had been cooking there for 30 years. We watched her knead bread that would be part of that day's lunch. I had just enjoyed some of the delectable treat in my homemade sausage sandwich served with tangy hot applesauce and sauerkraut. I also polished off an order of *rostli*—a fried pancake of shredded potatoes.

The Hutte remains the center of activity for the tiny town, the only restaurant for endless miles around. The wooden tables and other furnishings in the low ceilinged, rambling building belong to old residents. There's a wood-burning stove, and church bells ring regularly. For the full Swiss culinary experience, the enormous 15-item Sunday buffet called **Bernerplatte** should not be missed. Served at 5pm, Bernerplatte is loaded with items ranging from bratwurst and Hutte chicken to onion pie and curried pineapple.

"You think you're never going to get here, but you will," Eleanor Mailloux tells people as she gives them directions and warns against taking shortcuts. Helvetia is tucked away in the central mountains, surrounded by hemlock and spruce. Settled in 1869 as a Swiss colony organized by the Bennets of Weston, Helvetia once had population of more then 300, which now has dwindled to about a third of that number. The Swiss heritage is cherished and Helvetia was the first town in the state to be placed on the National Register of Historic Places.

Ramps

A native plant in the lily family, **ramps** are the first green shoots of spring, easy to find in forested ravines. They have broad, flat, spear-shaped leaves and a potent onion taste. A type of wild leek, they are an excellent source of vitamin C. Indians dried and ground ramps, using them as a substitute for garlic. Early settlers viewed it as a wonder, fresh and green after a winter of meat and dried foods. Ramp lovers, and the merely adventurous, should try the ramp wine made by **Kirkwood Wineries.** It has to be tasted to be believed. For ramp festivals and dinners, *see* "Far Out Festivals."

Trout: Grow 'em, Catch 'em, Eat 'em

Trout season never ends in West Virginia and native **trout** are found everywhere, from nearly 2,000 miles of pristine trout streams to countless restaurant tables in every corner of the state. Brown, brook and rainbow trout—some domestic and stocked, others wild—show up fresh out of the stream in wilderness frying pans and as trout cakes, smoked trout logs or specialty dishes. If you pay to have the stream stocked at the **Cheat Mountain Club**, they'll cook all the trout you catch.

Sweets & Treats

De Fluri's Chocolate manufacturing operation and storefront may be the best addition to Martinsburg since the B&O Railroad arrived in the 1840s. The people who consume the nearly 20,000 pounds of chocolate they produce each week would no doubt agree. Brenda left a high-powered economist career in London and started dabbling in chocolate. She married Charlie Casabona when she discovered he could run the machines and slapped her maiden name—DeFluri—on the product because it sounds like chocolate. She claims to be passionate about the chemistry of chocolate and various centers. I'm passionate about trying to decide whether raspberry jellies, Spanish orange peel or amaretto cream tastes best coated with dark chocolate. Then there is the dark chocolate cranberry bark that may be the best taste ever. Brenda created a special West Virginia wine chocolate truffle and her handcrafted candies now appear in various corners of the state as well as around the world. DeFluri's received a national award for their 18-piece collection of assorted truffles. Their latest cutting edge venture is vegan chocolate.

Austin's Homemade Ice Cream has been producing several hundred gallons of ice cream a week for more than half a century at their combination factory and shop in Ceredo. There's no eating-in at Austin's, only drive-through. Budget Saver Twin Pops are a national ice cream treat made famous by packaging a rainbow of seven flavors—and colors—in a clear plastic bag. They are the prime product of the nearly century and half old **Ziegenfelder Company** which cranks out half a million pops in their 'round the clock operation.

Distance is no object to find the increasingly rare bakery. A real bakery not a section in a supermarket. Two exceptional bakeries in the state would require serious driving since they are at the two furthest points possible. Two types of handcrafted German stollen, a traditional holiday bread, are made by the **Shepherdstown Sweet Shop Bakery** and sent around the world in special boxes featuring illustrations of local landmarks. Initially made only at Christmas and Easter, the stollen became so popular is it now available year 'round. The bakers are also famous for their cheesecakes baked in a hot water bath for three hours making them really creamy and dense. Guinness Stout Chocolate Toffee is the most popular of a dozen flavors followed by raspberry swirl.

Richters Maplehouse offers the bonus of an authentic maple syrup camp with both modern and antique mapling equipment along with their tasty products, including rare maple cream. Open all year, the camp has special tours during the Maple Syrup Festival, held annually in nearby Pickens on the third weekend in March.

Parkersburg weighs in with two local gourmet treats: **Mister Bee's potato chips** and **Holl's Chocolates.**

The 20,000 pounds of Swiss chocolates Holl's produces in a year are made fresh daily and use only the freshest ingredients. Holl came from Zurich in

1958 and brought recipes still used today for his family's traditional twice-dipped truffles and almond *gianduya*. The rich, deep and indulgently chocolate taste of Holl's candies attests to their pure Swiss heritage. Visit the shop, watch the process, and mix and match a selection to take home.

Mister Bee's chips are light and crisp with subtle favors. The only potato chip made in the state, Mister Bee's are delivered directly to the retailer assuring freshness.

Bonnie Belle's Bakery in Nutter Fort can produce a cake or cupcake with a computer-generated design in edible food colors. Orders come from all over the east and families are known to have every child's face on a cake in the freezer. Started in 1947, the family bakery makes everything from scratch using original family formulas. Only the digital robotics decorating is new.

Another family bakery where the third generation is thriving on original family recipes is **Spring Hill Pastry Shop** in South Charleston. They crank out more than 100 cakes on any given Friday.

Jeff's Breads near Lewisburg produces artisan loaves with outstanding crusts using a starter more than 400 years old.

More menu items

Green Glades Creamery uses milk from their herd of jersey cows to make a variety of cheeses including feta, havarti and cheddar.

Italian Heritage

A quick look around the state often gives folks the opinion that it's a "white bread" kind of place. There's a big portion of that white bread however, that has a crispy crust and goes by the designation of Italian. This substantial ethnic group is most distinguished by their culinary wonders.

The bottomless bowls of **Undo's** pasta are a food-lover's magnet in the old Italian neighborhood of Benwood just south of Wheeling. Red checked oilcloth covers the tables and the building is flanked by a Garabaldi's Lodge and a dead end industrial wall. This is the original Undo's, open in 1953 and complete with Undo himself, shuffling around offering patrons a taste of the house wine in plastic glasses. Incredible bread—little pizzas with garlic and oil as well as breadsticks—is served with an individual butter pot over a flame for dipping.

A reminder of Clarksburg's railroad heyday, **Julio's** is tucked away on the corner across from the train station. There are no menus or prices, only waitresses who recite the mostly Italian offerings.

Eat Here!

Tari's Cafe. Let me admit it upfront. Tari's is my hometown restaurant and the more years I log in at her tables the more I am spoiled for virtually everything else. And it's not just me. Ask anybody where to eat in Berkeley Springs and they'll point to the white and green storefronts in a pair of restored turn-of-the-century buildings, with Tari's name on the door. Folks regularly drive a hundred miles to eat there. People beg to have Tari's cater their wedding.

Yes, there is a Tari and she invented the cafe in 1989 with an unshakeable commitment to pleasing customers. In 2006, Tari sold the business to the young woman who had been working with her since opening day. The transition has been seamless. Recipes stayed as did chef Devin Lucas and the best crab cakes west of the Chesapeake Bay. The alluring Gallery Room is filled with local art and its windows hung with local stained glass. One of the best parts of Tari's in the public's view is that it is reliably open daily for lunch and dinner.

It is hard to believe that tiny Berkeley Springs could boast two of the best restaurants in the state but it's true. Presided over by chef Damian Heath, son of the town's most popular artists, **Lot 12 Public House** serves the best of American cuisine with a northern Italian twist. Intimate and elegant, in a 1913 house with porch seating in summer, Lot 12 has made its name with seasonal menus and favorite dishes like quail with polenta, roast duck with bourbon flavored juices, veal scaloppini with country ham and risotto and head-on trout. They have a much-praised wine list

and an intimate but popular bar. National attention began in 2000 when Lot 12 was selected by *USA Today* as West Virginia's "plate" for its gourmet ramp dish and continues annually as Heath is reliably the state's only James Beard regional finalist for best chef.

Ask Betty Lou Hovermale about her crusts and she'll tell you she makes them by hand (literally—with gloves) and knows by touch when they're right.

Any local politician recognizes **Betty Lou's Café,** tucked among the upscale places, as the place to meet and greet movers and shakers in Berkeley Springs. For decades, Betty Lou Hovermale made lunch every day for workers at her husband Roy's Service Station. Returning from winter in Florida a couple years ago, she found the family had opened a café at Roy's with her name on it. She makes 20 to 25 pies from scratch (including fillings) daily and spends two days before Thanksgiving making 300 more as an Eastern Star fundraiser.

★ Virtually every corner of the state claims a special barbecue joint. Take a time-tested recipe that earns the place cult-level carryout orders and add celebrities. The results make **Dee Jay BBQ Ribs & Grille's** expanded new place in the northern panhandle the place to eat.

★ Fishbowl size beer glasses and meatball sandwiches are staples at **Mario's Fishbowl** in Morgantown. At nearly 60 years in business, it has served generations of WVU students.

★ Irish breakfast with homemade Paddy Cakes and imported Irish sausage is served on the owner's Irish grandmother's lace tablecloths both morning and evening at the **Brazenhead Inn** near Snowshoe. Spud and onion soup is always on hand. Bass player and owner Will Fanning hosts impromptu jams and regular Saturday night music in the pub. Literally built from a dream Fanning had, Brazenhead also offers guests rooms and suites for folks who want no driving tasks to interfere with their taste for Irish beer. Brazenhead earns the right to call itself the only true Irish pub in the state.

★ Used to be there was nowhere to eat in Charleston. Now there is **Soho's** in Capitol Market. Not only is the northern Italian food excellent, but the company is notable. I've never been in the place that I didn't see folks I knew, not only capital city residents but visitors from various parts of the state. This is not the place for having a hideaway dinner.

★ Installing the famous Greenbrier staff as the management of Tamarack's food court—**"The Taste of West Virginia"**—was an inspired and tasty decision. The food court provides five-star eating in a cafeteria setting at prices that compete with the fast food chains. Lunch and dinner are served daily. From the dozens of lunch choices, Jack chose real sliced pork barbecue with no fake smoke, sweet and sour cole slaw, and new red potatoes in country style chunks. I indulged in chicken pot pie with big chunks of chicken, thick sauce and pre-made herbed crust that perched  atop the bowl. Tabletops in the food court were designed by a variety of state artists. As a bonus to our lunch, we coincidentally sat at the table whose top was made and designed by Berkeley Springs' jewelers and longtime friends, Carol and Jean Pierre Hsu. For more on Tamarack *see* "Art Wonders" and for the Greenbrier, *see* "Truly Incredible."

★ On the way to Peter's Mountain hawk observatory in Monroe County, we stocked up for lunch at two food shops, **Cheese n' More Store** and **A Taste of Eggcellence.** The first store was remarkably neat with bags of nuts, candies, spices, hard-to-get ingredients, and an array of nearly 50 different cheeses. Across the road is the bakery with a full supply of breads, cookies, pies and rolls—including pepperoni rolls.

★ It takes more than 60 trained chefs to turn out 4,000 meals a day in season at **The Greenbrier.** Most of the chefs have been trained at the resort's own Culinary Training Program, the first of its kind in America. This century's change from an American to European plan has added updated

cuisine, dramatic tasting offerings, global-decor restaurants and relaxed dining hours. Although the food remains outstanding and the main dining room is still traditionally elegant with epauletted waiters, some things were lost in the transition. Not to be repeated is our memorable experience with the bread lady, an ancient crone who surely had served Robert E. Lee during his regular visits, and was extending her life by drinking the famous spring water. Whatever her story, we watched entranced as she hobbled continuously around the huge room with its scores of tables, poised to drop a roll on the plate of any individual sending her the appropriate brainwaves. She never spoke, not even a whisper.

Historically, food has been a holy grail at the Greenbrier. In 1858, the 1,200-seat dining room in Old White was the largest in the United States. A splendid dinner in 1908 persuaded the C&O Railroad chief to buy the Greenbrier. Over the years, 26 U.S. Presidents have dined there. Today, the state's most important native athlete, basketball star Jerry West, has a namesake restaurant at the resort that includes a record-breaking 44 oz steak and walls hung with authentic memorabilia including West's 1960 Olympic gold medal and a career-full of jerseys.

The Greenbrier continues to make all its own breads, pastries and 26,000 pounds of chocolates each year. The resort's largest soup kettle makes 125 gallons fresh each day.

★ Food was the beginning for the **Bavarian Inn,** and continues as the centerpiece today. Although owner Erwin Asam no longer cooks daily as he did when the restaurant began, he does keep his spoon in the soup, tasting and suggesting adjustments to his son's team of chefs. The kitchen complex is designed for handcrafting superb meals for hundreds of guests a day. A bakery produces first-rate apple strudel and signature Black Forest cake; and a special meat room is used for "fabricating" custom cuts of meat.

The standard menu includes popular German staples like red cabbage, herring and the full-bodied *jaegerschnitzel*—hunter's veal loaded with mushrooms in a bacon-flavored sauce. Tiny red potatoes are often cut to look like mushrooms then roasted; mushroom mélanges appear in appetizers like *Shwammerl-wildpilze*—portabellos, shiitakes and white caps in a brandy sauce over a flaky puff pastry. Table-quality white wine contributes to the rich taste of most meat dishes as the liquid of choice when the chef deglazes the sauté pans, loosening taste morsels. Attention to detail even has the kitchen using only homemade veal stock in its veal dishes.

In addition to the year 'round German and Continental specialties, the Bavarian Inn's menu features a fall and winter "Game Festival." Although venison and other game must be certified and can be found only from a handful of suppliers, the Bavarian offers a wide range of exotic choices, from wild boar and marinated rabbit to roast pheasant with champagne kraut. Our late March dinner menu listed as spring specialties three different asparagus dishes and shad roe. In summer, vichyssoise and cold fruit soups are added. Excellent service is provided by a bevy of fresh-faced dirndl-clad waitresses and red-vested waiters who watch each table to deliver various courses at exactly the right moment.

★ Whether part of Adventures on the Gorge's meal plan or just a night out, **Smokey's on the Gorge** offers great buffets with dishes like barbecued wild boar ribs and quail. Eat inside the timber frame pavilion or on the deck but no throwing your scraps over the edge into the New River Gorge.

★ Monday night in any season is downtime in Canaan Valley. Fortunately, **Sirianni's** serves. Its authentic look of scrap-booked memory walls in a century-old former steamship office is enhanced by funky two-person wooden booths, tables big enough to seat a family reunion and an open-to-the-world kitchen as cluttered and alluring as the walls. Sirianni's is a pizza and pasta joint that rises far above the standard of the genre. The menu claims "no medium drinks," the decor shouts, "no pretensions," and the waitress announces "here's your beer," with no glass offered. What is not announced is that all dishes are overabundant providing plenty to take home for midnight snacks.

* If **DiCarlo's Pizza** in Wheeling was a person, it would be retiring. Instead, it still serves pizza good enough to rate 5th place on the national *Parade* magazine's pizza honor roll with a special nod to DiCarlo's tomato glazed hot crust-cold cheese method.

* The **King Tut Drive-In**, named for its founder Tutwiler and not the famed Egyptian ruler, has been a Beckley mainstay since the 1940s. Food items on the menu range from chicken livers and meatloaf to pot roast sandwiches and homemade pies

A Tradition Of Eating

I drove across the state to sample **Quinet's Court Restaurant** in New Martinsville, and I would do it again, and again. Founded more than a century ago, the main street eatery became Quinets in 1939 and has been popular ever since. Thousands of photos of famous and obscure diners cover the walls and scores of "regulars" make up breakfast groups and lunch bunches. The five dining rooms were added as needed and open one from another. Everyone eats from the 75-item buffet of all in-house cooked dishes including the breads and desserts. Before making the pilgrimage, I would never have believed it possible that every item on such an extensive buffet could be perfect. Highlighted in my taste bud memory were outstanding mushroom dressing, great fried chicken and fish and six types of pies. When I couldn't finish everything on my third—or was it fourth—plate, the waitress decided I really tried and let me off without the $1 fine.

Drink This

A spirits tour of the state may involve hauntings or it can focus on the kind of spirits you drink.

★ State-of-the-art equipment in a new 5,000 square foot production area with attached tasting room allows **Smooth Ambler Distillery** to produce small-batch spirits ranging from white whisky, gin and vodka to the state's only bourbon. A true grain to glass craft distillery, Smooth Ambler uses local corn and milled-on-site grains. High points range from silver fermenting tanks and a copper still that looks like a work of art to "bottling parties" when volunteers come help bottle, label and taste. Every drop of the hundreds of gallons they make each week is sold to outlets in more than a dozen states. Tours are conducted daily except Sunday.

★ Less alcohol but equally alluring is the impressive West Virginia wine industry with scores of popular vintages from a dozen wineries readily available at festivals and in shops around the state. **Lambert's Winery** could be billed as a wine theme park complete with tours and tastings. The mid-week pizza, wine  and jazz parties draw crowds. More attractions range from the hand-cut stone winery to an underground cellar, vineyards, event center and fire pit.

CHAPTER NINE

Million Dollar Views

If views were bankable, West Virginia would top the charts of wealthy states in this country. It is impossible to list all the vistas that make a casual traveler on a winding road gasp in wonder. Million dollar views of rolling hills, rivers, distinctive mountains or extravagant rock formations can be found in every corner of the state. Each season dresses the view differently. Frozen forests are winter fairylands, red bud and a million shades of green color spring, while summer begins with mountainsides of rhododendron. Fall is always a five-star occasion with endless hardwood forests ablaze in golds, reds, oranges and yellows.

Water vapor is the accessory of choice in many panoramas. Columns of fog rise along ridges and rivers; miles of clouds roll along the base of mountains, mists fill river canyons and veil mountain tops.

But the views must be viewed to be appreciated. No words can describe the ridges and peaks fading into the hazy blue horizon or the gilded light that seeps through thick forests.

There's no need to hype Mother Nature in West Virginia. There is, however, a need to protect her from those business interests that are trying to flatten the state—eating mountain tops and then spitting out the refuse to fill in the valleys. So, when it says Scenic Overlook—do. It's always worth it and you never know how long it will last.

Thomas Jefferson's Favorite

Many of the million dollar views are ancient and were certainly appreciated by tribal residents for thousands of years. Among the earliest historical praise by a colonial is a rapture written by **Thomas Jefferson** in his *Notes on the State of Virginia*. He wrote the passage about the view from a very high piece of land above the Shenandoah River at Harpers Ferry now known as **Jefferson Rock.** It reads: *The passage of the Potomac through the Blue Ridge is perhaps one of the most stupendous scenes in nature. On your right comes up the Shenandoah having ranged along the foot of the mountain a hundred miles to seek a vent; on your left approaches the Potomac in quest of a passage also. In the moment of their junction, they rush together against the mountain, rend it asunder and pass it off to the sea.*

Jefferson continued to exclaim about the rock-strewn Shenandoah and the cliffs upstream along the Potomac, proclaiming it all to be "worth a voyage across the Atlantic…to survey these monuments of a war between rivers and mountains that must have shaken the earth itself to its center."

Robert Harper, who, in 1748, first staked out the place that now bears his name, called the meeting of the rivers "The Hole." Carl Sandburg seemed to agree, although more poetically, nearly two centuries later when he wrote: "Harpers Ferry is a meeting place of winds and water, rocks and ranges."

Today the view of the Potomac Watergap from Jefferson Rock includes a railroad tunnel carved through a mountain, and the steeple, buildings and streets of Harpers Ferry National Historic Park. Painters and photographers flock to the scene. To capture the view in the most adventurous ways, try the zip line at River Riders which soars above the tree line, or walk the footbridge connected to the train bridge crossing the Potomac.

More Historic Endorsements

Blackwater Falls is another scenic marvel that has a long history of effusive travel prose. The most popular travel writer and illustrator of the 1850s was Porte Crayon, a pen name for David Hunter Strother. Strother was a native of Martinsburg and owner of a hotel in Berkeley Springs. He was particularly taken with the area in the central mountains, which he called "the Land of Canaan."

Saturated word images of the river and falls and detailed pencil sketches are found throughout Strother's travelogue of a visit to Blackwater. He described "a headlong current unceasingly fettered with masses of drift and monstrous boulders" and "massive jets and sheets from a common center falling in graceful curves into the black pool below.

"The stream makes a wild leap into the abyss of life," wrote Strother about the river's transformation into what the 19th century visitor knew as the Great Falls of the Blackwater.

While Strother brought the falls to the attention of the world, the first white men to see them were on a surveying trip in 1746 for Lord Fairfax and included noted mapmaker and presidential father, Peter Jefferson.

The falls remain as magnificent today but much easier to reach than in Strother's day. A sturdy boardwalk from the **Blackwater Falls State Park** lodge offers several vantage points of the 63-foot plunge of the river through a deep and rugged canyon. The water glistens in the sun with a nearly-black sheen, the result of natural tannins from fallen hemlock and red spruce needles as well as iron compounds. In spring, the densely forested canyon is covered with blooming rhododendron; in summer, it's lush and green. The roaring of the falls and the spray of their water give the views added dimension.

Since 1962, the annual **Wildflower Pilgrimage** pays homage to the unique flora. The weather ecosystem is also unusual with frosts having been recorded during every month of the year. For more on Porte Crayon, *see* "Remarkable Collections."

Romance trumped scenery in an 18th century tale involving George Washington's nephew and an overlook near Berkeley Springs that is still rated one of the best views in the east. Originally seen from Cacapon Rock higher up on the mountain, it is now reached by SR 9 and called **Panorama Overlook**. This scenic view was a favorite destination for George Washington when he visited Berkeley Springs to "take the waters." According to his own account, George's nephew Laurence Augustine rode to Cacapon Rock from the springs in 1796. From the summit he expected to see "one of the wildest, sublimest (sic) and most interesting views of mountain country, interspersed with cultivated valleys and rivers which our country afforded." Young Laurence's rapture at the "solitary hamlets with their circling columns of dense smoke and two beautiful rivers" was instantly swept away by a lovely 15-year-old Polly Wood, who was with another party of riders enjoying the view. After a feverish courtship, the two were married the following year and continued with undiminished love until Laurence died in 1824.

The panoramic scene of mountains, valleys and the joining of the wild Cacapon River with the more stately Potomac continues virtually unchanged from Washington's time, except for the paved mountain road curving down to the still solitary hamlet of Great Cacapon. A cliff of fluted Tuscarora sandstone hovers above the contemporary restaurant that faces the overlook.

Hawks Nest also had its historic boosters including traveler Francesco Arese who wrote in 1837: "This is one of the most beautiful natural sights I have ever seen. Under almost perpendicular rocks a thousand feet high, the New River flows rapidly through its very shut-in and very sombre valley." Arese goes on to complain that "not a single travel book, not a guide book or description mentions this place." The view remains; the obscurity has vanished.

Birds on the Wing

Hanging Rock Raptor Observatory perches at more than 3,800 feet somewhere near the middle of a 50-mile ridge of the Eastern Continental Divide called Peter's Mountain in Monroe County. In addition to the hawks and occasional bald eagles that cruise the area, the view from the top is a panorama of timeless animal trails, now roads, winding sinuously through neat Monroe County farms. Virginia is to the east; a retreating horizon of West Virginia mountains extends to the west; and the rock spine of the divide extends north and south to either side.

Open daily except Sundays, the area affords hikers a chance to enjoy an exclusive lunch site in a small frame building with benches and a table. We feasted on Mennonite taste treats from the two shops in Gap Mills—pepperoni rolls and caraway cheese—the day we made the 45-minute hike into the observatory. Volunteers record more than 200 hawks a day during migrations in September.

We climbed 1,230 feet on North Mountain to giant Oriskany sandstone outcroppings on a boulder-strewn peak populated by giant black turkey buzzards. Spread at our feet was the rolling countryside of Hampshire County. Winds swept the cliffs and the birds rode the waves. The rocky perch known as **Raven Rocks** *is part of the Ice Mountain Nature Conservancy. See "Mother Nature's Wonders" for more on Ice Mountain.*

New River Vistas

The ancient **New River** cuts its way through tree-covered mountains that rise over a thousand feet on either side, creating a spectacular gorge with miles of stunning views. The views are enjoyed by the folks hiking, driving or rafting the gorge and the river's once inaccessible length. The 53 miles of river are West Virginia's only National Park, which include deserted mining towns, bridges, rock-strewn rapids and sheer sandstone cliffs dotted with beehive ovens—along with basic raw beauty. **Canyon Rim Visitors Center** offers different perspectives, including a boardwalk down to an overlook of the New River Bridge. Further upstream, **Grandview Visitor Center** is famous for a riotous spring rhododendron display. For more on the New River Gorge, *see* "Mother Nature's Wonders."

The southern view from today's **Hawks Nest Overlook** along the New River Gorge includes cliffs covered with hemlock and rhododendron forests, and a railroad bridge carrying eighteen to twenty trains a day. The view to the north is of the boulder-strewn riverbed of the New, its water dammed into Hawks Nest Lake since 1934. Most of the flow has been redirected through a tunnel to a power plant on the other side of the mountain. The immense, 1,000 foot rock column, prominent long before the dam, was once named

Marshall's Pillar for the noted Chief Justice who visited in 1812 as part of a delegation exploring the possibility of a canal along the New River. Nearly 1,300 feet high, the overlook can be reached by Cliffside Trail from the lodge or by a short loop trail off US 60.

The same vista is particularly stunning in the morning with clouds hanging low over the river and mountain peaks protruding above them. Stairs from the lodge to the observation deck seem to plunge into the gorge.

Sandstone Falls, the largest on the New River, spans the river in a 1,500-foot wide cascade eight miles north of Hinton, dropping 10 to 25 feet. The best view is from above. A boardwalk leads to river-level views and islands in the middle, where there is an observation deck by the 25-foot waterfall. A scene in the 1994 film *Lassie* was filmed here.

The Beautiful River

Known to Indians and early settlers as "the Beautiful River," the **Ohio River** provides countless endearing waterscapes as it marks out 277 miles of West Virginia's western boundary from Chester to Huntington. **Anne Royall**, 19th century journalist and Monroe County native described the river, "justly celebrated for its beauty and utility...if the reader can imagine a vast mirror of endless dimension, he will have an idea of this beautiful river."

There are currently 20 lock and dam structures along West Virginia's stretch of the Ohio, as well as abundant river traffic, mostly tugboats shepherding long barges of coal, oil and chemicals. Only the Mississippi River is busier. After only a couple hours of indulging in a favorite sport—barge watching—you can discern the "rules of the road."

The Robert C. Byrd Dam and Locks on the Ohio River in Mason County is a multi-million dollar view—$224 million to be exact. In 1938 the Gallipolis Locks and Dam, the largest roller dam in the world, with eight rollers, was built in the same location. The Army Corps of Engineers renovated the

dam and locks in 1992, rededicating them to West Virginia's legendary U.S. Senator. The "workings" of the complex are located on a river island with its own bridge and a flock of geese hanging out on the lawn. The observation deck at the visitors center is open daily.

Priceless Panorama

East River Mountain Overlook at 3,500 feet barely surpasses the collection of mountains that surround Bluefield in all directions. Most impressive, however, is what's underground—the incomparable 24-foot high seam of the Pocahontas Coal Field.

Layers of bluish-gray shale and reddish sandstone in Bluestone Canyon, accessorized by a jumble of densely forested mountains, populate the spectacular vistas at Pipestem State Park. Prime vantage points include the **Pipestem Observation Tower** at 3,000 feet, as well as decks around the lodge and the tram down into the Canyon.

In southern West Virginia, all mountaintops are created equal and hover at about 2,500 feet. It's easy to get a panoramic view with only a short tower. At **Twin Falls State Park,** a simply constructed open wood tower looms about ten feet above the elevation of White Horse Knob which in turn rises about 100 feet higher than its neighbors. The result is a stunning 360-degree view of the surrounding forested mountains.

Looking due east at the first line of the Blue Ridge, the orchards and farms of southern Berkeley County spread out left and right below the pull-off at **Bucks Hill**—the intersection of SR 45 and 51. It was April and the daytime colors were red bud and peach blossom pink. That night as I headed back across the mountains there were clear skies overhead, a huge bank of cumulus clouds hovering over the mountains, and a dazzling light show of flashing lightning bolts illuminating the clouds from behind. I stopped at the overlook to watch Mother Nature show off. It was a popular choice—at least a half dozen cars were already there.

Sheer cliffs, enormous boulders and the wild water of the Cheat River as it pours through the gorge 1,200 feet below are stars of a spectacular view in **Coopers Rock State Forest.** That the view is enjoyed from a dramatic sandstone overhang is a bonus for the crowds of people  who visit each year. Impressive stones show up in more than just the view. There are wood-railed fences with stone pillars, huge stone slab walkways and roofed pavilions made from stone by the Civilian Conservation Corps in the 1930s. The high quality, extra large flagstone used in the trails and pavilion floors was quarried from the Snake Hill side of the canyon below.

It is not called Snake Hill for imaginative reasons. During the 1920s, the area was the home of Colonel William Cramer who kept and milked rattlesnake venom which he sold to pharmaceutical houses. He would serve the snake meat to his guests posed as chicken. Not surprisingly, he died of a rattlesnake bite in 1929.

For the best photo opportunities at Coopers Rock, select the afternoon light.

Saddle Mountain has been a landmark from prehistoric times, visible from mountaintop overlooks along the game and hunter trail that is now US 50. Geologically, it is a wind gap abandoned by the stream that originally defined it. Legend claims that Abraham Lincoln's mother, Nancy Hanks, was born on the east side of Saddle Mountain in 1782 although there is no proof. Based on the more than 50 other locales that also make that claim, she was born more places than George Washington slept.

Large flat rocks invite you to climb down and see up close the two cataracts that flow over a pair of ledges and form the broad, rapid falls of the Tygart River in **Valley Falls State Park.** Twice a year, tiny saw whet owls are banded and released there.

Kanawha Falls are the largest in the state and among the largest in the nation stretching almost 1,700 feet across the Kanawha River just downstream from where the Gauley joins the New. The spectacular view of these roiling waters is easily visible from both US 60—the Midland Trail—and a park that borders the river.

Eternal Watchtowers

Another timeless landmark noted on the oldest of Appalachian maps, is the pair of 900-foot rock chimneys known as **Seneca Rocks**. Curves in roads for miles in all directions reveal glimpses of them protruding from bare rock upthrusts of North Fork Mountain. Porte Crayon described them in the mid-19th century as "the loftiest and grandest specimen of the peculiar rockwork to be found" in the North Potomac Valley.

There's a panoramic valley view of the surrounding Seneca Creek area from the steep but walkable trail on the west side. It's a true summit with only one way up—climb it. The narrow top offers an exclusive view. There are horseback rides from **Yokum's Stables** to the top of the trail and folks have ridden up to get married. My personal favorite is the airborne view. We would circle Dolly Sods and Spruce Knob, the tallest peak in the state, then fly around the pair of rocks and wish we dared fly between them. In the late '90s, an easy trail was created. It goes almost but not quite to the top as befits a trail complete with interpretive signs.

When the first climbers reached the summit in the late 1930s, they found an inscription dated 1908, reportedly made by a surveyor working in the region at the time. Few climbers followed the pioneers and from 1943-44 mountain climbing American soldiers were trained on the rocks in the army's only low-altitude assault climbing school.

Today, several hundred folks a year go through the original **Seneca Rocks Climbing School** attached to John Maxwell's Gendarme Store. In session from April through November, the classes range from three-day basic to mountain rescue courses. With the growing popularity of indoor walls and gym climbing, would-be mountaineers need the school to remind them that in addition to better views, climbing real rocks is harder. All technical equipment is provided by the school.

The **Gendarme Store** also serves the great rock, selling equipment and offering a social center. The rough-sided outbuilding porch is usually cluttered with climbers or their remnants and posted with notes about hazards on various routes. The interior is jammed with esoteric equipment needed to climb.

In April 2000, the $6.5 million **Seneca Rocks Discovery Center** opened near the site of two pre-historic Native American settlements. Although the native stone building is impressive, the true highlights are its series of decks and patios offering stunning views of the twin rocks and Seneca Creek. An indoor rock-climbing wall prepares climbers for the real thing visible just beyond the windows.

The real thing can also be explored while tethered at one of America's rare Via

Ferrata built at nearby **Nelson Rocks Preserve**. This is a mountain climbing route for beginners with a permanent safety system and minimal need for equipment. There is a swinging bridge and ladder rungs are built into the rocks.

For more on Seneca Rocks, *see* "Truly Incredible" and "Mother Nature's Wonders."

CHAPTER TEN

Mother Nature's Wonders

Over countless millennia, nature's forces have made West Virginia a one-of-a-kind place, a state in constant homage to natural quirks and deviance. There are arctic ecosystems too far south, ancient mountains surrounding even more ancient rivers, and wilderness scenes unmatched east of the Mississippi.

Trees cover 75% of the state's area including nearly 1.5 million acres in federal and state forests making it a truly green place almost year 'round. The Monongahela National Forest alone is larger than the entire state of Rhode Island. West Virginia has more species and subspecies of birds—299—than any other area of its size in the world. West Virginia's nickname could be the Tree State or the Bird State as easily as its current moniker, the Mountain State.

And then there's the weather. In winter, the weather ecology can change in the space of a few hundred feet—up, down or sideways. Other than the flooding dangers inherent in 32,000 miles of rivers and streams—many flowing through narrow confines of canyons and gorges—there are no threatening weather occurrences, but there are oddities. The west side of the mountain slopes along the Eastern Continental Divide rack up 60 inches of rain a year, while their other side, lurking in a rain shadow, can muster up only half that amount.

The Oldest New

The **New River** and the 14-mile gorge it carves through 330 million year-old Nuttall sandstone are Mother Nature's overachievements in West Virginia. Geologists agree that the mysteriously named New River is, in fact, second in geologic age only to the Nile. Some white water devotees contend the New is older. Age may explain the river's rather deviant path. The New River, along with the Monongahela River in the northern part of the state, are two of the three North American rivers that run south to north. The New outdoes the Mon however in bizarre flow patterns. The Eastern Continental Divide is a natural barrier that runs along the top of the Alleghenies. Rivers rising to the east flow into the Atlantic Ocean; those to the west flow into the Gulf of Mexico. Except for the New. It rises east of the Appalachians in the Carolinas, and then cuts through the mountains to empty its water into other rivers that end up in the Gulf of Mexico.

Travel flaks hype the **New River Gorge**—which is up to 1,300 feet deep and a mile wide—as the Grand Canyon of the East, although its cliffs are tree-covered. Inaccessible until the late 19th century, the deep cut of the gorge ultimately led to its exploitation by giving lateral entrance to the area's rich coal seams—another prerogative of geologic age. Its "salt sands" also produce oil, gas and brine. Railroads followed the natural pathway of the gorge and opened it to mining in 1873. Booming coal camps quickly filled the area. In less than a century they were gone, leaving behind quaint ruins and cliffs. These are pockmarked with beehive ovens carved from the rock, and used to turn coal to coke on the spot.

Today, 53 miles of river, cliffs and gorge are protected as West Virginia's first and only National Park. The river is ranked Category 1 by the U.S. Fish and Wildlife Service for its abundance of unique and irreplaceable aquatic species. Great blue heron abound alongside rock climbers who flock to 1,400 documented rock climbing routes.

The National Park Service's **Canyon Rim Visitors Center** explains all these rarities, as well as offering a close-up view of the river, gorge and world-class bridge from a sturdy boardwalk.

Goldilocks Welcome

When I began soliciting suggestions for way-out wonders in West Virginia, one response dominated—**Beartown State Park.** We immediately scheduled a trip to the Pocahontas County wonder and were able to proclaim the suggestions right on target. Beartown is unique.

The 107-acre state park is well disguised. The entry road begins at the black and white log Mt. Olivet Church then passes an undistinguished collection of houses and farmland. Even the initial stretch of park boardwalk gives few hints of what's to come: the remarkable assemblage of house size boulders and astonishing rock formations broken from the sandstone cap of Droop Mountain. Hemlock and rock cap ferns bathe the area in iridescent green complementing the pervasive quiet as the boardwalks meander around the rocks. A half-hour walk takes you in, through and out of the wind—and rain—eroded rock city, with different views at every twist and turn.

Whether bears actually hibernated among the fanciful rock formations or not is a disputed point, but the notion gave rise to the name long before the park was established in 1970. Beartown State Park was created from land donated by Mrs. Edwin Polan of Huntington, in memory of her son Ronald, a student employee of the state parks who was killed in Vietnam in 1967.

Bizarre Botanicals

West Virginia boasts the most varied flora and fauna in the United States including more than a hundred species of trees, virtually all hardwoods, 36 species of orchids and more than 2,000 wild plant species. **Panther State**

Forest in McDowell County is touted as the most biologically diverse in the state. On Kate's Mountain in the Greenbrier State Forest are found 14 of the world's 15 plant species confined to shale barrens.

Virgin stands of timber with trees hundreds of years old are rare anywhere on the planet, but even more so in West Virginia, which was virtually denuded of trees by timber companies during the past century. The unique feel of virgin stands—weighty, old and pure—can be experienced in two locations.

Gaudineer State Forest owes its 50 acres of old growth red spruce to a surveyor's mistake in 1859. Incredibly tall and straight, some of the trees are over 300 years old. A scenic walk just off the road offers a breathtaking panorama of surrounding mountains and forests, with nary a bit of human habitation to be seen.

The ultimate forest primeval is **Cathedral State Park**, a registered natural landmark just off US 50 east of Aurora, and the only stand of mixed virgin timber left in the state. Its 133 acres includes virgin hemlocks—huge, straight blue-green giants with lacy needles that are the remnants of vast Appalachian hemlock forests. Some are 500 years old. Very accessible, you can drive through Cathedral or walk along a forest floor where rhododendron and ferns are the only underbrush. For tree huggers, this is the ultimate destination. These trees are so big around—up to 21 feet—it takes two people to hug one.

Though glaciers came to West Virginia's front door, they never made it into the state. The arctic climate they brought along, however, left behind vegetation that still thinks it's north of the 50th parallel.

The 750 acres of spongy bogs in the high Alpine bowl that make up **Cranberry Glades** kept the atmosphere cool enough to seduce rare glacial plants from leaving after the Ice Age. This misplaced tundra includes the southernmost extent of many arctic flora, including reindeer moss. Barrier-free boardwalks criss-cross this national natural landmark, and tags identify exotic plants like the insectivorous sundew and snake-in-mouth orchid. As we drove out of the Glades, a bearcub ran in front of our car, confirming that abundant cranberries serve as a bear-magnet.

Fifty-five square miles of the backcountry surrounding the Glades was declared the **Cranberry Wilderness** in 1983, permanently off-limits to cars and commercial activities. Shelters along the river are fought for on a first-come, first-served basis and the only concern is that it's also a black bear sanctuary.

The treeless heath barrens of **Dolly Sods** at 2,600 to 4,000 feet are home to glacial plant life and lots of woodland creatures from hawks and bobcats to beaver and flying squirrels. In fall, the acres of wild blueberry bushes turn a fiery red. The southernmost habitat of snowshoe hare is also found among Dolly Sods' 10,000 acres. Happily, motorized vehicles and bikes are not.

The Cranberry River flows through the Wilderness and is a sought after trout stream for fishermen from more than a thousand miles around.

The original spruce and hemlock forest, with its thick humus floor, was grazed and logged to destruction then burnt down to the rock. Further humiliation rained on the area along with artillery from World War II practice runs. Most of the bombs left behind have been removed. Today, the eerie windswept high plains support boulder fields and wind-stunted vegetation as well as abundant blueberries and cranberries. Natural landmarks are scarce, so hikers and berry pickers must remain alert.

North Fork Mountain lies on the rain shadow side of the Eastern Continental Divide, making it the driest place in the state with grass balds like the Smoky Mountains. Extensive dwarfed pine barrens are the southernmost trace of red pine and include a virgin stand at Pike Knob. Clumps of arctic vegetation and rare animals have also been discovered. Westerly winds on the summit of **Spruce Knob** create one-sided red spruce stands; at 4,860 feet, it's the highest point in the state.

The southernmost extent of the great spruce forests that once covered America was found in the high country around **Canaan.** At one time the forest floor was so dense that there was hardly room to walk on the more than eight-foot "duff" layer of shed vegetation. Tragically, the area was lumbered and burned away in a generation around the turn of the 20th century. Today, the spruce forest is once again flourishing, replanted by the Civilian Conservation Corps in what many believed was an impossible project.

The **Pipestem bush** has hollow stems that were used by Indians and early settlers to make pipes. It gave its name to Pipestem State Park. Identified by this name only in books of West Virginia flora, the bush is technically *spirea alba*.

The worldwide standard for yellow apples is the **Golden Delicious**, which originated from a chance seedling of a tree on Porter's Creek near Odessa in Clay County. The mother tree was found in 1905 by the Mullins family, who turned it over for development nearly a decade later to Paul Stark of Stark Brothers Nursery. The big, yellow and delicious fruit that Luther Burbank called "the greatest apple in all the world" received the apple world's premier medal—The Wilder—in 1919, the only yellow apple to ever do so. After producing apples for nearly fifty years, the mother tree is now remembered by a plaque at the site.

West Virginia's most famous contribution to horticulture, the Golden Delicious, was superior to an earlier yellow apple also found in the state. The **Grimes Golden** apple originated around 1800 in Brooke County on the farm of Thomas Grimes reputedly from a seed planted by Johnny Appleseed in 1796. Grimes was sitting on a local jury and pulled an apple out of his pocket to eat. When fellow jurors asked its name, he had no answer. The jury weighed in and named it Grimes Golden. Today, the notable beginning is celebrated by a watering trough and two stone pillars in a Wellsburg park, the world's only known monument to an apple.

Mother Nature gets a nudge from Jim Exline whose two-acre patch of "poor man's orchid" is color-coded. This means bearded iris of the same color are not planted next to each other, which is easy with more than 30 to choose from including orange, black and the popular "broken" color. More than 650 varieties are numbered along the garden paths. The six week season at **Exline's Iris Garden** near the Potomac River just outside Berkeley Springs peaks on Memorial Day.

February-blooming hellebores native to Russia but cross-pollinated by hand into a unique West Virginia variety flourish at **Sunshine Farm**, where rare-plant breeder Barry Glick, King of the Helleborus, provides the perennial to the world. More than 600,000 hellebore plants cram his mountaintop greenhouses in spring. Best feature of the plant? Deer don't eat them.

Too Hot/Too Cold

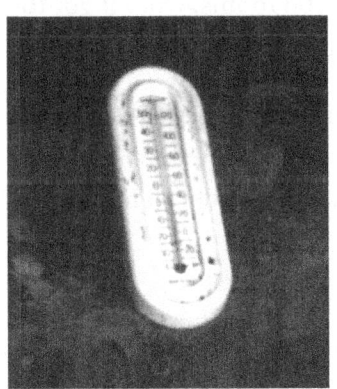

Historic reports claim ice was cut year 'round at **Ice Mountain,** described by one writer as "a huge sandstone refrigerator." Samuel Kercheval, 19th century author of *The History of the Valley of Virginia*, described *pure and crystal looking ice, at all seasons of the year...in blocks of from one or two pounds to fifteen or twenty pounds in weight. If this be true, it renders this place still more remarkable and extraordinary. The order of nature in this immediate locality, seems to be reversed; for when it is summer all around this singular spot, here it is covered with ice of winter and vice versa.*

Contemporary descriptions claim there are about 60 small vents and openings at the base of a 1,250-foot rock talus that release cold air all summer with ice present well into May. On my trip to the rare and sensitive cold producing mountain slope along the North River in Hampshire County, I found the ice to be non-existent and the chill to be far less dramatic when I stuck my hand into one of these vents. It looked like an animal burrow surrounded by clusters of misplaced arctic flora—bunchberry, Siberian prickly rose and twinflower—all in their lowest elevation and southernmost location. Allegedly 38 degrees, it felt no colder than good air conditioning. I found no ice. No core samples have ever been taken and no one knows why the area is cold producing.

Ice Mountain is a 149-acre Nature Conservancy area designated a national natural landmark in 2012. Twice a month, the group conducts an appealing hike among poplars, rare Appalachian wood ferns, blue cohosh, fossils, rhododendron, cucumber magnolia and witch hazel to the banks of the river and the cold vents. The hike continues up to **Raven Rocks**. *See* "Million Dollar Views."

Another story of peculiar natural cooling comes from the southern coalfield city of **Bluefield** that bills itself as "nature's air conditioned city." Demonstrating that the title is more than hype, Bluefield serves free lemonade anytime the temperature is over 90 degrees. The gimmick began with Lemonade Lassies in 1939 and has continued ever since in spite of the grueling summer of 1952 when lemonade was served free 24 times! What did not continue after the first attempt in 1937 was the giving away of free hotel rooms. Once it got too hot at the same time a state convention of Oddfellows was in town.

Another weather oddity is **Elkins'** claim to having the 7th worst weather in the United States and the worst in West Virginia. Elkins averages 171 rainy days and 211 cloudy days per year. Folks with Vitamin D deficiency should stay as far away as possible.

Goings-on Underground

What's beneath the surface in West Virginia has often been more valuable than what's on top; this includes rich deposits of coal, oil and gas. Two-thirds of the land in the state is under laid with coal seams. In **Wyoming County,** there are three acres of coal for every acre of surface. The unimaginably rich, nearly 1,000 square mile **Pocahontas coal field** has a 24-foot high coal seam, rather than the commonplace 24 inches.

Of greater recreational interest are the state's **caves**. Limestone deposits along the eastern edge of the state led to a region riddled with caves, more than a thousand in Greenbrier County alone. Many are long and large because of the unique uninterrupted quality of the limestone deposits. Today, spelunkers count more than 4,200 caves in West Virginia, with wild ones being discovered every day. The number includes 6 of the 25 longest caves in the country.

Gandy Creek disappears into a cavern for about a mile near Spruce Knob Lake. The surrounding area, known as the **Sinks of Gandy**, is filled with sinkholes and caves that can be explored, although the land is privately owned. There are reports that a Native American ghost in full war dress occasionally appears around the caves. Porte Crayon wrote about the sight in 1872 describing the upstream entrance as "a gaping mouth which swallows the little river at a gulp."

Lost River goes under Sandy Ridge near Wardensville, and comes out two miles on the other side of the mountain as the headwaters of the Cacapon River, which then travels 100 miles north to empty into the Potomac.

A commercial cave in Greenbrier County, **Lost World Caverns** is home to several unique features. In its former incarnation as the wild Grapevine Cave, the huge, multi-room cavern was known worldwide through the tabloid press as the original home of "bat boy." The world also focused on the cave and its star rock formation when two guys named Bob decided to stalagmite sit in 1971. The half million year old War Club is a stalagmite 28 feet tall with a base diameter of two and a half feet. Bob Addis of Parkersburg built a platform attached to War Club and sat for 15 days, 23 hours and 22 minutes for what he claims is the Guinness World Record. His partner, Bob Liebman would bring Mexican food from Clem's Diner in Lewisburg. The Greenbrier East High School band came to play and enjoyed the great sound in the cavern.

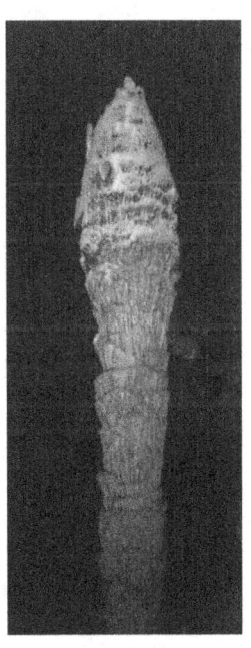

Although the cave was not discovered until 1942, bear bones over 10,000 years old were found in what is now Lost World Caverns. Registered cavers can still drop 120 feet by rope through the natural entrance.

At the turn of the 20th century, workers digging post holes for a livery stable in the heart of downtown **Charles Town** made an incredible discovery. The limestone underpinnings of the town George Washington's brother built were riddled with caves. The workers also discovered a 60-foot deep, three-acre lake. Opened in the 1930s as a tourism destination, boat rides were given on the underground lake. Today the entrance is hidden, riveted beneath a metal plate on the floor behind the lunch counter at the Liberty Street Cafe. The tiny blue building—and it is assumed, the underground expanse—are owned by the town.

Underground caverns also riddle the limestone foundation of **Lewisburg.** Yell into the giant street grate at the corner of Court and Foster streets and you'll hear the sound echo through the huge cave below.

There are neither boardwalks nor staircases in a wild cave. **Scott Hollow** is a developed wild cave in Monroe County. Discovered in 1984, Scott Hollow has over 20 miles of passages that have been mapped through the black voids of the Mystic River. Once upon a time it was open for four to five hour guided trips. Now it is closed. The current owners built a very unique trap door structure over the cave entrance. It's a sort of doggy door for cavers so they can come around the clock and take the wild entrance by dropping through a culvert under the trap door. There's a large metal door on the basement level for those choosing to walk in.

Read about Organ Cave, in "Historic Oddities" and "Tours and Trips." *See* "Superlatives" for information on Smoke Hole Caverns and Seneca Caverns.

Nature Chunks

There's not much water in West Virginia, and most of it is geologically trapped in springs, rivers and streams. There are ten man-made lakes in the state but only one natural lake. It's actually a two-acre sinkhole in the limestone rock of Hardy County named **Trout Pond** for the great fishing.

Part of a shallow sea millions of years ago, **Bluestone Canyon** is named for the gray-green shale readily visible along the road in the bottom of the canyon. Geologically, canyon walls rose around the river which drops 1,700 feet in its 77 miles. Indians called it Big Stone River because of the boulders found throughout its riverbed.

The canyon road is the morning walk of choice for guests at **Mountain Creek Lodge.** A tiny fawn trailed me for a mile or so along the road then back to the lodge where it stood waiting on the lawn. When I opened our balcony door and told Jack it was there, the fawn looked up to find my voice.

At the **Falls of Hill Creek** (*right*)**,** Mother Nature had promotional help from humans. Hill Creek drops over rock layers of sandstone and shale in three waterfalls as it passes through a narrow gorge. Three quarters of a mile of maintained boardwalks, steps and four overlooks make it easy to appreciate the sight. In summer, even the light is saturated with green. The lower falls at 63 feet are the second highest in the state.

Just east of Bramwell is **Pinnacle Rock** (*lower right*), a 364-acre state park built around a 2,700-foot remnant of an ancient geologic fold. Climbing a rugged stone staircase nearly to the top, one is rewarded by a panoramic view of the swath of mountains along the Virginia border and Jefferson National Forest.

Eight rivers flow out of the mountains of **Pocahontas County** heading in all directions. No rivers flow in. The eight are: the Greenbrier, Gauley, Elk, Cranberry, Williams, Cheat, Cherry and Tygart.

The Elk, at 180 miles, is the longest river located entirely within the state. It is home to an exceptional diversity of fish as well as a crayfish type—cambarus alkensis—found nowhere else in the world. **The Elk River Water Trail** offers ten access points for serious fishermen, thrill-seekers and lazy-day drifters. Year 'round fishing is so impressive it caught the notice of Ernest Hemingway who tagged the Elk as a big two-hearted river full of challenges.

Few explorers from George Washington on have missed describing the amazing stretch of the Ohio River as it winds its way south from Paden City to Parkersburg. In less than 100 miles, more than 40 islands litter the river, ranging from less than an acre to more than 400 acres. Many have sandy beaches. There is only one bridge—from St. Mary's to Middle Island—that connects the **Ohio River islands** to the mainland, and none connecting them to each other. Their prized wildlife ecosystems include bald eagles, peregrine falcons, beaver, mink, muskrat and over 30 species of freshwater mussels including the endangered pink mucket and fanshell. Fifteen of the West Virginia islands are currently part of the **Ohio River Islands National Wildlife Refuge.**

All West Virginia state parks are built around a natural wonder as a means of preservation. The centerpiece of **Twin Falls State Park's** 4,000 acres in Wyoming County is easy to guess. What's not so obvious is that Marsh Fork Falls and Black Fork Falls are seasonal. If you make a summertime visit, chances are all you will see are piles of rocks in the streams. When the streams are full, you can climb over rocks and experience the uninterrupted flow of negative ions by sitting beneath the arched shelf over which the lower waterfall plunges 25 feet. Further downstream, you can clamber over a moss and fern covered mill foundation. The upper reaches of the Mississippi watershed originate in the streams of this same park.

Evolving from a 1923 game farm, the **West Virginia Wildlife Center** at French Creek has a more than a mile long accessible trail featuring cougar, bear, and boar as well as large areas for elk and bison.

Seneca Rocks guarantee West Virginia's mention in the annals of geologic wonder. However, the 10,000 climbing pins left in the ancient 900 foot cliffs which map out 375 major climbing routes suggest a lessening of the great rocks' great karma. For more Seneca Rocks, *see* "Million Dollar Views" and "Truly Incredible."

The main street of Pineville would be directly on the rapid-filled Guyandotte River if it weren't for the dramatic 100-foot pinnacle of layered sandstone that sits in the middle of town. Called **Castle Rock**, it has two levels (*right*). The first, reached by 55 uneven steps carved from the rock, is a plateau with a picnic table and walkway around the base of the penultimate point that rises the final 50 feet to the sky.

No lighting a match near the boiling spring on **Trace Fork Canyon Trail** in South Charleston. It is odorless natural gas that makes the water bubble in one of the few "burning" springs remaining. Caves, mill remains, odd rock formations and a waterfall mark this slice of wilderness just a block or two from a major shopping center.

Located on private property, the nearly 200 foot long sandstone natural bridge in Roane County is one of the longest in the East.

Water current is in charge of round trips in **The Jug of Middle Island Creek**. It makes it possible to circumnavigate a large, inhabited island in the creek all day long by scarcely lifting a paddle. The Creek itself is notable for being the longest stream in the state not to be called a river.

Weird Apparitions

Catch the moon about midnight at 165-acre **Lake Sherwood,** and the reflection of the water looks like a giant cliff. The illusion often has an accompaniment of hoots and howlings, which break the

Hard to believe it's natural but government geologists claim it's so. The grid pattern on the 300 million year old **Waffle Rock** *prominently displayed at Jennings Randolph Lake is fractured and leached sandstone.*

predominant sound of you sucking air. **Hopkins Vista** is nearby with a mysterious spot for UFO landings. For a more traditional approach, try the 300-mile Allegheny Trail.

CHAPTER ELEVEN

Remarkable Collections

The magnificent obsession that marks great collections is well represented in West Virginia. Some evolve from the history and industry of the place while others are driven by individual hunters and gatherers.

A sparkling sample of contemporary collectors was the inaugural exhibit at Hurricane's Museum in the Community in May 1998. Among the automobiles, string holders and Pez dispensers was a small but colorful array of former *Graffiti* editor Michael Lipton's more-than-eighty-item electric guitar collection. Lipton's quote could be the universal theme for all collectors. "If I had a twenty dollar bill and saw a twenty dollar guitar, I'd buy the guitar and know I'd have it longer than I would have had the twenty."

Whether the motivation for collecting is buried in childhood memories or devotion to a particular facet of life, it all adds to the treasure store of things worth keeping.

Ancient Wonders

Seventy display units—hand-built wooden and glass cabinets more than six feet tall—line more than 60 feet of wall in the basement of the **Blennerhassett Museum**. The cases were built in the late 19th century for the Native American collection of Thomas Stahle, a music teacher and amateur anthropologist who immigrated to Parkersburg from Germany just after the Civil War.

Stahle interpreted as well as collected, telling stories section by section. He developed the displays and hand-lettered the explanation of each. There are extensive samples of musical flutes, toys, whistles, hematite cosmetics and "paints," drills, cutting tools, pipes, ornaments and more. A pair of 5 by 3 inch shell masks with etched facial features stand-out among the thousands of rare artifacts.

Stahle's collection was inspired by the rich deposit of Native American artifacts buried on Blennerhassett Island, some of which date back nearly 14,000 years. Other local collectors donated their finds to his work. The Blennerhassett collection is also home to the Cedar Rocks petroglyph, which was found near Wheeling. This arrangement of human and animal forms surrounding an abstract geometric pattern is a rare portable petroglyph, carved into a 3 by 2 foot sandstone slab rather than the more typical exposed bedrock.

See "Historic Oddities" for more on Native American sites.

X-Files Foreshadowed

For more than twenty years, Clarksburg was a major center for UFO devotees thanks to world-famous UFO expert Gray Barker. Today his work is featured on countless websites, and the **Gray Barker UFO Collection** is open to the public in Clarksburg.

Born in Braxton County, Barker's life was changed in 1952. That's the year when sightings of flashing lights in the sky, glowing objects and the mysterious "Flatwoods Monster" was turned into a story for *Fate* magazine. Barker pursued his writing, becoming well known in the flying saucer world of the 1950s and 60s, writing and publishing *Saucer News* and later, the long-lived *Saucerian*.

As an astrologer, I have lots of friends in the UFO community. I was intrigued by West Virginia's connection, and set out to see Barker's collection at the Waldomore in Clarksburg. Built by the Goff family in 1839, Waldomore is the Greek Revival mansion housing parts of the Clarksburg Public Library including the Barker collection. Librarian David Houchin was reluctant but knowledgeable as he unlocked the door to the Gray Barker room. Barker's assemblage of publications and papers have been part of the special collections of the Harrison County Public Library since his death in 1984.

A card catalog guided me through 35 drawers of Barker's files and notes, a journey that includes forged letters, references to his persecution by "Men in Black"—the first known use of the phrase—and bogus saucer films. The model saucer allegedly used by Barker to falsify photographs is in the collection, along with the typewriter he chopped up and hid in a stone wall to avoid an FBI probe. Most of his published works are there including: *They Knew Too Much about Flying Saucers*, *Book of Adamski*, and *Secret Terror Among Us: Silver Bridge*. More than 500 books and copies of 75 magazines and periodicals from the *Fortean Times* and *Flying Saucer* to *Saucer Space & Science* and *Star Log* are present.

Barker supported himself, as I do, operating a movie theater. He ran Lovett's Drive-in for 30 years.

UFO activity tends to be reported from numerous people in the same geographical area. The Indian mounds of the Ohio River valley are one such area. Point Pleasant was a hotbed in the mid-1960s with scores of UFO sightings as well as the appearance of the mysterious "Mothman" in 1966.

The Flatwoods Monster aka Braxton County Monster lives on through the Internet. Originally seen by three young teenage boys, consensus describes it as having a glowing red spade-shaped head and green clad body about ten-feet tall. Its vehicle was a pulsing red ball. Dismissed at the time as a meteor and owl, the Flatwoods Monster has a following although never to the scale of Mothman.

West Virginia has a cottage industry in UFO films, including *Whispers from Space*, an independently produced documentary which questions Barker's belief in the saucer phenomena he exploited, and Bob Teets' *WV Close Encounters in the Mountain State*.

For more on Mothman, *see* "Truly Incredible."

The "Official" State Story

A makeover turned the **West Virginia State Museum** from a dusty collection in the basement of the Cultural Center to a well-scripted tour through state history supported by more than 60,000 authentic artifacts in appealing exhibits. Train tracks are followed into darkly lit coal mines and walls are filled with banjos, fiddles and West Virginia glass bottles. A surveying telescope of George Washington's, a long rifle used by Daniel Boone and John Brown's noose are now featured and interpreted.

One of the most eccentric and popular treasures from the museum's former life was able to find a place. Professor Hechler's Flea Circus now greets visitors in the entrance hall. The well-dressed Emmiline and Alexander, stars of the circus, remain on display in a colorful circus car. When alive and in their prime, the quarter inch-long creatures could pull nearly 700 times their weight. Their stunts included hauling carts and wagons, jumping through hoops, dancing, juggling and leaping nearly a foot in the air. The famed New York performers came to West Virginia in 1906.

West Virginia Glass Mother Lode

The world's largest punchbowl (*see* "Superlatives") is one of more than 3,000 pieces of Wheeling glass identified and displayed at **Oglebay Institute's Glass Museum**. In an adjacent room, nearly 200 pieces of Wheeling-made china and porcelain are housed in elaborate cases from a downtown jewelry store. The prized feature of the collection is not glass but a "hologram" of glass chemist, William Layton Jr. Stand in front of the display and the seated Layton will explain how his father, working in Wheeling, revolutionized the glass industry in 1864 when he added bicarbonate of soda to the mix of sand. Layton's change in formula resulted in a substance that was cheaper, easier to work and resulted in better, clearer glass.

Glass from major Wheeling companies—Ritchie, Sweeney, Hobbs, Brockunier, Central and Northwood—is the collection's main focus. The collection, plus glass studios where visitors can watch glass artists at work, is housed downstairs in the Carriage House Glass Center. Upstairs, the glass is for sale.

John Henry in Wood

The **John Henry Collection** displayed on a long table dressed up as a stretch of railroad dominates the Railroad Museum in the Summers County Visitors

The **West Virginia Museum of American Glass** in Weston has another impressive collection with more than 11,000 pieces on public display and even more in open storage. It houses the National Marble Museum, a research library and more than 125 scholarly monographs on sale produced by museum members and bearing titles from Kings Crown Pattern Glass to Rich Cut from WV Glass Houses.

Center. The 120 hand-carved wooden figures radiate primitive artistic power.

Charlie Permelia was an injured coal miner from Lester. Completely self-taught, Permelia spent eight hours a day for seven and a half years creating detailed foot-tall versions of West Virginia's legendary steel-drivin' man and his mates. The figures and train cars are carved from 56 kinds of wood--black and white walnut, ash, cherry, chinquapin, buckeye, sassafras, basswood, magnolia, paw paw, bamigallian, spice wood, cucumber, sourwood, tamarack, red brush, arbor vitae and more--all depicting John Henry and his friends "workin' on the railroad."

Roadside Attraction

It snuck up on us as we drove east on US 50 in Preston County. The long, low wooden building was a traditional roadside stop of the 1930s and 40s, with a sign stretching across the front listing at least 50 items sold inside. We had no plans to stop. We did not need a cider operating press or sorghum molasses or ammo; nor did we need tomahawks, auto supplies or fertilizer. Then we saw the spinning twenty-foot-tall metal waterwheel and dozens of wheeled antique farm implements parked behind the fence.

There is no charge to wander among the scores of old machines at **Cool Springs Park**. No interpretation or signs either. A rare steam tractor is parked with a half dozen other antique tractors; a block of railroad track supports three cabooses and a freight car. Peacocks and curious mini-donkeys share the park with the rusted metal.

Songs and Sketches

Over 1,000 individual collections assembled since 1933 are housed in the **West Virginia and Regional History Collection** at West Virginia University, making it the state's most extensive collection. Here are countless political and historical papers, including all those of the "loyal" Virginia government, as well as Civil War diaries. It also contains the largest collection of West Virginia photos and newspapers in the state. All are on microfilm.

Gems include the Chappell Collection, more than 2,000 songs and tunes recorded originally on aluminum disks and now transferred to nearly 700 tapes. Assembled by Lewis Watson Chappell, these are the first sound recordings of American folk songs and were done in the field between 1937 and 47.

More than 500 sketches and some paintings by David Hunter Strother comprise another prized collection. The celebrated 19th century illustrator and author—pen name: Porte Crayon—was a household word in America due to his work in *Harper's New Monthly Magazine*. The Strother Collection includes dozens of illustrated travelogues for *Harper's*, Civil War recollections, and a ten-part series—*The Mountains*—on the rural character and folkways of the new state of West Virginia. Strother was a native of the state and lived most of his life in Berkeley Springs, where he and his father before him were innkeepers. He chose the North and became an Adjutant General in the Civil War. Strother used woodcut drawings to illustrate his travelogues. He is buried in Martinsburg at Green Hill Cemetery which he designed.

The Pale Blue Army

Along with spaghetti and comfortable guest rooms named for archangels, Peg Perry serves up icons, statues and paintings of the Blessed Mother at Maria's Garden in Berkeley Springs. The restaurant entryway has a stone wall set with an image of one of the first Mary apparitions—Our Lady of Guadelupe in 1531. The grotto in the outdoor garden was a natural for a shrine according to Perry. "I always associate niches with the Madonna," she said.

The **Marian Museum** at Maria's features more than a hundred images of the

Virgin Mary received as gifts as well as private stories of wondrous meetings, roses growing in winter, and whirling statues.

Powder Horn Bonanza

From 1910 to 1940 Elkins builder H.M. Darby compiled a "magnificent conglomeration" of prehistoric and early American artifacts, which he assembled and deeded to Davis & Elkins College in 1941. After nearly thirty years in various attics, the college began to preserve and research the collection in 1969. During this process, the huge collection languished in cardboard boxes.

Darby was not a traveler. He called himself a "dealer in curios" and his letterhead announced "Darby's Pre-Historic and Early Pioneer's Art Museum." He collected through advertisements and people who brought him various pieces. He kept meticulous records of uses, history and price of all the objects in his collection. Fate dealt Darby's ghost a blow when the years of being stored in random attics around the college led to the loss of documentation for countless pieces in the collection. For decades, Dorothy Lutz worked to reconstruct the information, carefully tracking down clues as to the use and source of various artifacts. Researchers and scholars come from all over to see the collection, and to help Lutz with the work of identification.

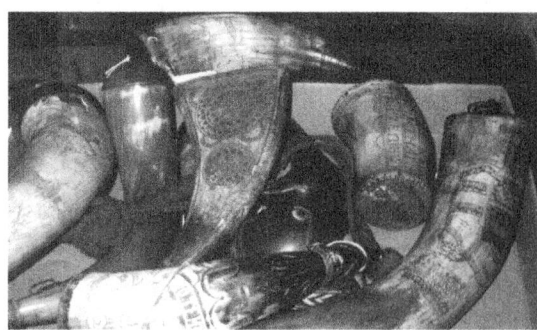

The Darby collection of more than 200 colonial powder horns is one of the largest in the world. While it is doubtful that anyone (other than Darby) has recorded the full extent of the collection, there are more than 5,000 Indian points and primitive stone tools dating back nearly 10,000 years. Countless thousands of other artifacts range from tobacco mills, numerous lamps, early American tools, magic cult objects and bizarre relics, to ordinance, pistols, swords and kitchenware.

In 2012, the college moved the enormous collection from display at Graceland and Halliehurst, the twin mansions of Elkins to a more public and permanent home in the Myles Art Center. Now housed in glass-fronted cabinets in a large room, the size of the collection requires rotation through the display exhibits. No one will ever again be visually overwhelmed at the scale of the collection.

Badges Of Honor

Several military collections are found in various corners of the state.

The **Mountaineer Military Museum** in Weston recently opened a new addition. Thousands of artifacts are showcased in theme cubicles including Civil War and a MASH unit. Highlights of the museum are its structure—the former Colored School made of local brick—and an impressive photographic hall of local veterans past and present.

Rowlesburg's **World War II Museum** is dominated by dozens of realistically sculpted mannequins in authentic and detailed uniforms.

What People Cherish

Some of the most unique collections are those assembled by an individual based on their personal passion. Most are open by appointment only.

Mike Perry's personal passion is the more than 500-acre **Heritage Farm Museum and Village,** an award-winning collection of 17 restored buildings filled with everything from steam tractors and a 1908 electric truck to blacksmith tools and home implements. The state's largest private collection of historic items is open year 'round for guided tours. Re-enactments for the *History Channel's* companion documentary *America's Greatest Feud: Hatfields and McCoys* were filmed here.

Huntington physician, Joseph Touma, assembled what may be the world's largest collection of ear trumpets. More than 300 of the primitive hearing devices are featured in his varied collection of thousands of items. Other prized artifacts are a meticulously restored 1926 Model T Doctor's Coupe, several Civil War amputation sets, leech jars, a tonsil guillotine and other medical arcana. More than 1,000 books include rare 14th and 15th century copies of ancient texts. There's even a Quackery Department and a collection of bed pans. Every incoming class at nearby Marshall Medical School comes for a tour of the private **Touma Medical Museum**. Marshall has its own world's largest collection: the **West Virginia Biological Survey Museum** of cataloged specimens of animals native to West Virginia.

Collectible Bits And Pieces

The mother lode for coal research is found on the second floor of Craft Memorial Library in Bluefield. Thousands of photos, tools, rare books, coal camp scrip, blueprints, oral histories, films, and diaries make-up the vast collection of the **Eastern Regional Coal Archives.**

West Virginia's State Archives are a treasure trove for genealogical researchers, with hundreds of volumes of state, census and military records as well as county, community and family histories.

Scholars travel from all corners of the globe to examine the folk music treasures in the **Augusta Collection** at Booth Library of Davis & Elkins College. The collection includes more than 2,500 sound recordings, as well as a growing number of videoed performances and workshops from the annual Augusta Heritage program. Histories, interviews, field recordings and photographs from Gerry Milnes' field work for Augusta are included along with tapes from early West Virginia Folk Festivals and the Mars family gatherings.

On two floors of a restored Victorian schoolhouse in Wheeling, tens of thousands of vintage toys including one-of-a-kind store samples are lovingly displayed at the **Kruger Street Toy and Train Museum**. Many are from the nearby Louis Marx and Company which closed in 1980. Guides at the museum are as fascinating as the toys.

Parkersburg's place in history as the first producer of oil and gas in United States is documented in an extensive collection of equipment, documents, maps and stories at the **Oil and Gas Museum**. An inviting pile of metal and machines including giant wheels and pumps are housed in the yard next to the brick museum building. The Museum's park in nearby California features ruins of the California House as well as memorializing the site of one of the world's first two oil wells.

Henderson Hall is a three-story Italianate mansion with an intriguing silhouette overlooking the Ohio River. It was a center of social and political life for nearly two centuries. Three Native American burial mounds on the property testify to its prehistoric significance.

The original Federal portion of the house was built in 1836; the mansion was added just before the Civil War to make a total of 29 rooms. The house was occupied by descendants of the original family until 2008. It retains all of its contents, and is open to the public under the new ownership of Parkersburg's Oil and Gas Museum. The rare clocks, rosewood piano, silver and china, twelve-foot gilt mirror and other unique pieces are not antiques; they are the daily furnishings of successive residents. Fortunately for modern visitors, the Hendersons kept everything from dresses and portraits to correspondence from everyone they knew—and they knew everyone important at the time. Artifacts on display range from the original deed signed by Patrick Henry and ballots from the Lincoln-Douglas election to two centuries of family portraits. There is a cherry stair railing that runs continuously from the first to the third floor. The floors are all the original wood. The major change was the addition of electricity early in this century.

Between the extensive collections of both the Huntington Museum and Marshall University, Huntington can lay claim to the state's largest collection of art books.

Thousands of rare and unique artifacts are displayed in **Wymer's General Store Museum** in Wheeling's downtown Artisan Center. More than 10,000 pieces from Wheeling's past include a complete salesman's sample of every type and size nail made by LaBelle Cut Nail Factory, decaled pottery steins and Marx Toy Company figures. Others are part of an 1880s general store.

Telephones circa 1890 to 1960--the days when they were only a means of hearing voices over wires--are the core of the **Bice-Ferguson Museum** in Shinnston.

The award-winning **Museum of Radio & Technology** fills six display rooms in downtown Huntington and is home to the WV Broadcasters Hall of Fame. The largest radio museum in the United States, it has hundreds of old radios from the 1920s to 50s, the only 1939 RCA-TV camera in existence and a radio station studio from the 1950s. The gift shop and its posters and reproductions are Nirvana for radio buffs. Best of all are the radio-geeks who hang out at the Museum delighted to chat with all comers.

The World War II vintage **Stifel Field Terminal at Wheeling Airport** houses a spectacular collection of aviation related artifacts collected by Tom Tominack, airport czar. Original wood doors lead you into the terminal. Rest rooms are as 1940s as the rest of the building with period urinals and the ladies room boasting a dress form. Exhibits include mementos of Jimmy Doolittle's rumored flight under the Wheeling Suspension bridge in 1927 and Charles Lindberg's visit to nearby Glendale field the same year. Of local interest is the display honoring Joan Stifel, one of fewer than 500 female pilots in 1938, as well as the exhibit on Fokker Aircraft. A dramatic mural of *The City of Wheeling*, a Capital Airlines plane flying over the Wheeling skyline as it did on November 1, 1946 when the airport opened, dominates one wall of the terminal. "We weren't able to find an artist we could afford to do the mural so I built a model, then had some photographic experts superimpose it on a postcard of Wheeling from that period," said Tominack. They used a hair dryer on the propellers to make them seem as if they were moving.

The **Tyler County Museum** began its life as the first county high school in the state. When its educational career ended in 1993, the community turned the building into 16 rooms of history including a farm and industry room, a barber shop and an early 19th century church.

The only real dinosaur in the state—even if it did come from North Dakota—is on display in the **West Virginia Geological Survey Museum** in Morgantown. Why not a West Virginia dino? Rocks in the state are too ancient to have dinosaur skeletons in them. To see a world class rock unearthed in-state, visit the 800-pound Oriskany sandstone crystal in the **Museum of the Berkeley Springs.** Another rock in the museum purports to be a survey marker bearing George Washington's signature, not completely improbable since Washington surveyed much of the surrounding area.

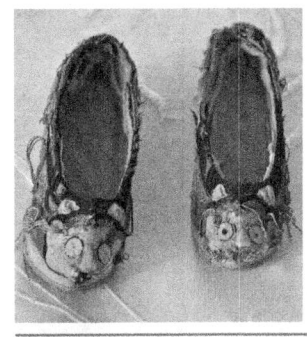

The restored **Pearl Buck Birthplace** *showcases the novelist's 85 books including signed and first editions. Some of her books are for sale in the gift shop. Buck was the first American woman to win the Nobel Prize for Literature. Built in 1858, the white frame Stulting House was always known to Pearl as her mother's house. As part of his crusading work to "plump" for the wonders of his beloved West Virginia, Jim Comstock, publisher of* The Hillbilly *bought the house and gave it to the state as a tourist attraction.*

The state's only plant conservatory is housed in a specialty wing of the Huntington Museum of Art. The Art Tower is a glass sculpture created exclusively for the conservatory space by Dale Chihuly.

The Herman Dean Firearms Collection has its own room at the **Huntington Museum of Art.** *Hundreds of items range from early pistols and powder horns incised with maps to a breech loading rifle made by John Hall of Harpers Ferry. There are outstanding examples of decorated weapons including both pistols and a Kentucky flintlock rifle.*

The **West Virginia State Farm Museum** *just north of Point Pleasant houses some interesting taxidermic oddities—a two-headed calf and General, the world's third largest horse.*

CHAPTER TWELVE

Shopping Treasures

Power shopping is all in your point of view. For some folks, the hand painted sign on a roadside market in the mountains outside Elkins announcing COLD BEER • TANNING • LOTTERY covers all the bases. For the more discriminating, there are unique products, historic shops, notable buildings and unparalleled bargains.

High Fashion

Stylish women in West Virginia are proud of getting a knock-out look at knock-down prices. They tell more stories about **Gabriel Brothers**' bargains than about five-figure designer gowns.

A foxy Lisa Starcher Collins was the hit of an arts gathering with her dazzling layered look, head to toe from Gabe's for $13. Rosalyn Queen wheedled a photo with the Pope in Rome thanks to her Gabe's bargain suit. Lined black satin mini-skirts with a Donna Karan label at $5 each outfitted the entire staff of a local restaurant at a cost less than dinner for two. The price tag on my Enzo Angelini leather bag read $248; at Gabe's it was $12.99. Nothing is ever more than $100; often ten dresses can cost less than $300. Women fly in from all over to shop.

Even better than the price tags are the challenges of the hunt.

New batches of low-price closeouts and irregulars in men, women and children's clothing appear daily in more than two dozen Gabriel Brothers' stores in six states. In true bargain basement style, there is minimal order and selection is limited.

Practitioners boast of daily pilgrimages and hitting five Gabes—Parkersburg, Fairmont, Clarksburg, Morgantown and Washington, PA—in a single daylong power shopping surge.

It takes practice and skill to work Gabe's for the ultimate bargain. Regulars know to guard their treasures while collecting them and to check each item thoroughly. Individual items may be flawed or damaged, and there are no guarantees. Even at $7, the glittery designer sweater I bought was no bargain when I put it on for the first time and discovered one sleeve was six inches shorter than the other.

This palace of cut-rate clothes shopping sprang from the ambition of Z.G. Gabriel, a Lebanese peddler operating from a truck in Pennsylvania. In 1961, Gabriel and his sons settled into their first store in the downtown building now housing the West Virginia Brewery in Morgantown. Gabriel Brothers' has always been a family store with good stuff at good prices for the area. They bypass wholesalers, dealing directly with store liquidators, who often seek out Gabriel Brothers because of their good reputation.

It's still family owned and operated, but currently there are two businesses, caused by a family split in the mid-'80s. Brothers James and Arthur became Gabriel Brothers and kept the West Virginia stores. Today, their nine children and more than 2,500 employees operate the family clothing store chain. Stores are open daily except traditional holidays. Hours are a standard 9am to 9pm.

Buying at the Source

A producer of fine china in the state since 1907, **Homer Laughlin** created inexpensive and colorful **Fiestaware** in 1936. The only of its products sold

to the retail market, **Fiestaware** is one of the most collected in the world. The retail outlet at the factory has a large seconds room where a rainbow of Fiesta bowls, pitchers and plates are stacked in huge bins for sale at extreme discount. During our visit, I was able to buy a collector friend a new design, a small Fiesta pitcher that was a clock. More than 25,000 china patterns have come from Homer Laughlin, many custom-made for noted clients, including the Greenbrier. A third of all dinnerware ever sold in this country has come from its kilns, and it was the first totally lead-free pottery in America.

A large showroom was built in 1921 to rival those of Europe. Today its ceilings, covered with ornately carved ceramic tiles cast at Homer Laughlin, arch over broad walnut shelves filled with displays of the company's many patterns and pieces.

The Fiestaware Outlet in Flatwoods adds a location outside the factory for broad selection, a seconds room and occasional tent sales with exceptional bargains. Limited production of hand decorated pitchers and mugs are sold only at **Tamarack** and the gift shop at the Cultural Center.

For more on touring the Homer Laughlin factory, *see* "Tours Not To Miss."

Glass and More Glass

West Virginia's first glass factory started in 1797. By the 19th century, glass manufacturing was a major industry with scores of factories and new techniques that transformed the making of glass. Today only a few major producers remain, as well as fewer than a dozen small studio factories.

Blenko Glass Company is famous for its deep vibrant colors and contemporary designs. They also have the best outlet store with seconds in dozens of popular pieces. For serious shopping, come early before the buses arrive.

Blenko's colored glass sheets, blown only at night, make it a mecca for stained glass workers all over the United States and Japan. They come searching for raw material among thousands of sheets in more than 1,400 colors racked in a large warehouse behind the factory. Cheap scraps of brilliantly colored glass are also abundant.

William Blenko came to America from London to produce hand blown glass for stained glass windows. In 1929, he started producing hand blown decorative glassware. Winslow Anderson who designed his first piece for Blenko in 1946, and his most recent in 2003, is recognized as America's first original glass designer.

They aren't named **Marble King** for nothing. Producing a million marbles a day almost all from recycled sources that include discarded colored glass from nearby manufacturer Fenton, the Paden City factory is one of only two full-scale operations in the country that produce marbles. It is also the first toy manufacturer to receive the "Made in the USA" certification. They created the first American-made cats eye marble. Tucked away in a nondescript industrial park, Marble King has an interactive museum and a shop—both inhouse and online—where you can buy their products from a pouch full and toys to jewelry and handmade collector marbles, even some that glow in the dark. What you cannot buy is a can of spray paint. That rattling you hear when it is shaken? A Marble King marble.

It's A Store. It's A Theme Park

Cabela's #10 store outside Wheeling has so many entertaining attractions that it's hard to imagine finding the time to actually shop. The 175,000 square foot facility has a 30-foot mountain in the back complete with waterfalls and ponds, various exotic life-size animals and a small plane soaring overhead. There are rows and rows of firearms including rare ones just for show, walls of aquariums and a world-class whitetail museum boasting more than 150 deer posed in various habitats. Among countless thousands of visitors was then-President George W. Bush who stopped during a campaign tour in 2004.

In 2012, Cabela's opened a second store in Charleston. Although small by Cabela's standards—it's only 80,000 s.f.—the camo Disneyland flavor is there. Response to the opening stunned Cabela execs. Nearly 40 people spent the night camped outside. The crowd swelled to more than 500 four hours before doors opened, the largest opening crowd in Cabela's history.

Old Timey Stores

There is nothing plastic in **O'Hurley's General Store**, just three rooms crowded with time tested merchandise known for quality and price, ranging from black powder guns and hats to baskets, clothes and wooden toys.

In the rear of the former family gas station, Hurley has a 19th century machine shop where he crafted the working model of James Rumsey's 1787 steamboat. (For more on Rumsey, the hapless inventor, *see* "Historic Oddities.") Hurley's iconoclastic empire in Shepherdstown includes the Great Hall, a true timber-frame structure completely hand done. The working fireplace is floor-to-ceiling 19th century brick, and is used both to heat the room as well as to bake johnnycake in its traditional built-in bread oven. Tongue and groove wide oak planks on the floor include some cut from a 33-foot oak log. The room is lit by 120 candles, literally, held in five-foot turned oak chandeliers made in Hurley's shop. Every Thursday night it is the scene for a free music jam.

Founded in 1908, **Berdine's** is the oldest, continuously working 5 & 10¢ store in the United States. Original oak shelves and display cabinets are chock full of interesting items, including Berdine's specialty, metal mechanized toys. An old timey candy counter laden with new candy is strategically placed.

Berdine's is the place for buying all the important stuff like cap pistols, trinkets, West Virginia glass, school supplies, paper dolls and thread.

For an authentic century-old hardware store that still supplies all the needs of a thriving community, you have to visit **Hunter's Hardware** in Berkeley Springs. There's a backroom filled with baskets of nuts, bolts and rare plumbing supplies, as well as seed bins supplied each spring with the makings for peas, lettuce, beans and spinach.

You get sucked in by the red covered "kissing" bridge and a tiny car with a wind-up key on it; you stay for the stories, local products and antiques. More than a century old and still in the family, **Sharpe's Country Store** in Slatyfork retains the 1926 gas pumps (non-working) and community gathering place atmosphere.

Shops that stand out in a crowd.

★ **Stages** in Wheeling is ideal for costume dressers looking for a good selection. Feather wigs, medieval robes, masks, and a huge vat of stage prop swords await you. Just south of town is **Imperial Teacher's Store**, a warehouse filled with everything from write-on inflatable globes to almost life-size posters of George Washington.

★ Housed in an 1847 restored bank-style barn originally built by Samuel Harper complete with stone foundation and hand-hewn beams, the **Lost River Artisans Cooperative** showcases more than 60 juried artists, books, wines and local foods. There's a local museum on the lower floor and one of the trendiest neighborhoods in the state surrounding it.

★ In Berkeley Springs, the **Ice House** is a century-old former cold storage building turned art center. A co-op of more than three dozen local and area artists and artisans, ever-changing gallery shows, and locally designed logoed products make this the first stop before heading out to other art shops and studios in this town with a national art reputation.

★ For holiday shopping year 'round, the bright red **Greenbrier Christmas Shop at the Depot** offers five rooms overfull with exquisite ornaments, decorated trees and gifts. Located in White Sulphur Springs across from the Greenbrier, the Depot stocks new items in October.

★ Eddie's signature trucks haul tires from Berkeley Springs to a dozen outlets elsewhere in West Virginia and three other states. But it is the **Eddie's Tires** mother store, south of Berkeley Springs, that draws the customers. They drive from all over for the rock-bottom price, the broad selection from a variety of brands, and most of all for the service. "They can't believe we can get them in and out with new tires, all balanced in twenty minutes to a half hour," said Debbie Dhayer—daughter of Eddie, the late founder—one of the pillars of the family-owned empire.

Eddie and Louise Stotler parlayed a roadside gas station into a tire business in 1951. When word was out that Eddie was coming in from a factory run with tires to sell, folks would gather and wait. A half-century and millions of tires later, Eddie's continues to keep the rubber on the road.

It's a cross between a museum and a game check center. The rows of whole animals and mounted heads at **Spencer's Taxidermy** *hints at the importance of game in the state. Three men are kept busy stuffing the prizes in the backroom workshop.*

★ Vintage stringed instruments and the mountain music they are made for are the focus of **Fret 'n Fiddle** in St. Albans. In addition to buying and selling instruments all over the world, the shop is the home of a monthly jam session of the Appalachian Fiddlers Association.

★ In Wheeling the paramount site for produce shopping is **Jebbia's Market**, in the biz since 1886 and still operated by the family. Everything from Amish eggs to personally selected Idaho potatoes are available for both retail and wholesale. Daily lunch specials are posted on a monthly calendar.

Gangs Of Shops

★ Sprawled along I-64, **Huntington Mall** in Ona is West Virginia's biggest mall.

★ **Old Central City** in Huntington is focused on West Fourteenth Street. At an average of five antique shops per block, the exhaustive collection numbers more than twenty locations. If your shopping demon wants more, there's a Big Lots nearby.

★ More than 50 addresses are listed in a handbill for Hurricane's **Citywide Garage Sales** in August. Everyone participates. Also check out Charleston's **East End Yard Sale** held annually in May.

★ **Mountain Heritage Arts & Crafts** happens twice a year—in mid June and late September—on hundreds of acres of Sam Michael Park outside Harpers Ferry. Nearly 200 artisans are invited to participate making it one of the top 20 fine arts and craft shows in America. Over the years, my personal finds have ranged from a hand carved bone star pendant and one-of-a-kind pine needle baskets to Wild Woman pins that started a mini-craze in the state.

★ Since 1997, dozens of vendors and shops have called Charleston's **Capitol Market** home. Many more appear in pleasant weather when the outside area features regional farmers. West Virginia food products are highlighted ranging from cheese, fish and wine. Nearby is the historic site of a farmers market.

See "Truly Incredible" for information on the Gendarme Store, "Tours" for Fenton Glass and "Art Wonders" for Tamarack.

CHAPTER THIRTEEN

Superlatives

For a state that perennially turns up at the bottom of lists measuring some sort of economic progress or another, West Virginia also manages to have a number of firsts, biggest and bests to its credit.

Best Bridge

The **New River Bridge** was the world's longest single arch steel bridge when it opened in 1977, but the Chinese built the Lupo Bridge 105 feet longer in 2003, relegating the New River Bridge to longest in the Western Hemisphere. Its main span is 1,700 feet long and the total length is 3,030 feet. Suspended 876 feet above the New River, it is the highest bridge east of the Mississippi; second highest in the United States. Building the bridge cut the time needed to cross the New River Gorge from 45 minutes to 45 seconds. The bridge, which cost almost $37 million, was deliberately left unpainted so it would be less obtrusive against the scenery, and would not require constant repainting.

The bridge is the site of one of the world's most unique events. On **Bridge Day** hundreds come to jump off the span while thousands of others line up to watch.

The railroad bridge in Point Pleasant is the longest in the country. It spans two rivers—the Ohio and Kanawha—and the entire town.

All these reasons, and the sheer beauty of it, earned the New River Bridge a ranking among the 10 top all-time bridges from *Roads and Bridges* magazine. Now that there is a walking bridge suspended beneath the road bridge, thrills are readily available everyday without the need for a parachute. For more on Bridge Day, *see* "Far Out Festivals."

Also rare but on a much smaller scale, the Rainbow Bridge in Mingo County is the only single span formed concrete arch bridge in the eastern U.S.

Tunnel To Anti-Terrorism

Thousands pass it daily driving on I-64/77 south of Charleston. The **West Virginia Memorial Tunnel** started life in 1954 as part of the West Virginia Turnpike. It was unique then being the first tunnel in the U.S. monitored by television. The two-lane, 2,800-foot highway tunnel required moving 30 million cubic yards of earth. A little more than 30 years later, it was bypassed and closed. Even before 9/11 made every local government into an anti-terrorism outpost, the National Guard had staked out the abandoned tunnel. A congressional mandate was given to establish it as a counterterrorism testing and training center and conversion began in 2000.

Surrounded by 10,000 acres of semi-wilderness, the **Center for National Response at Memorial Tunnel** is a one-of-a-kind training facility. Users may choose scenarios ranging from post blast rubble with hazards or three labs of weapons of mass destruction (always referred to as WMD) to subway train and station.

The most gleeful person in the state about this resource may be the film commissioner who is merrily shopping it to moviemakers with disaster scenes. Watch for the tunnel at a multiplex near you.

Coasters and Corn Dogs

Camden Park is a stop on the pilgrimage of roller coaster devotees, prized for its two historic wooden coasters. The "Little Dipper" is the only kiddie coaster made of wood still operating in the United States. The younger "Big Dipper" is another classic wooden coaster, ranked in coasterdom's top 100 and included in American Coaster Enthusiasts Hall of Fame. It is one of the few in the country that still uses manual brakes and where you can ride without seat dividers or individual lap bars meaning the force can lift you out of the seat. The classic carousel was the first ride in the park, and has kept spinning since it debuted in 1907.

Camden Park was built at an exchange point on the trolley line with an eye toward boosting streetcar traffic from Huntington. At one time there were prizefights, cockfights and hot air balloon ascensions at the 26-acre amusement park that has not missed a summer since it opened in 1903. Today, there is still more than thrilling rides. The park's Pronto Pups are rated by many as the world's best corn dogs, and it may be the only amusement park with an authentic Indian mound. It even has a dinosaur exhibit. Bargain prices are the icing on the cake of West Virginia's sole remaining amusement park.

Golf Here First

Russell Montague had a private estate named Oakhurst just down the road from the Greenbrier. In 1884, he added six holes of golf and formed **the first golf club in America** for his rich and fancy friends. For six successive Christmas days they met in the "Oakland Medal," the **first series of annual golf tournaments** in the United States. The club was disbanded in the early 1900s. In 1959 Lewis Keller bought the course from Montague's son at the urging of his friend Sam Snead and eventually restored it. Oakhurst Links was recently purchased by the nearby Greenbrier which plans to continue a traditional operation with fairways mowed by grazing sheep, replica hickory clubs, gutta percha balls made from tree sap and a museum demonstrating how golf was originally played.

Not only did Montague have the first organized golf club, he also had the **first golf club made in America.** His handy man, Frazer Coron, fashioned it with an apple wood head and a hickory handle.

Star-studded golf made its way to the **Greenbrier** by 1913. President

Woodrow Wilson was one of the first to tee-off. He played there often and other luminaries followed in his trail, including the Duke of Windsor both before and after his abdication as Edward VIII of England. The Greenbrier was one of Dwight D. Eisenhower's favorite golf retreats and JFK's sister, Pat Kennedy, won an amateur tournament there.

Sam Snead began and ended his remarkable career as the Greenbrier's pro, and he and Ben Hogan had repeated match-ups during the 1950s when both were in their prime. In 1957, Snead played the most competitive round of golf in history at the Greenbrier, a feat commemorated in the resort's Sam Snead Museum. Bing Crosby played there and Bob Hope shot his best round of golf at the Greenbrier.

Today, guests may choose from three championship golf courses including the famous Greenbrier Course, the only resort course in the world to have hosted both the Ryder and Solheim tournaments. In 2010 golf's PGA Greenbrier Classic arrived at the Old White Course and was soon named by the tour as its Best in Class Tournament.

Another one-of-a-kind course is the **Peter Dye Golf Club,** near Bridgeport, which boasts a coal tipple and 22 coal-filled mine cars, as well as three lakes and a large stream. A portion of the cart path from hole six to seven passes through a section of mine tunnel. Its 18 holes are built on land that has been both deep and strip mined. It hosts the West Virginia Classic, part of the official PGA National Tour. **Twisted Gun** in Mingo County is also built on reclaimed mine land.

Glass Champs

The **world's largest punchbowl** is in fact the world's largest surviving piece of cut lead crystal and it is no sideshow oddity. The punchbowl stands four feet ten inches tall, weighs 225 pounds, and holds 16 gallons of liquid. Lit for dramatic impact by Oglebay Institute's theater designer, it is front and center at **Oglebay's Glass Museum**. Point and shoot and the story unfolds.

The bowl was called a vase by its designer, Thomas Sweeney of the noted Sweeney Glass Company. Thomas and his brother Michael made the bowl in 1844. A smaller version, made for Henry Clay, was broken in 1916 and the pieces lost in a 1930 house fire. The larger Sweeney punchbowl disappeared during a family squabble and did not turn up until 1875, when Thomas found it encased in granite pillars at his brother's grave with an inscription claiming that the bowl was made by Michael alone. It was finally removed from the gravesite in 1949 to protect it from vandalism.

There are five pieces to the original punchbowl. In the glass shop above the museum 12-inch models with removable lids are made for sale by Fenton Glass.

West Virginia was the #1 glass producer in America, with its home-turf advantages of white silica sand, limestone and natural gas. Two manufacturing processes invented in Wheeling revolutionized glass making and contributed to the state's ascendancy. William Layton added bicarbonate of soda to the mix of sand in 1864 and Michael Owens invented the bottle-making machine in 1904.

Newest Boy Scout Camp on the New

Because the New River Gorge is the coolest, most action-packed area in the country, the Boy Scouts of America chose it for the biggest and most impressive project in their history. The 10,600 acre **Summit Bechtel National Scout Reserve** is BSA's 4th High Adventure Base and permanent home of the National Scout Jamboree. The Reserve includes mountain bike courses, zip lines, man-made climbing, shooting ranges, water sports and an incredible skateboard park plus access to the 70,000 acres of the New River Gorge National River Area. All in all, a worthy project for nearly $100 million in donations.

Holidays Invented Here

In 1868, Julia Pierpont initiated **Memorial Day** in Fairmont as a means of honoring Civil War dead. She was the wife of loyal Virginia's Civil War Governor Francis Pierpoint.

Forty years later, Anna Jarvis fulfilled her mother's wish for a day to be set aside to honor all mothers and daughters with a public celebration on May 10, 1908, the anniversary of her mother's death. The ceremony was held at Andrews Methodist Church in Grafton where Mrs. Jarvis taught Sunday school, and **Mother's Day** was introduced to the world. By 1914 it was a national holiday. Today it's the day when more greeting cards are sold and more people eat out than any other. Anna Jarvis spent the rest of her life objecting to this commercialism that began almost immediately after the holiday became official.

In 1962, the **International Mothers Day Shrine** was erected at the church. Each Mother's Day, special services are held there at 2:30 pm.

The mother-daughter devotion that inspired Mother's Day shines in almost identical faces staring from portraits of the two at the **Anna Jarvis Birthplace House**. Once used as headquarters by General McClellan, the wooden house is a museum, with Mothers Day festivities and renovation-naming opportunities honoring individual mothers. Anna was honored by being the first woman to have a bronze bust in the lower rotunda of the Capitol.

Fathers were not forgotten. In July 1908, the first **Father's Day** celebration was held in Fairmont, motivated in part by the Monongah mine disaster.

Teddy Bears in Real Life

We all know that Teddy Bears originated with President Theodore Roosevelt. What is less well known are the West Virginia roots of that all-American toy. As the story goes, a young girl in Greenbrier County rescued a baby bear from a forest fire and treated it as a pet. A candidate for public office with connections to TR's wife had promised to send her children a bear. He decided the rescued cub was just the thing and sent it off to then-Vice President Roosevelt. The press corps wrote about Teddy's bear and a classic was born. The bear soon became too much to handle and was sent to live out its life at the New York Zoological Gardens.

Far Out First!

★ **The first motorized plow** was built in Charleston in 1915 from a push plow and Indian motorcycle parts by Benjamin Franklin Gravely. A photographer by trade, Gravely needed to raise food for his family so he tinkered with garden implements. Local legend claims that Gravely was actually inventing a post hole digger that ran away from him and plowed a furrow in the garden. Eureka! Gravely International remains a major manufacturer of garden implements.

★ The first pilot plant of commercial size to **produce nylon** was erected at Belle.

★ The small town of Beverly claims the **first public cemetery west of the Alleghenies** with burials dating from 1768. Soldiers from every American war short of the 1991 Gulf War are buried there.

★ The **first brick paved street** in the United States was Summers Street, financed in 1872 by Dr. John Hale, a Charleston businessman, at his own expense. Fellow West Virginian, Mordecai Levi, had recently invented the system of brick paving that allowed Charleston this singular honor. A third West Virginian, John Porter, contributed the unique vitrified brick needed for street paving.

★ **Arthurdale** became the **first resettlement community of Federal Homestead Act** in 1933 with 165 houses built on 2,400 acres. It was a favorite project of Eleanor Roosevelt and considered one of the greatest social experiments of the time. By 1938, the population of the experimental community was more than 1,000. That year, FDR gave his only graduation address as president at Arthurdale. Tours of the community today point out examples of the original structures that remain. Federal funding ran out in the early 1940s and all are now private homes. The New Deal Homestead Museum operates in five of the original structures including the forge. Littlepage Terrace and Washington Manor were the **first low-income housing project application**. The buildings still provide housing in Charleston. Another social experiment found the first food stamps issued in 1961 in Paynesville.

★ The notion of delivering mail directly to rural homes occurred to William Wilson, Postmaster General of the United States in 1896. He chose his hometown of Charles Town to launch the **first RFD, rural free delivery,** on October 1. The Charles Town Post Office is still open for business.

★ Marlinton in 1747 became the **first recorded settlement** west of the Alleghenies.

★ Occasionally being first is not all it's cracked up to be. In 1921, West Virginia was the first state to **enact a gross sales tax.** As if making up for this abuse, the gimmick of **Dollar Day** as a time of sales, was invented by a Preston County man who immigrated to New York. Sometime around 1913, the state passed the first **workman's compensation law** in the United States.

★ In 2000, West Virginia became the first state to offer its drivers an **official Nascar license plate.**

★ Like George Washington, Thomas "Stonewall" Jackson was everywhere in the state. Born in Clarksburg, he grew up near Weston with his grandfather who planned the town. As a military professor at Virginia Military Institute, he chose the South and took his cadets to war. Tall, awkward and badly dressed, Jackson was not a romantic general in the vein of Robert E. Lee. He was, however, one of the figures who modernized warfare with his tactical brilliance and battlefield innovations. Wounded by his own troops, Jackson died in 1863. In 1921, Stonewall Jackson's family farm in Weston became the **first state 4-H camp in the United States.**

★ Salt making was a prehistoric industry along the Kanawha and Little Kanawha rivers. Indians would boil the brine from salt springs along the rivers to evaporate the salt. Kanawha "red salt"—its color derived from iron impurities—was treasured for its superior quality in curing meats and making butter. At the turn to the 19th century, the Kanawha Valley was the largest salt production area in the country and it spawned several industrial "firsts." In 1806, **America's first deep well** was drilled at the Old Ruffner Saltworks to bring up salt water and in 1817, salt makers at the Kanawha Salines (today's Malden) met to form the country's first trust—the **Kanawha Salt Trust**. Salt production continued in the Malden area until 1985. Although salt production has virtually disappeared, the presence of this raw material is the basis for the Kanawha Valley's world-class chemical industry.

★ When 18-year-old George Washington arrived in 1750 with his older brother Lawrence in tow to "take the waters at Bath," there was already a well established spa society during the summer season around the famous warm springs later known as Berkeley. Today's Berkeley Springs is **the country's first warm water spa.**

★ The **first National Recreation Area** so designated by the U.S. Forest Service was the 100,000 acre **Spruce Knob-Seneca Rocks NRA** in 1965. It includes both the highest point in West Virginia and the only true rock pinnacle summit east of Devil's Tower, Wyoming. In 1911 legislation was passed allowing for purchase of land not already in the public domain. Two years earlier West Virginia had consented to federal purchase of lands in the state for what became the Monongahela National Forest.

★ The world's **first golden trout** to emerge in captivity originated from a single yellow-mottled fingerling in the state hatchery at Petersburg in 1955. It was a mutation from the more common rainbow trout. Known as the West Virginia Centennial Golden Trout, the state first stocked streams with it in 1963. From August through October, the nature show features the trout in stages from spawning, to hatchling, to ready-for-the-streams.

★ Beginning in the late 1870s the first moveable dams in the United States were built on the Kanawha River. By 1898, the lock and dam system was completed making it **America's first complete river lock and dam system**.

★ In 1811, Alexander Quarrier invented the **world's first automobile** in Charleston. It used a steam engine. Twenty years earlier, James Rumsey, true inventor of the steamboat, patented a vehicle that looked suspiciously like a horseless carriage. For more on Rumsey, *see* "Historic Oddities."

★ A fashion industry hero! James Gibbs, invented the chain stitch sewing machine on his Pocahontas County farm at Mill Point near McNell Mill. He showed it to great acclaim in 1854 at the precursor of today's state fair then held near the present site of the WV Osteopathic School in Lewisburg.

★ In 1989, the Secretary of the Army designated **Morgan's Grove Park** "birthplace of the U.S. Army," by virtue of the Bee Line March to Cambridge in 1775. Colonel Hugh Stephenson marched his company from here to Boston in 24 days to be the first troops to join George Washington's Continental Army.

★ The world's first concrete street was laid in Webster Springs in 1903.

★ Philippi might lay claim to the first land battle and first limb amputation of the Civil War (*see* "Truly Incredible") but Grafton had the first casualty when Private Thornsberry Bailey Brown was the first Union soldier killed by a Confederate soldier. He is buried in the state's first national cemetery in Grafton where Brown was shot. It was in Parsons (Corricks Ford) where the first general of the war was killed on July 13, 1861—General Robert Garnett. The first American soldier killed in the Korean War hailed from Pineville. His statue stands today in front of the Pineville Courthouse. Another military first took place in 1863 when Fayetteville was the scene for the first use of indirect artillery fire in warfare.

★ Martinsburg was the location in 1955 for the first civil defense test in which the government actually left Washington taking account of radioactive fallout. The Old Federal Building, now housing the Art Centre, was designated for Department of Justice top officials. Attorney General Robert F. Kennedy requested that he be relocated to the Martinsburg site. Shepherd College was designated as relocation site for the FBI. Plans to take over the college were extensive and an FBI microwave telecommunications station was built on the grounds of the mansion that now serves as the president's house. All these plans were in the days before underground bunkers at locales including the Greenbrier.

★ The first **bluegrass music college degree program** in the country, probably the world, is at **Glenville State** with famed fiddler Buddy Griffin at the helm. An impressive list of successful graduates can be found in all aspects of the bluegrass world.

Biggest! Highest! Longest!

★ Mountains ring the 14-mile long Canaan Valley. At 3,200 feet, it's the **highest valley east of Mississippi** and home to several natural wonders. With a climate that mimics northern New England and guarantees 150-200 inches of snow a season, Canaan Valley is prime ski country. It is also an unusual and fragile Arctic ecology, with the second largest inland wetlands in the United States and the ridge top running Blackwater River. Nearby Davis is the **highest incorporated town east of the Mississippi**. This exalted elevation brings out the reds in the trees earlier than elsewhere in the state making it the ideal setting for the September Leaf Peepers Festival. The **highest courthouse east of Denver** is found in Princeton. The whole state is sublimely elevated. Its mean elevation of 1,500 feet makes it the **highest state east of the Mississippi.**

Folks like to say that if the mountains were pressed flat, West Virginia would be bigger than Texas.

★ West Virginia's unique geography places it on the Allegheny Front, a formation that generates constant wind currents. No surprise that the huge **Mt. Storm Wind Farm** with more than 130 turbines and counting is the largest in the east. The graceful and otherworldly wind towers are a startling visual addition to mountain peaks, overlooks and rock formations.

★ A 200 by 55-foot Civil War bombproof structure at Fort Mulligan, near Petersburg, may be the largest in existence. There is a unique overlapping entrance near the water tank.

★ **The Blues Revue**, the world's largest blues magazine is written and published in Salem by Bob Vorel.

★ The **State Capitol** in Charleston was completed in 1932 after two earlier

★ **Droop Mountain** *is the site of the* **largest Civil War conflict in West Virginia.** *Union victory here in 1863 secured most of the state for the duration of the war at a cost of nearly 600 casualties. While the park was under construction by Civilian Conservation Corps members in 1935, workers were unnerved by forests of dead chestnuts and sink holes filled with bodies.*

ones burned in less than a decade bringing the total of buildings that served as the capitol to six—plus two steamboats. It was designed by noted architect, Cass Gilbert, and built with a dome taller than the U.S. Capitol and larger than any other state's. In a rash of flagrant display, the 293-foot high lead dome was coated first with copper, and then with gold leaf. It kept flaking off until a 1991 restoration that used 30,000 square feet of gold leaf resulted in the dome Gilbert envisioned. It took two years to re-gild it in 2005-6 during which time the plastic wrapped dome look like an ad for a safe-sex commercial. At the same time, the House of Delegates Chamber was restored to Gilbert's original paint job of cream, beige, crimson and sky blue from the former trendy but garish maroon, pink and teal. A two-ton chandelier of more than 10,000 pieces of Czech crystal hangs 180 feet above the floor in the dome's Rotunda, reached by climbing 48 steps, one for each state at the time of construction. In a nod to numerical symmetry, there are 333 rooms in the Capitol.

The east and west entries of the Capitol are protected by the heads of Roman gods and goddesses worshipped by few in the Mountain State. Mercury, Minerva, Neptune, Ceres, Vesta and Vulcan are all represented. Far more West Virginians pay homage to the winged tire that hangs over the entrance to the Department of Motor Vehicle building across from the Capitol's west entrance.

To demonstrate the difference in status between the small Senate and larger House of Delegates, the Senate's carved eagles have their wings open, in the House chamber they are closed.

★ The Greenbrier River is **longest free-flowing river** in the eastern United States as it flows south from its birthplace along the Continental Divide in Pocohantas County into the New River at Hinton. Fish species unique to the New River watershed make for one-of-a-kind fishing.

Running along much of the river is the 76-mile **Greenbrier Trail** for hikers, bikers, horseback riders and cross-country skiers. It is considered among the top ten hiking trails in the United States. *See* "Adventure Driving" for more.

★ Middle Island Creek, which drains most of Doddridge County and then flows 75 miles west into the Ohio, is called the **longest creek in the world.**

★ Plopped into an intersection just north of downtown Chester, the **world's largest teapot** announces that fact, making it an ideal photo opportunity. A former hogshead barrel from a root beer sales campaign, the tin skinned teapot has been more or less in place since 1938.

★ The **world's largest sycamore tree** is on Back Fork Trail one mile east of Webster Springs. The **largest hemlock** east of the Mississippi is in **Cathedral State Forest**. Named Centennial, it is more than 120 feet tall and is estimated at nearly 500 years old. With its 63-inch diameter, the **world's largest chinquapin oak** is in captivity at West Virginia's **Core Arboretum.**

★ Rainelle United Methodist Church is the world's largest room made from wormy chestnut wood.

★ Wheeling is filled with big things. La Belle was the **largest cut nail plant** in the world. Up until its closing in 2010, it operated in the same buildings with the same machines and a staff blacksmith making old-style square cut nails of American steel much the same way as it did when established in 1852. Wheeling Island is second only to Manhattan as the **most heavily populated inland river island** in the United States. Largest of the Ohio River islands, it has 5,000 people, a glittery casino and greyhound racing at Wheeling Island Racetrack and Gaming Center and a wildlife refuge on its point.

The incredible **Oglebay Resort** with panoramic views of its more than 1,700 acres, three 18-hole golf courses, lakes and a 65-acre zoo is operated by the Wheeling Park Commission making it the **world's largest municipal park**. More than a million people visit Oglebay's winterlong "Festival of the Lights," making it one of the state's most visited attraction.

★ The **world's longest ribbon stalactite** hangs from the ceiling of **Smoke Hole Caverns** and weighs six tons. Nearby are unusual side-growing helectites and the second highest ceiling of any eastern cavern—274 feet. The caverns have always been popular, used by Seneca Indians to smoke meat, by Civil War soldiers to store ammunition, and by moonshiners who appreciated both the abundant supply of spring water and the single entrance cavern. Visitors on guided tours, given every half hour, can watch formations taking shape drop by drop in this still-active cave.

★ Contemporary weddings are held in **Seneca Cavern's** Grand Ballroom, the **second largest cavern room** in world. The caverns were discovered in 1760.

★ Weirton Steel became the **largest employee-owned plant** in the United States in 1982. It stretches for miles between SR 2 and the Ohio River. Along the southern edge of the state, U.S. Steel has the **world's largest preparation plant** in Gary.

★ The NBA superstar is a bona fide homegrown sports hero. The **largest**

public collection of Jerry West memorabilia, including his 1960 Olympics gold medal, is on display at the steak restaurant named for him—**44 West at the Greenbrier**. The restaurant also offers one of the state's supreme pieces of beef, a 44-ounce porterhouse.

★ Located on the Ohio River, Huntington is the **largest inland port** in the United States based on tonnage.

★ Tucked away in the Ceredo Museum is the **Ceredo Petroglyph**, largest and best preserved in the country.

★ The place to go for a lobotomy in the early 1950s was the **Trans-Allegheny Lunatic Asylum,** base of operations for lobotomy technique initiator, Walter Freeman. One of the exhibit rooms on the TALA tour of historic medical horror is a room tricked out for treatments.

Dam Dams

When huge **Summersville Dam** was begun in 1960 by the Army Corps of Engineers, they faced a serious dilemma. Usually the Corps names a dam after the nearest post office. They chose to break tradition and forgo having Gad Dam.

Summersville Dam is 390 feet high and the **second largest rock-fill dam** in the east. It has more than paid its $48 million price tag through the whitewater epiphany caused when water from the Gauley River is released via 29-foot wide tunnels. *See* "Fast Living."

The Army Corps of Engineers built its **first concrete-faced dam** at R.D. Bailey Lake on the Guyandotte River in the 1970s. The unusual, 18-acre rock-filled structure is a quarter of a mile across and 310 feet high—the second highest in the state. The intake structure is designed to mix varied temperatures of water to enhance the fishing. Perched above the 630-acre lake the dam created, a visitors center provides great views.

Tygart Dam in Grafton is the **oldest and largest concrete dam** east of the Mississippi. It was built by the CCC and completed in 1938. Tours are given in the summer.

Burnsville Lake Dam does not feel degraded by serving as the outfield wall for the recreation area's baseball field, surely a rarity in dam-world.

It Is The Oldest

★ Sitting inside the tiny log building with rough benches and a balcony along two sides, it is easy to imagine Francis Asbury, America's first Methodist Bishop, standing on the raised platform and preaching in the space two years after its dedication in 1786. **Rehobeth Church and Museum** is the **oldest church building** in existence west of the Alleghenies. Dedicated while Shawnee still terrorized the frontier, it was hidden in a sinkhole for protection. Surrounded by an 18th century cemetery, it is one of ten dedicated Methodist shrines in America.

★ The imposing **Old Stone Presbyterian Church** in Lewisburg is the oldest church building in continuous use west of Alleghenies. The two-story native limestone building was constructed in 1796 for a congregation organized in 1783. Tradition claims that women of the congregation carried sand for the building on horseback from the Greenbrier River. The church has an old slave gallery and cemetery. It served as a hospital during the Civil War.

★ **Marsh Wheeling Stogies** have been manufactured since 1840. That made the company the **oldest American cigar manufacturer** still operating under its original name in the city where it was founded until it closed in late 2001. Now, only the distinctive sign remains. Mifflin Marsh started the business by selling his thin, hand-rolled cigars from a basket—four for a penny. By 1879, Wheeling was teeming with nearly 100 stogie factories complete with "readers" to entertain the workers while they rolled.

★ Built in 1770, the **Graham House** between Hinton and Alderson is the **oldest log home** on its original site in West Virginia.

★ Stretching far back into the mists of time, archeological digs have confirmed **St. Albans** as the **oldest continuously inhabited location** in both Americas.

★ The **oldest tower clock** in the state is found at **McMurran Hall** in Shepherdstown. Still wound by hand twice weekly, the clock is one of only three known to be made by noted 19th century watchmaker, A.L. Dennison of Boston.

*The **oldest continuously active military unit** in the United States Army is the 201st West Virginia Army National Guard which began as Captain Morgan Morgan's Company of Volunteer Militia in 1735. Today's West Virginia Guard has been named best in the country.*

★ The **oldest family reunion** in America is that held by the Coles and Skaggs in Fayette County.

★ The **oldest dated quilt** in the country was made in 1795 at Clear Fork in Wyoming County.

Just Plain Special

★ The **world's largest draw knob organ** built by native son Allen Harrah found an appreciative home at Forest Burdette United Methodist Church in Hurricane. The **Harrah Symphonic Organ** has 456 draw knobs, six keyboards, 64 computers, 26,000 pipes and more than 20,000 digital notes. It can produce sounds ranging from drum rolls to trumpet calls, can simulate an entire symphony orchestra and unleashed could blow the stained glass windows from their frames. Total cost: about $1 million.

★ Kimball World War I Memorial in Kimball ranks as both the **first black American Legion building** in the United States as well as **the only existing monument of African-American participation in World War I.** Dedicated in 1928, it was designed in the classical style by Welch

 architect Hassel Hicks. It is not surprising to find this monument in McDowell County. When the coal mines were booming, African-Americans made up half of the county's population and 1,500 blacks left from here for World War I. Gutted by fire in 1991, only four walls remained. It was restored and re-dedicated in 2010.

Hicks also designed the **first multi-level municipal parking garage** in the United States located in Welch, as well as the **Williamson Coal House**.

 ★ While a small but choice play area cut into the hillside earns Ritter Park acclaim as **one of the ten best playgrounds** in the United States, there are several other magnificent attributes to Huntington's 78-acre municipal park.

In the playground, larger than life stone columns, arches, triangles and sand box are joined by a wonderful collection of slides and tunnels—including an Alice in Wonderland hole—where kids can crawl, tuck, hide and climb. Nothing is plastic. The several block-long stretch of green that extends from the playground area is always filled with walkers, baby strollers, joggers, bikers, bench sitters, folks with dogs and even elderly 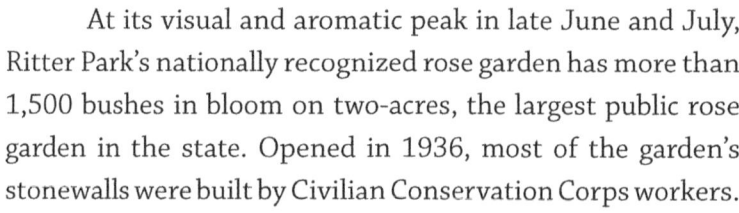 gentlemen practicing their golf swings. The addition of a magnificent fountain dresses up the 10th Street entrance.

At its visual and aromatic peak in late June and July, Ritter Park's nationally recognized rose garden has more than 1,500 bushes in bloom on two-acres, the largest public rose garden in the state. Opened in 1936, most of the garden's stonewalls were built by Civilian Conservation Corps workers.

★ The original compound was built in 1774. The reconstruction of **Prickett's Fort**—16 cabins, meeting hall and storehouse—is considered the most authentic and accurate portrayal of a frontier refuge fort in existence. Even the interpreters are authentically clothed. In April, The School of the Longhunters trains folks to live like frontiersmen, offering seminars ranging from powder horns to 18th century clothing. Folks attend in costume and sleep in period tents.

★ America's **largest indigenous Christian denomination**—Disciples of Christ—developed and thrived in **Bethany** through the Campbell family. They founded Bethany College, built the historically significant nearly all walnut Alexander Campbell Mansion, and lie in state surrounded by spectacular hand-hewn stone block walls.  Today's Bethany is dominated by an early example of American collegiate Gothic Revival architecture—the Old Main with its distinctive 140-foot clock tower. Begun in 1858 and completed in 1871, Old Main was designed by Cincinnati architect, James Key Wilson. Another significant structure is Pendleton Heights, built in 1841-42, once a site on the Underground Railroad and often used to house the college's president. All in all, the campus is an architectural paradise and the tiny town nestled on the campus outskirts is nearly free of recognizable development and modern intrusions.

Bethany claims two other distinctions. The national fraternity **Delta Tau Delta** was started there in 1859 and the **telephone was invented** at Bethany.

★ NASA's **Classroom of the Future** is located in the Challenger Learning Center at Wheeling Jesuit University. It pioneered streaming video in the Clinton White House.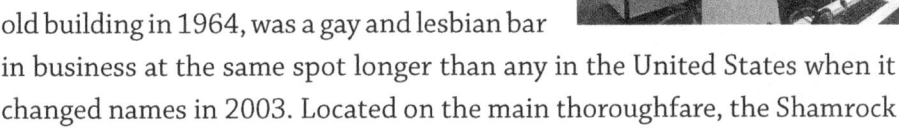

★ Bluefield's **Shamrock**, opened in a century-old building in 1964, was a gay and lesbian bar in business at the same spot longer than any in the United States when it changed names in 2003. Located on the main thoroughfare, the Shamrock was known primarily through word-of-mouth until Carol Burch-Brown, a professor at Virginia Tech, decided to document the life of a working class gay bar in photographs and interviews. Included is the famous drag queen Miss Shamrock Pageant. Burch-Brown's material is available at the Smithsonian's Museum of American History archives.

★ The **only privately owned interstate toll bridge** in the country can be found just west of Paw Paw on SR 51 to Oldtown. It's a bargain at 50¢.

★ That West Virginia has had the **lowest crime rate** in the nation for a quarter of a century speaks volumes about our quality of life.

★ Coal reserves in West Virginia are considered to contain the **best bituminous coal** in the world.

Aviation First!

The Wright brothers' first airplane was made from Cheat Mountain red spruce. *The Aviator*—a statue of Weston native Louis Bennett Jr. organizer of the West Virginia Flying Corps who was shot down during World War I—was the **first memorial to an aviator in the United States.** Showing Bennett in a pair of enormous bird-like wings, it was dedicated in Wheeling in 1925.

On display at **Wheeling Airport's terminal museum** is the flight suit of Wellsburg tail gunner, Staff Sgt. Donald Crosby who was the **highest scoring aerial gunner in the European theater** during World War II. Also featured in the museum is Lawrence Lambert, a West Virginia native who was the **first American to successfully test an ejection seat**. Lambert executed his feat from a Black Widow P-61 flying 302 miles per hour at 7,800 feet.

The state's first aviator, Paul Peck, died in a plane crash before he was 25.

There are other superlatives scattered in other chapters throughout the book. These are a few of the cross-references to check:

★ *See* "Amazing Architecture" for:

Trans-Allegheny Lunatic Asylum—largest hand-cut blue sandstone building in the United States

Our Lady of the Pines—smallest church in United States

Camp Washington Carver—1st African-American 4-H camp in United States.

★ *See* "Art Wonders" for the *Robey*—oldest continuously operated movie theater in America.

★ *See* "Historic Oddities" for *Grave Creek Mound*—largest conical earthen mound of its kind.

★ *See* "Mother Nature's Wonders" for:

first Grimes golden and *first golden delicious* apple trees discovered.

world's second oldest river—the New!

world's highest coal seam—the Pocahontas Coal Field.

CHAPTER FOURTEEN

Things That Used To Be There

The importance of things that are no longer is underlined in West Virginia by the commonplace method of giving directions: "turn at the corner where _____ used to be." It happens all the time.

Some of these important—or infamous—buildings, businesses and historic marvels still have sights to see; others are relegated to photographs or drawings. All play a part in the fabric of life—past, present and future—that is West Virginia. These are a small sample.

Springs Society

For more than a century, society took their leisure while they took the waters at a string of resorts that lined the edge of the Blue Ridge. The spas shared cycles of prosperity and decline that were caused by common factors. Blue Ridge spas flourished in the first half of the 19th century when they were all in Virginia. The Civil War dealt spa society a disastrous blow and divided the circuit into Virginia and West Virginia. The railroads brought another burst of activity from the 1870s through the early part of the 20th century.

Only three in West Virginia survived the fire, flood and economic bad times to flourish today—Berkeley Springs, Capon Springs and the Greenbrier, and only the latter continues in the grand tradition. All that remain of the others are waters and ruins. *See* the spring's tour in "Adventure Driving."

The red brick and white columned splendor of the **Sweet Springs Hotel**—designed and built in 1833 by William Phillips, a talented builder at the University of Virginia—sits empty and unused, patiently waiting for wise restoration. Three two-story brick guest houses added in the 1850s remain in varying degrees of disrepair. Long rows of chinking-less log lodging rooms with stone fireplaces that resemble a 19th century motel are, in fact, remnants of slave and servant quarters. The first hotel built on the spot in 1792 is long gone.

Sweet Springs had notable guests and presidential visitors from George Washington to Franklin Pierce. The Civil War knocked Sweet Springs from its pinnacle, although the railroad filled the resort with thousands of guests in the 1870s. West Virginia bought the property in 1945, using it successively as a tuberculosis sanitarium and a home for the aged. Today it is privately owned and the topic of ongoing conversations about revival.

The exotic bath building, across the lawn from the hotel, would clean up well. All brick, there is a central open-air pool where active springs can be seen bubbling. Historically the springs were famous for their acidic briskness and cures for rheumatism and nerve disorders. Today, water from the springs is bottled and sold. It has won repeatedly at the Berkeley Springs International Water Tasting.

Capon Springs originally was a splendid pre-Civil War mountain spa and a favorite part of the summer springs tour. Today, Capon Springs is a pre-World War II family resort, with just a tinge of its illustrious antebellum heritage. When built in 1849, four-story Mountain House with its long colonnade was one of the largest structures in the South. Its oval outdoor swimming pool was the largest in Virginia. Mountain House burned in 1911; the pool still serves today.

Contemporary Capon Springs has nearly a dozen white Victorian buildings, a comfortable main hotel and a spa. It is arranged as a 19th century resort village on both sides of a main thoroughfare. The hot, cold and steam bath houses are now residential. Virtually in ruins during the 1920s, today's resort is a registered historic district. For more on Capon Springs, *see* "Great Plumbing/Unusual Places to Stay."

Nothing remains of the century-old spa that once was a large summer resort with a grand hotel. More than 3,000 acres of the land is now Lost River State Park, and the whitewashed log cabin of original owner Light Horse Harry Lee is a museum. Across the stream, the noted sulphuric spring is captive under glass in a pavilion labeled with the name given in the 1890s—**Lee White Sulphur Springs.**

Lee, the father of Robert E. Lee, acquired more than 60,000 acres of land and the sulphur springs in 1796 as spoils of war. It was land a young George Washington surveyed as part of the original Fairfax Grant. In about 1800, Lee built a boarding house of white oak on a stone foundation. He lined the spring with imported marble. Later, he reportedly built a large log hotel. The family continued to use the hotel as a resort until the Civil War. The springs and hotel became a commercial resort after the war. The resort was expanded in the 1890s and then destroyed by fire in 1910 on the day that its widowed owner took a new bride. Perhaps the ghost of the first Mrs. Carr objected to the hotel's prospective new hostess.

Turn-of-the-century accounts of the water claim it is cooler and medicinally superior to the Greenbrier's sulphur springs. They were used in the classic fashion—to relieve the discomfort of excess.

There are three different springs along Indian Creek where once stood the grand resort of "Old Salt"—**Salt Sulphur Springs:** sweet, salt and sulphur. Thousands came to "take the waters" for brain diseases including headache and mania. The original stone hotel built in 1820 still stands along with several other stone buildings built at the same time. Now a private home, it is the largest pre-Civil War stone building complex in the state. A 15-foot wooden clock tower and the Chapel of the Salt along US 219 alert you to the upcoming remains. Gone are the 72-room Erskine House on the ridge, brick cottages and legions of guests that continued until the resort finally closed in 1936.

Shannondale Springs was founded as an estate on a horseshoe peninsula of the Shenandoah River in the Eastern Panhandle by Lord Summerfield. Reportedly, Summerfield fled to America to escape a scrape he had gotten into on the Continent. Popular in the first half of the 19th century as a haunt of presidents and old world aristocracy, Shannondale claims to be the unofficial summer White House of presidents Hayes, Garfield and Arthur. By the early 20th century, fire and decay had destroyed the large brick hotel and surrounding cottages, which at the resort's peak could house 120 people. Although there were once plans to preserve the sole remaining intact bathhouse and springs to protect them from development, those plans were destroyed by fire in 2004.

Hotels and Bathhouses in Berkeley Springs

Colonel John Strother built a grand, 400-room hotel between 1845-48 on the south end of the park surrounding the famed warm springs. Strother was replacing an earlier hotel on that spot destroyed by fire in 1844. The hotel was centerpiece of a golden age for the historic springs and called successively the Pavilion, Strother and finally **Berkeley Springs Hotel.** Strother's noted son, author and illustrator David Hunter Strother—aka Porte Crayon—grew up at the hotel and later operated it. Among the hotel's most memorable guests were the men and horses of Stonewall Jackson's army, who trashed the place when they bivouacked there in 1862. David Hunter Strother had chosen to side with the North.

The Berkeley Springs Hotel was famous for its lavish entertainments and end-of-season balls during its second golden age following the Civil War. Those who enjoyed the German musicians in 1897 did not know it would be the last season. The great hotel burned in 1898. Its rival Fairfax Inn succumbed to fire three years later and the town went into decline.

The covered bathhouses of Berkeley Springs, the country's first spa, have also come and gone in successive waves. Grand Victorian baths built in 1888, designed by local inventor Henry Harrison Hunter were torn down for an outdoor swimming pool in the late 1940s. Two original bath buildings from 1784 and 1815 remain in use at Berkeley Springs State Park. The traditional spot for the grand hotel is occupied by The Country Inn built in 1933.

Hotel, Prison, Hotel, School

Prehistoric buffalo herds searching out the unique water of Pence Springs left their indelible mark by cutting a still visible trace in the hillside. The water was first bottled in the 1870s, then a hotel built in 1897. It burned, was rebuilt and became a hot spot complete with casino in the 1920s.

The next reincarnation for the Pence Springs Hotel was as the State Prison for Women from 1947 to 1983. Ashby Berkeley, whose mother worked at the prison, saved the structure from destruction and resurrected it as a hotel, leaving metal bars and poetic graffiti on the third floor for conversation pieces. Under Ashby's reign there was great food and outrageous stories about underground tunnels, brick-lined hidey holes for bootleg liquor and a bar piano that belonged to the notorious Bricktop, a jet-setting Alderson native well known on the international club circuit and late night television talk shows. She was reputed to be Charles DeGaulle's mistress as well as the owner of a Rome nightclub, established—the story goes—so she could be near the Pope.

When Ashby retired to train a new generation of hospitality workers, he sold the historic structure to a private school. The springs continue to flow and someday, perhaps, another alumnus will revive the hotel again.

Coal And Railroads Left Their Mark

Over 500 small company towns in southern West Virginia did not exist until some railroaders and industrialists in the 1880s discovered coalfields in the hills and began to mine their mineral wealth. Once the coal was gone, company stores, churches, miners' homes and coal tipples vanished too, leaving ghostly remnants and deserted town sites for hikers and rafters to contemplate. In some places, like Welch, the town still remains; it is simply the bustling population that has disappeared. The National Archives millennium display of 100 photographs of the 20th century included only one from West Virginia. It was a crowded Saturday night in Welch, circa 1948, showing three movie theaters, the main street jammed with cars and the reason why the city was called "Little New York."

There are many structures still standing at the huge Kaymoor coal mine including an almost pristine stone powder house. The mine operated from 1899 to 1962 and had a total of 202 coke ovens. It's not much more than an easy two-mile hike to the mine site from the **Kaymoor Trail** head in the New River Gorge. Or you can float down the New River. Steps take you from the trail to the town site.

The town of Watoga along the Greenbrier railroad is gone. All that remains are a few foundation stones and a bank safe, located along the **Greenbrier River Trail** eight miles south of Marlinton. **Carswell** fared better. The mine closed in 1950 but several cut stone structures remain including a powerhouse that was one of the largest in the state, an office and 200-foot brick smokestack.

The town of **Thurmond** had no main street. It was created as a steam railroad town in 1873 and the buildings of the business district opened directly onto the tracks. It was a booming place, called by some the Dodge City of the East. More than 15 passenger trains a day carried 100,000 passengers to Thurmond in 1916—more than Richmond and Cincinnati combined.

Across the New River in Southside, Glen Jean's founder—Thomas McKell—built the fabulous hundred room Dun Glen Hotel, home of a legendary 14-year poker game. He was forced to create a separate city for his hotel since he wanted liquor sales and gambling, a no-no in Thurmond whose namesake founder was a strict Baptist. Fire destroyed the hotel in 1931, and the coming of diesel locomotives lessened the demand for coal and water along the route.

Today, the National Park Service displays historic exhibits in the restored **Thurmond Train Station**, which also serves as an Amtrak stop. Ruins of four buildings that were once Main Street await restoration. One of these buildings used to house "Mrs. McLure's Restaurant," world famous for her free dinners to servicemen passing through on troop trains during World War II. The state's smallest incorporated town is Thurmond, with seven full-time residents. It stood-in for the town of Matewan in the John Sayles film of that name.

The coal barons and railroad men who made their fortune off the abundant Pocahontas coalfield decided in 1885 to create a haven for themselves in a tiny town they called **Bramwell.** Once considered the richest small town in America, Bramwell was home to 14 millionaires and had three trains a day to Manhattan. In 1917, America's first Liberty Bonds were sold here. Located in the midst of major coalfields, company payrolls moved through the Bank of Bramwell. According to local memory, the money was moved from the train to the bank in a wheelbarrow with rifle and machine gun-toting guards.

The millionaires built opulent mansions for their families and smaller mansions for the coal company physicians on Doctors Row, some of which were destroyed, along with the downtown business section, by a devastating fire in 1910. Extravagant details among the various mansions remaining include a green-toned copper roof and indoor swimming pool, stonework by Italian masters, carved mahogany panels, walls of hand-tooled leather and ebony porch floors. The Depression ended Bramwells' wealthy reign and today it is a quiet town of historic mansions, brick streets, and the meandering Bluestone River. Only the **Corner Shop** remains of the business district. It has more than 60 feet of century-old wood and glass display cases along the wall. Ice cream sodas served from an original fountain cost a buck and a quarter. The Bramwell Millionaire Garden Club hosts twice a year house tours, and several mansions now operate as B&Bs.

At the turn of the 20th century, West Virginia's more than 3,000 miles of logging railroads topped all other states. **Cass** was a log boomtown with huge milling operations developed by lumber interests in 1900 lured by the virgin timber on Cheat Mountain. Nearby was another new settlement, the railroad

The Cass Museum at the train depot includes a scale model of the built-from-scratch railroad company town at the turn of the 20th century.

and pulp mill town of Spruce, highest town in the eastern United States, and a town that never had a road. Today Spruce is a ghost town and what remains of Cass are 11 miles of restored tracks, sawmill ruins, an old engine graveyard and big log-hauling locomotives. The few remaining buildings include identical white frame loggers' houses now used as rental cottages, and one of the country's largest company stores now selling souvenirs. The state has owned and developed Cass as an historic attraction and train excursion since 1961 after the logging and mill operations ceased. For more on the Cass Railroad Excursion, *see* "Tour and Trips."

Pleasure Centers

When Big Bertha's Gentlemen's Club near the Capitol Theater on Main Street closed in 2000, it marked the whimpering finale of the vice and gambling heyday that Wheeling enjoyed for nearly a century and coined the phrase: "That Wheelin' Feelin'." A wide-open river town, one of seven national Ports of Entry in the early 19th century and perched on a major route west, Wheeling's back room poker games were standard fare in city saloons by the end of the 19th century as was the well-established red-light district. During World War I, Wheeling became known as the city of nightclubs. It boasted the only totally open bookmaking parlors between New York and Chicago, and the only burlesque theater in the state. For a lot of young men heading on trains out to war, "that Wheelin' Feelin'" was a favorite memory.

Beginning as a bootlegger during Prohibition, Big Bill Lias rose to become the Wheeling crime boss for a scene that included gambling casinos, bordellos and gang wars. When the federal government seized his assets for back taxes in the 1950s, they ended up with his racetrack—and hired Lias back to run it! By the time the scandal hit Congress, Lias was the third highest paid federal employee, close behind the President and Chief Justice of the Supreme Court.

During World War II, everyone who came from West Virginia was asked if they knew **Cinder Bottom.** Located in the town of Keystone, Cinder Bottom was a extensive area along the railroad of whorehouses and saloons—noted for offering girls of every color.

For nearly two decades at the beginning of the 20th century, the settlement across the Greenbrier River from the logging town of Cass—known as East Cass—was home to every known vice from gambling and prostitution to opium dens. There was even a Dirty Street. Fires and flood have removed all vestiges of sinful living.

Last of Their Kind

Once there were countless ferries crossing the Ohio River from Pennsylvania to Kentucky. Today only two remain. **The Sistersville Ferry is the only one based in West Virginia.** Established in 1847, it is now owned by the city. It plies its way back and forth across the river whenever a car or rider appears on the dock between 7am and 5pm daily from April through Christmas. The tiny, red, diesel-fueled paddle boat holds four cars and has a seating deck. Recently, the city bought a new diesel ferry, renovated towboat and eight-car barge. More authentic and less expensive than a carnival ride, the five-minute crossing costs pedestrian riders only one buck. If you're really lucky, the pilot will let you hang out in the wheelhouse. Although the Ohio destination has a name—Fly—it's the skyline of Sistersville that draws the eye, with its commemorative Victorian-era oil derrick and fine Methodist church tower.

The earliest history of the region was connected to the French and Indian wars of the mid-18th century. During this time, Governor Dinwiddie authorized a chain of forts to protect the western Virginia frontier. George Washington was the young officer entrusted with the task. Today, only **Fort Ashby** remains of Washington's 23 wooden palisade forts. Built in 1755, the tiny log building was restored in 1939, and provides a main attraction in downtown Fort Ashby.

Early Industry

Several furnaces are remnants of West Virginia's early 19th century iron industry.

The **Peter Tarr Iron Furnace** in Weirton produced cannonballs in the 1800s, including those used by Commodore Perry in his battles on Lake Erie in the War of 1812. Built in 1794, Tarr was the first blast furnace west of Alleghenies. The 20-foot circular structure was restored in 1968 and is now in a subdivision. A 30-foot stone structure in the shape of a truncated pyramid is all that remains of the **Henry Clay Iron Furnace.** Once surrounded by a community of log houses, a school and company store, the cold blast furnace was constructed about 1835. It operated until 1847 producing iron for the cut nail industry. Today's ruins are an attraction of the scenic trail in Coopers Rock State Park. Another single stack furnace like Henry Clay, the water-powered Virginia Furnace produced six net tons a day of foundry and forge pig iron beginning in 1852 along the falls of Muddy Creek. The **Bloomery Iron Furnace** operated from 1833 to 1881, floating its iron on rafts and flatboats down the Cacapon River to the Potomac. It can be seen in a tiny roadside park near Romney. The restored **Valley Furnace** was built in 1848 and produced 4.5 tons of iron daily.

Virginius Island in the Shenandoah River at Harpers Ferry was an industrial powerhouse during the 19th century with Hall's Rifle Works and other water-powered factories located on its shore. Along the Potomac on the other side of Harpers Ferry stood the 20-building complex of the U.S. Armory. The Civil War destroyed many of the industries, while later floods finished off the rest. Today, the picturesque ruins of the Shenandoah Pulp Company Mill are part of hiking and picnicking on Virginius Island.

All phases of Harpers Ferry's long social and industrial history are captured in today's National Historic Park and the thriving tiny town. *See* "Amazing Architecture" and "Historic Oddities" for more on Harpers Ferry.

During World War II, explosives were made in **Point Pleasant** and stored in grass-covered concrete domes. After the war, the explosives reportedly were removed and the domes given or sold to local government and area chemical companies.

The rows of concrete igloos captured the imagination of John Keel who reported on UFO and Mothman sightings in what he called "the **TNT area**." Keel further reports that the U.S. Government admitted to storing atomic waste material in the concrete domes.

Eyewitnesses of the Mothman appearances in the late 1960s claim the seven-foot winged creature used the domes as a perch. It being West Virginia, scores of folks came out to try and shoot it. Today, the domes are part of a wildlife station, eerie and grown-over with brush and trees.

For more on Mothman, *see* "Truly Incredible." For more on UFOs, *see* "Remarkable Collections."

"Warning: Gas Pipeline" signs announce the prevalence of the oil and gas industry around the state—a surprise to many. **Spencer Heritage Park** celebrates its connection with an oil derrick. The **Rathbone Well** in **Burning Springs** was the first drilled solely for petroleum in West Virginia in 1859, just months after the first in America at Titusville,

Organized tours of the area where Mothman was sighted can be arranged, often with an eyewitness guide. Even without the giant creature appearing, it's an eerie adventure.

PA. In 1863, Confederate soldiers set the stored oil ablaze, destroying one of the world's only two oil fields and more than 300,000 barrels in a single day. This made Burning Springs the first military oil objective in the history of warfare. Astonishingly, there was a virtual press blackout of this notable event. Cleaned and refitted in 2001, Rathbone is once more producing oil. A 19th century drilling facility is in the works. The shallow oil pool tapped by various wells in the region was one of the richest ever known.

Mills

With all its fast running streams, West Virginia was a natural location for mills. Many are gone now, often the victim of fires. Mills would burn when an inexperienced miller created sparks by letting the huge granite millstones grind against each other. Dust created from the grinding is highly explosive.

Reeds Mill continues to function commercially, grinding wheat, corn and buckwheat in the 19th century tradition. The Midget Marvel Flour Mill machinery is still housed in the building along with other examples of mill mechanisms. Once more than 30 mills of various sorts, ranging from grist, to woolen, to powder, existed along Second Creek as it tumbled from the mountains northwest toward Union.

Bunker Hill Mill (*left*) is the only one in state with dual water wheels. The old stone building was reconstructed in 1875 on a 1738 mill site. The district in which it was located had a huge concentration of mills, ranging from grist and fulling to chopping and sawmills.

Built in 1794, Blakely Mill was moved from Greenbrier County soon after it ceased operation in the 1950s and reconstructed at **Jackson's Mill.** The gristmill grinds weekly and sells its share of the resulting meal at the general store, including Bloody Butcher cornmeal which makes your cornbread pink. There is a rare barrel packer in the mill. The site's original grist and sawmill erected before 1800 by Stonewall Jackson's grandfather still stands along the river as a museum.

Reconstructed from three mills, **Glade Creek Grist Mill** in Babcock State Park grinds cornmeal, buckwheat and whole wheat. Its real claim to fame is as one of the most photographed scenes in the state.

The Old Mill at Harmon dates to 1877. Built as a gristmill and powered by water turbines from Dry Fork River, it is now a working mill museum.

One of the largest cast-iron overshot waterwheels in world is located at **Thomas Shepherd's gristmill**, constructed in Shepherdstown in 1763. The 40-foot waterwheel dates to 1891, and can be seen from Mill Street along with the waterfalls of Town Run, a tributary of the Potomac. The mill is privately owned.

Gone But Not Forgotten

Bones in Greenbrier County caves demonstrate that wooly mammoths, sabre tooth cats and giant cave bears called West Virginia home 12,000 years ago. More recently extinct are the once huge herds of buffalo and elk. The last bison were seen in 1825; the elk were gone by 1843.

Mountainsides of giant chestnuts were wiped out by blight in the first part of the 20th century, remaining only in buildings that used their corpses. Old fence posts and building materials of chestnut are frequently "recycled" by woodworkers into furniture because of the rarity of the wood.

In 1938, the giant **Mingo Oak** died and was cut down. At that time it was judged to be the largest white oak in the world. Ring counters assert that it was 582 years old, the oldest living thing in the state. The 146-foot white oak giant produced 15,000 feet of lumber.

A road marker at an overlook is all that remains of the **Pringle Sycamore** down on Turkey Run. A sprout from the original tree root marks the spot. An 11-foot-wide room in the trunk cavity of this giant among the giant sycamores that once populated the state served as the abode of the two Pringle brothers from 1764 to 1767. Deserters from Fort Pitt who had quarreled with their trapper companions, the brothers eventually settled in the region.

When you see the sign for Roanoke on I-79, it's normal to expect that there actually is a town at that exit. Wrong. There used to be a town but it was flooded when Stonewall Jackson Lake was created. Now, former residents mount the good fight to keep the road sign as a memorial to their homeplace.

Frank Thomas was a working artifact. For more than fifty years his **"Poor Man's Flying School"** turned out pilots from the dogleg runway he literally hacked out of the Fayetteville countryside and operated as Fayette Airport. Until he died in his seventies in 2001, Frank flew folks around the New River Gorge in his Cessna, often reciting poetry while they soared and dipped. The bargain price earned him the title of "Five Dollar Frank." His distinctive voice guided pilots through the gorge with terse replies. Once on the ground, his stories and flying museum kept him talking.

CHAPTER FIFTEEN

Tours and Trips Not to Miss

A surprising variety of organized excursions are offered in West Virginia, from industrial tours to train rides. Always worth trying are numerous quirky local tours—some self-guided—about unique local treasures.

Touring the Pen

The **West Virginia Penitentiary tour** is authentic. The horrifying innards of the infamous prison have not been cleaned up and improved by the new occupants—the Moundsville Economic Development Council (MEDC). If anything, the wholesale dismantling of mechanical systems and hardware by the departing correctional authorities makes the graffiti-decorated environment even bleaker. Only the emotional pain is missing from the place inmates called "Blood Alley." However, the tour guides—several of them former guards—add that missing element by reciting day-to-day

There is something endearing about exploiting the true soul of a place, even when the soul is as sinister and macabre as **Moundsville** *prison's must be, considering that nearly 1,000 people died there.*

prison horrors and gory details of past executions like beheadings and hangings. They also point out that serial killer Charles Manson was born just up the road in McMechen.

Once a prison official told me that the worst part of prison was the loss of freedom and that it would be awful even in a hotel. A great theory but time in a Hilton sounds lots better than time in the "the Alamo," the maximum cellblock of the maximum-security facility and the bottom level in the grotesque stone and steel hell of Moundsville.

The prison was built on a 10-acre site in 1866 to house the state's most dangerous felons. It was the second public building of the new state of West Virginia. The first was another stone dungeon—**Trans-Allegheny Lunatic Asylum.** Moundsville's forbidding block-long Gothic structure was built by convict labor of hand-cut gray sandstone quarried at Grafton and Wheeling. Five acres were captured inside stonewalls four feet thick at the base, sunk six feet into the ground and climbing 24 feet in the air. Four towers, parapets and a walkway completed the medieval architecture. It was used for almost 130 years, and is now on the National Historic Register, probably the only structure on the Register that is also noted as one of the world's scariest places.

Noted author Davis Grubb referred to the pairing of burial mound and prison as an "ambiguous and dreadful brotherhood... each full of its secrets, riddles and whispers of ritual killing."

The Penitentiary is located directly across from the Grave Creek Mound, on what was at the time of its construction, the edge of town.

Since it costs nearly $2 million annually to heat the place, today's penitentiary tours are often conducted through an unheated building. Sliding along narrow corridors and moving into closed cells scarcely big enough to turn around, it's almost impossible to imagine that the last inmates left this prison as recently as 1995. According to the guide, 2,700 men under the control of 300 guards once crammed the place.

A puff of steam announces hydraulic doors opening and closing as bus tours are herded through the facility, after being fingerprinted and photographed. Being treated like inmates is part of the experience. The cage-like steel revolving door at the entrance is one of only two in existence. The other is in Manchester, England.

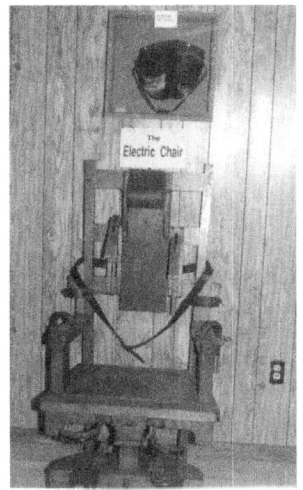

One of the final stops is the prison gift shop, where visitors can buy tin cups, handcuffs and prison caps while examining the electric chair. West Virginia couldn't afford to buy an electric chair, so prison officials took two inmates to Ohio to inspect theirs. When they returned, these handy inmates built **Old Sparky**, the deceptively flimsy looking mechanism that killed nine men before retiring in 1965.

In addition to public tours, the prison hosts the National Corrections Training Center, a state-of-the-art crime mapping lab and the country's largest mock riot for more than 1,000 law enforcement personnel and equipment manufacturers. The last real riot at Moundsville was in 1986, when 200 inmates held 16 hostages for two days. Three convicts died, killed by other convicts. It's one of the stories told on the tour.

Every October, Moundsville high school students operate the truly horrific 12-day **Dungeon of Horrors** haunted prison tour that takes no more than 15 people at a time through a 20-room maze. It is populated by more than 60 actors, all sorts of monsters, a casket ride and frights illuminated by top-notch lighting effects. After a half-hour or so of horror, adults and children tumble out through heavy metal doors into the prison yard shrieking and sobbing. Organizers turned over tour admission to Ticketmaster after there were near riots trying to obtain tickets in 2000. Imagine, people rioting to get INTO a prison!

Judged to be one of the most supernaturally active places in the country, the prison starred on an MTV cable television show in 2000 aptly entitled "Fear." The mission was to determine whether the prison was haunted. Six areas were targeted for exploration: three in the North Yard, three in the south. Since then, overnight ghost hunts—with guests spending a gloriously uncomfortable night in the prison—have become extremely popular and are held on at least a monthly basis.

Tour guides like to tell folks that the L.A. Times said the Moundsville tour was better than Alcatraz. I told my guide I'd been to Alcatraz. "Well, what do you think?" he asked me. "Moundsville doesn't have the boat ride," I responded.

You Don't Have To Be Crazy To Go To Weston Anymore

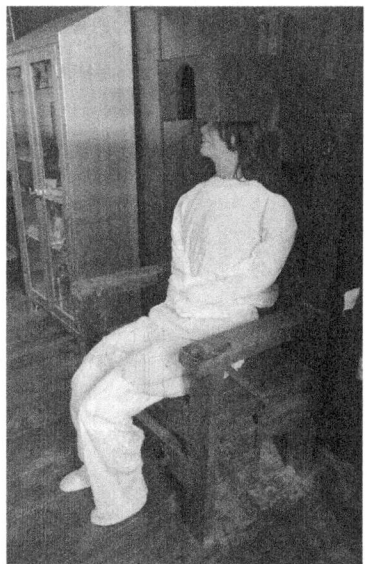

Contender and moving up fast to capture the title of best tour in the state is the **Trans-Allegheny Lunatic Asylum** under the inspiring and energetic leadership of its recent owner, Rebecca Jordan Gleason. Costumed as Civil War nurses, knowledgeable docents guide the extensive menu of year 'round heritage tours. Flashlight and paranormal tours along with an elaborate haunted house fill October. It all climaxes in the state's largest costume ball on Halloween weekend.

Room after room, wing after wing of the multiple buildings on the expansive grounds are transformed or soon to be into specialized exhibit rooms. Victorian living quarters for resident doctors are as fascinating as eerie empty halls and artifact-filled mental health treatment rooms that would qualify as torture chambers.

Fortunately, unlike the good old days, you can check in—and check out.

The mid-19th century Gothic splendor and unique history of the Trans-Allegheny Lunatic Asylum make it a truly chilling place for a ghost hunt that includes an overnight stay. For more *see* "Amazing Architecture."

Cliffs, Eagles & Edibles

Some places are made to be seen by train, and **the Trough** of the South Branch of the Potomac River is one of them.

Up until the train started running between Romney and Moorefield in 1910, the 17 miles of rocky cliffs and steep canyon known as "the Trough" were inaccessible according to visitors including young George Washington. He wrote in 1748 that "the Trough is a couple of ledges of mountain impassable… and the river down between them. You must ride around the back of the mountain to get below them." Even today it is still just the river and the tracks.

The **Potomac Eagle excursion train** rides back and forth through the Trough in season, leaving and returning to Romney's Wappocomo Station. June is the best time for spotting the giant birds as they're raising their young, but spotting is virtually certain on any trip.

Eagle spotting is the game on the **Potomac Eagle excursion train.**

Eagles soaring through rocky cliffs above a rippling river are only one part of the scenic package. Passengers also see miles of cattle in lush bottomland, old riverside plantations, stone ruins, fishermen in the river, and historic settings spanning the century from the French and Indian War to the Civil War.

First among the sights from the Potomac Eagle is **Wappocomo,** a large brick colonial house built in 1774. It has a unique orientation, facing the mountains rather than the river. The house has been in Parsons family hands for seven generations and remains a private home today.

The path of the Potomac Eagle follows the same route taken by a group of millionaires back in 1910 when they first started passenger service to their exclusive **Hampshire Club.** Since 1945, the club property has become the **Peterkin Conference Center** of the Episcopal Church, which boasts an altar made from the slate tops of two Romney pool tables.

Passengers ride in standard open window coaches from the 1920s, bought from a Canadian railroad. There's a 52-foot open gondola car for the ultimate photo opportunities and a Classic Club Car for high rollers.

Potomac Eagle trips run from three hours to all day. There are extra trains during October leaf season, and special trips include a re-enactment that has the train stopped and mildly terrorized by a group of marauding Civil War troops. Since Romney was a historical battleground in the War Between the

States, changing hands a reputed 56 times, re-enactors from either side would be accurate.

Facilities are basic, as is the food. Bring your camera and arrange to ride the river side one way and the cliff side the other.

Boat Ride To The Past

The sternwheel riverboat trip along the broad Ohio River to **Blennerhassett Island Historical State Park** from Point Park in Parkersburg from May through October is worth the modest price. Touring the ancient island and reconstructed mansion is a bonus. Two nights in October, the sternwheel ride culminates in candlelight parties at the mansion.

Held sacred and inhabited for almost 10,000 years by Native Americans in the Ohio River Valley, the island was the 18th-century home of the famous Delaware Indian, Nemacolin.

Cases of ancient artifacts taken from the island are on display in the **Blennerhassett Museum** back on the mainland. *See* "Remarkable Collections" for details.

The historical romance phase began in 1797. Harman Blennerhassett was an English aristocrat who lived in Ireland. He married his niece, young Margaret Agnew. They left behind the social ostracism to make a life in America. They bought the island, called it Isle de Beau Pre, and built a fabulous mansion with a ten-room central section and circular wings for Blennerhassett's extensive library and scientific laboratory.

The pair stuck out like a sore thumb in the isolated outpost, so when Aaron Burr came looking for wealthy partners in his scheme to acquire an empire in the Spanish southwest, Blennerhassett Island was a natural stop. Whatever their involvement, the couple left the island when Burr's scheme crumbled under accusations of treason in 1806. The mansion was plundered soon after and finally burned to the ground in 1811.

Archeologists uncovered the mansion site in 1973. It was faithfully rebuilt on its foundations, furnished and established as the centerpiece of Blennerhassett State Historical Park during the 1980s. Margaret and her son, Harman Jr. are buried on the island and a small piano from the original mansion was recently added to the furnishings. The 20-minute boat ride, tour of the mansion and entry to the mainland museum, is one of my favorite West Virginia bargains.

Taming Glass

Glass factories share three qualities—they're hot, metal and male. Nowhere was this more obvious than at Fenton Glass where I watched their master blower tame molten glass with his breath. He had the attitude of an Olympic athlete.

I was shocked when the tour at **Fenton** took us directly onto the expansive factory floor, close enough to wilt under the heat of huge furnaces filled with molten glass. Deafening noise, glass, dust and heat met the tour group as we moved within touching distance of the men working the floor. There were no warnings or guardrails.

Shock turned to fascination as we moved into place on the perimeter of the blow shop and watched a lean, intense man turn, twist and blow gobs of molten glass into art forms with his breath. The team of gatherers, blockers and assorted "boys" served the master blower who stood on the traditional blowers platform, hand on hip, staring a challenge at the crowd, waiting to blow the next phase. He was heat personified and obviously a star; he's even on Fenton's postcards.

Traditional tools and processes are used at Fenton, where the first piece of glass was blown in 1907, two years after the factory opened. Fenton's best-known contribution to the glass industry was the development of gaily-covered carnival glass.

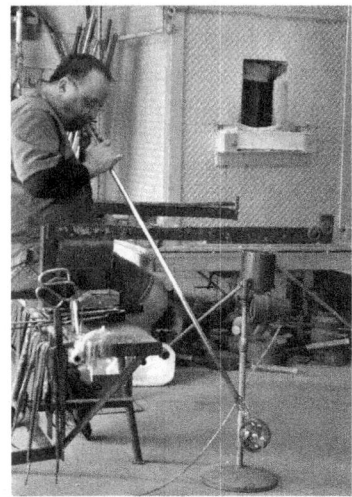

It's not giant furnaces at thousands of degrees of heat, but intimate glass blowing and shaping demonstrations can be easily arranged at Appalachian Glass in Weston.

Soon after the 100th anniversary, Fenton faced a crisis built on high labor costs, overseas competition and a declining collectibles market. There were months of announcements of pending closure of the factory. Taken to the brink, Fenton stumbled and was forced to close the industrial-scale manufacturing. Today, the gift shop is king and Fenton-made beads and teardrop earrings are the focus of tours though not with the high drama and heat that came with hot furnaces and glass blowers.

Congress Goes Underground

When the "big one" fell, the President of the United States would give the word and 1,100 members of Congress, staff and top government officials would be whooshed by jumbo jet to the Greenbrier. There they would enter the **Government Relocation Center,** a secret bunker below the world-famous resort hotel, and proceed to run the government using stored documents for payroll, retirement and health benefits.

A full electronic media production room allowed the buried members to stay in touch with whatever constituents survived. The Capitol dome backdrop for televised messages had both a fall and spring version. No one considered what the audience would think about the uniform green jumpsuits all the Members of Congress would be wearing in their contamination-free hideaway.

Part Cold War paranoia and part golfing fantasy, the bunker was built in the late 1950s by President Dwight D. Eisenhower at a cost of $10 million. Although the world disappointed planners by not going up in mushroom clouds of flame and radiation, that was never an issue at the bunker, which was maintained at top readiness for 34 years. Magazines in each of four lounges were replaced constantly. A single Greenbrier employee got all the subscriptions making him a world-class junk mail magnet. The complex mechanical systems that provided water, heat and the cleanest air on the planet were turned on and run for six hours every Wednesday. A 60-day supply of freeze-dried K-rations, wine and alcohol was stored and rotated. There were no cigarettes; bunker-world was smoke free.

Accommodations were expensive, but not posh: a bathroom for every 120 people, mass bunk rooms with a locker for every four bunks, a 12-bed hospital ward with lab and dental chair, and a pharmacy well-stocked with anti-depressants. There were plenty of clocks to help keep people regular and 800 active phone lines. The trash incinerator was set so it could double as a crematorium. For 30 years, every piece of new technology that remotely fit the purpose of life after nuclear war was installed at the bunker.

One deception led to another. A jet airport with the longest runway in West Virginia and a control tower chock full of instruments most cities don't have was plausible pork. Cable television was brought into the tiny, rural valley to provide a cover occupation for the shadowy Forsythe Associates, who had the only key to the bunker's gun room and therefore were the guys in charge. The infamous "television repairmen" from Forsythe were also in control of straight jackets stored in the "jail."

Parts of the top-secret bunker were used by the Greenbrier regularly. The meeting room set up to mimic the floor of the House of Representatives served as the resort's theater. The hall planned for congressional staff was used for exhibitions; the abundance of pillars needed to shore up the 70 feet of dirt piled on top of the secret structure was explained away as an architectural quirk. The famous **Dorothy Draper** decor, with its busy patterns and bright colors, worked perfectly to hide doors and cuts in concrete.

The party line claims the bunker was top secret, not even showing up in Soviet intelligence files. Hundreds of Greenbrier County residents, hotel workers, and other personnel have years of bunker stories that show at least local folk knew what was hidden in plain sight. They just saw no need to tell the outside world.

The Greenbrier was paid well for being the only hotel in the world with a contingency plan for the destruction of civilization. Tax dollars built the West Virginia wing, literally the cover for the bunker buried under Kate Mountain, which was then leased to the Greenbrier for a modest annual fee of no more than $50,000. When the bunker was conveniently revealed in mid-1992, in time to be placed on a base-closing list, it was given to the hotel. The cafeteria and fully equipped kitchen is now site of the Greenbrier's world famous cooking school, and tours are conducted regularly with fees used to cover maintenance.

Tours begin as a 25-ton steel door, cut into the side of the mountain and perfectly balanced to be moved by the hand of a single person, shuts behind the group. A well-informed guide—ours was a former Central Intelligence Agency employee—leads the group down a 433-foot tunnel lined with food supplies to the first stop and begins the incredible tale.

Move Over Casper

For more than three decades, Shirley Dougherty gave tours of the scariest places in **ghost-ridden Harpers Ferry** weekends from April through November. Now the longest running ghost tour in the country, living historian Rick Garland as O'BeJoyFull conducts it. The tour assembles on the piazza of St. Peter's Church. Shirley's stories are collected in her book, *Ghosts of Harpers Ferry*, and remain the basis for the tours.

Daily Bread

Wandering through Huntington's Old Central City, my nose suddenly caught the scent of fresh bread as I saw hundreds of loaves rolling past at eye level in the windows of a large concrete block building painted brick red. I tracked down the entryway and attached myself to a group of school kids just departing on a regular hour-long tour of **Heiner's Bakery.**

From the moment I slipped on the required white hairnet, I was swept back to childhood memories of bakery tours in my hometown.

Heiner's Bakery started in 1905. The aroma and recipe are unchanged. Piles of flour are still turned into bread dough and stacks of pans still stand at the ready. Even with new silicon chip directed machines, the process remains a mechanical wonder of breaking down every step needed to make bread and inventing a machine to do it. Little balls of dough zoom around at just the right speed, getting rolled then dropped into a pan. The measured rising time complete, mechanical arms lift gangs of pans into huge 58-tray bread ovens. A young man watches the wall of dials, lights and chalkboards filled with loaf counts. The purpose of staff is realized mostly when the mechanical and silicon systems fail. Human hands will reach in and reload plastic bags or straighten a loaf of bread as needed.

Every day 100,000 loaves of Heiner's bread accumulate countless miles of travel time sailing around on conveyor belts just under the ceiling of the building. Every loaf travels for an hour to cool off before slipping into its plastic wrapping at the rate of 84 each minute.

Heiner's Bakery is a cog in several local economic wheels, providing rolls for the famous Stewart hot dogs on the other side of town, (*see* "Local Food") and giving away waste dough to a man that feeds it to his hogs.

Secret Methods

The company's ever-popular **Fiestaware** has earned the daily bread for the **Homer Laughlin Factory** for more than half a century. It is made within the more than mile-long compound in a building separate from the main factory.

A fourth generation family-owned business, Homer Laughlin is the world's largest pottery plant, and during most years the largest manufacturer of dinnerware. It was the first American pottery to be totally lead free, and the innovator of tunnel kilns. There are regular tours of the enormous main factory, and I was fortunate to have noted studio potter Pam Parziale along as a companion.

No tours of the separate Fiestaware production building are allowed, presumably to protect trade secrets surrounding the prized pottery.

We watched their newest machine molding a perfect plate from raw clay in six seconds. "It takes me twenty minutes," said Pam. The rest of the operation is just as streamlined with new 12-hour kilns that allow the pottery to turn a piece of china around from design to finished product in 24 hours.

The tour ends in a museum room filled with rare and historic Fiestaware pieces, where everyone is given a small commemorative plate and released into the outlet shop. To learn more about buying the product, *see* "Shopping Treasures."

Dig Deep

Jeff Moorefield is a robust and rollicking former miner who delights in tales of methane gas burning off eyebrows and rats eating unprotected lunch pails.

He was our guide at the **Beckley Exhibition Coal Mine**, taking us through a gaping hole in the mountain into 1,500 feet of dark tunnels only slightly larger than the standard three-foot seam of coal once mined there. We were riding in a man-trip mine trolley pulled by a battery powered locomotive. This is not an excursion for those who avoid close spaces.

The exhibition mine was worked by a local family around the turn-of-the-century; commercial development began in 1905 and ceased in 1953. The old drift-mine offers an authentic example of what coal mining once was when working in ankle deep water to move three or four tons of coal a day with a pick and shovel was the norm. It does not represent today's mechanized industry where miners suit up like astronauts and direct "continuous miners" by remote control to chew up and move several tons of coal a second. Only the maze of low tunnels and the usefulness of the product remain unchanged.

There's also a self-guided tour of other authentic coal camp buildings reconstructed above the mine including a church, miner's house, superintendent's house and a tiny single man's shed.

Jefferson's Sloth

One of the largest in the country, **Organ Cave** stretches for more than 40 miles and has 200 leads not yet surveyed; more than could ever be mapped in this lifetime. Opened commercially in 1835 and never excavated, it has daily tours. Sites along the tour include Indian artifacts, calligraphy from 1812, Civil War graffiti, veins of saltpeter that glow when lights shine on them, sea coral and fossils. Bones of a saber tooth tiger were also found. Live creatures include eight species of bats, fresh water shrimp and a dozen hibernating black bears that moved in one winter when the gate was left unlocked.

Well-trained teenage guides discuss factual material rather than anthropomorphizing rock shapes—and there is much to discuss. Tours begin at an unusually large main entrance, one of eight into the cave. They follow the original path Civil War soldiers took down into the large room to mine. Electrified old time lanterns provide unobtrusive lighting and every third person on the tour carries a candle or light. The historic saltpeter hoppers, made with peg and hole method of construction, are exactly as they were left in 1865 in the deepest and driest section of the cave, nearly 480 feet below the surface.

The indentation of a giant sloth's huge head cavity can be seen although Thomas Jefferson removed the fossil, the first known of a three-toed sloth.

Like the nearby bunker at the Greenbrier, the cave was outfitted as a fall-out shelter in the 1950s where 500 people could stay for five weeks.

Nature's Tours

★ The Spotted Salamander is the paved, level trail with Braille interpretive nature stations in **Kanawha State Forest** at the edge of Charleston.

★ The state publishes a **fall color map** allowing folks to follow the leaves, beginning with the Highland counties in late September, rolling west in early and mid-October, and finishing with the southern tier and Eastern Panhandle in late October. The map is a thoughtful gesture, but one that will not stop repeated calls in June or July by potential leaf peepers asking which day the leaves will peak.

★ In 1905, Governor William MacCorkle built and lived in **Sunrise,** a mansion atop a hill across the river from downtown Charleston. He often welcomed visitors at the train station, located at the bottom of the hill along the river. To accommodate the traffic, MacCorkle built the **Carriage Trail.** Designated a national recreational trail in 2012, Carriage Trail is a favorite city walk through dense woods switching back and forth around giant rocks across the Kanawha River from the State Capitol. A marker designates the spot where two women tried as spies by a drumhead court martial in 1863 were brought, shot and buried. Speculation has it that the two were probably prostitutes someone wanted to discard. **Tramps Walk** is a parallel sidewalk down the hill.

Riding The Rails

★ The extensive forests of West Virginia once supported a booming timber industry and 3,000 miles of a logging railroad line. **Cass Scenic Railroad,** operating on the same line built to haul logs in 1902, is the last whistle-screaming, smoke-pouring 11 miles left.

Some of the final steam-powered Shay locomotives invented to haul logs down the steep curves now take folks up a sheer climb of up to 11% grade through several switchbacks and red spruce forests to the million dollar view at Bald Knob, second highest peak in the state at 4,800 feet. Built in Ohio in 1905, and working at Cass ever since, engine #5 is believed to be the only Shay still operating on the tracks for which it was originally purchased. Traveling at five miles per hour in red and green open-window passenger cars renovated from old log cars, the trip to the top takes more than four hours and requires a stop at a spring for water. A shorter trip to Whittaker Station takes two hours. Operating from late May to the end of October, there are dinner trains and a special fall color schedule. The brakemen will answer your questions.

A couple insider tips. For the best photo opportunities of the engine taking on water choose the car farthest from the engine going up and closest going down. No matter which trip you take, save time for shopping at the impressive gift shop.

The setting at Cass is so stylish, it was the site of a multi-page fashion shoot in Italian *Vogue*.

★ **Mountain Rail Adventures** bundles a group of five unusual, nostalgic and scenic train rides through the heart of the state's mountains using both the Durbin and Elkins depots.

The **Cheat Mountain Salamander** has a new, extended seven-hour ride on the highest mainline rail system in the East. The excursion still offers dramatic scenery, eight bridges, tunnels, black bears, the High Falls of Cheat and the abandoned timber town of Spruce. A buffet dinner in the dining car is a new feature. The train is named for the small, endangered woodland creature that lives in the Cheat River—its sole habitat.

Vintage wooden cabooses and a Roaring Twenties era coach are pulled by the **Durbin Rocket**, a rare Climax #3 steam engine built in 1910, on a memorable two hour ride along the Greenbrier River. The ten-mile round trip leaves from the restored century-old Durbin Depot.

The **New Tygart Flyer,** an elegant, streamlined passenger train, takes its passengers on a very slow but thrilling passage through the Cheat Mountain Tunnel, closed for regular passenger traffic since 1959. Cut by hand a quarter mile through the mountain in the mid-19th century, the tunnel has an S-curve in the center denying passengers the clichéd, "light at the end of the tunnel." The ride culminates in the High Falls of Cheat. It departs and returns to the historic Elkins Depot and includes a buffet lunch.

Newest of the train rides takes pajama clad children in November and December from the Elkins Depot to the North Pole where they are greeted by Santa Claus. It's a licensed *Polar Express* adventure.

Art at Work

Artist-organized studio tours on specified weekends are a staple in the Eastern Panhandle where a well-planned route can bring you to more than a dozen; or you can come back the next year.

The Father of the Modern Steel Drum turns out his prized instruments from a warehouse workshop outside Morgantown. Ellie Manette, a native of Trinidad, is now artist-in-residence at West Virginia University and staffs his

Manette Steel Drums manufacturing operation with student apprentices. Tours envelop you in heat, hammers and the relentless sound of banging.

Odd Rides

Besides mountain bikes, rubber rafts, kayaks, trains, horses and ATVs, there are a couple odd things to ride.

★ The 3,600-foot aerial tram is often obscured by morning mists as it drops nearly 1,100 feet from the rim of Bluestone Canyon to Mountain Creek, **Pipestem's** lodge along the Bluestone River at the canyon bottom.

"I had no idea it would be so aerial," said my pilot husband as we rode up and down through the clouds. He was clearly impressed with the expansive windows of the four-person gondola. Doing the trip in the dark is another adventure, highlighted by the heritage comedy of a well-lit still nestled in an overhang on the side of the mountain.

The tram ride is free to guests of Mountain Creek, a bonus for staying down in the canyon. For more *see* "Unusual Places to Stay."

★ **Snowshoe Resort** has unique rides for both the traditional—horse-drawn sleigh rides to watch the sunset each evening, and the contemporary—a six-wheel Hydrotaxx all terrain vehicle that can go anywhere all year long.

★ The state's only lake tour is at the posh state park **Stonewall Jackson Resort** where a 75-foot cruise boat takes passengers at daybreak and midday to all the secluded nooks and crannies on the way to the dam and back. Weekend evenings have a romantic dinner cruise. Keeping to the theme, the boat is named Little Sorrel after Stonewall's horse. Guess he didn't have a cruise boat.

CHAPTER SIXTEEN

Truly Incredible

A handful of places transcend any category and can only be described as truly incredible. Each of them could serve as centerpiece of an advertising campaign entitled: "Surprise! It's West Virginia."

Mummies in Philippi

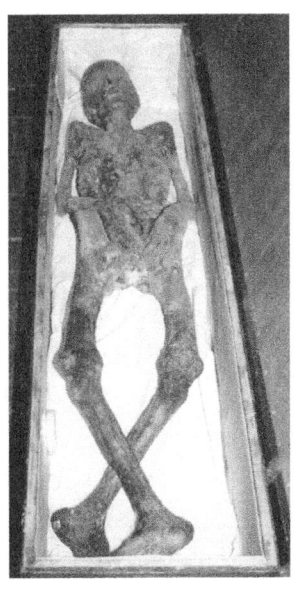

It was the #1 choice for weird from online insiders when I posted the call for "way out" suggestions. There was no background information, only the intriguing mention of the mummies in Philippi. I could not imagine how that could be. Visiting became a top priority.

The mummies are housed in the small, Mission-style **Barbour County Historical Museum** next to the famous Philippi covered bridge. Purely by chance, we arrived on the first day the museum was opened for the season. There was a major crisis. The mummies had grown mold over the winter from water leaks in the building. Town employees were consulting a museum curator about the best method for cleaning them. "They're a hundred years old," she warned the men who were planning to wash the mummies down with bleach. "Wear gloves."

While the cleaning crew deliberated on what to do, I slipped into the back room where the mummies were. Two tiny wooden boxes lay on the floor. Feeling like a tabloid journalist, I opened them and quickly snapped pictures of two leather dolls with splotches of green mold. Then I set out to gather their story.

Graham Hamrick was a Philippi shopkeeper and undertaker with a hankering to outdo the Egyptians. To this end he developed and patented a mummification process. After trials with vegetables and animals, he needed to test it out on humans. In 1888, Hamrick obtained two unnamed female corpses from the Hospital for the Insane in nearby Weston and tried out his formula. According to records, he also mummified a hand, a head and a baby; all three erroneously thought to be lost forever. His pair of females, called the Hamrick mummies after their creator, became famous world travelers touring Europe with P.T. Barnum in 1891.

Hamrick received patent #466,524 for an intricate formula including water, saltpeter and sublimed sulfur set afire. In his patent request, he identified the process as a simple and economic way for anyone "without special skill" to effectively preserve a body in its natural condition for a long time. Fumigating the bodies in a closed box, Hamrick gave the two corpses immortality—and a permanent leather complexion. Eventually, rights to the formula were sold to a Pittsburgh embalmer. Crates holding a dozen jugs that may or may not hold ingredients and completed embalming fluid, are housed in the museum along with the mummies.

Barnum returned the mummies to Philippi, and sporadic sightings were reported through the years. Noted *Hillbilly* publisher, Jim Comstock, had the mummies on loan in his short-lived Mountaineer Hall of Fame in Richwood where Pearl Buck saw them and was fascinated. Anyone over 14 could pay to see them at the Philippi Street Fair in the mid-1960s. They then disappeared until the flood of 1985, when they were found after floating from their storage area under the piano of Frank "Bigfoot" Beyer, the owner of the mummies prior to the town of Philippi. The alleged missing mummified hand came to my attention on a book-signing trip to Charleston. Beyer's daughter informed me that she still had the hand. I've yet to rid myself of the image of a gnarled, leathery claw perched on the dressing table of this proper matron, her many rings stored on its fingers.

In some misguided attempt at decorum, the mummies are currently displayed in glass-topped cases, modestly draped with white cloths and sporting sprigs of artificial flowers. I'm glad I got to capture their images naked except for the mold.

Hamrick's mummies are not the only bizarre attraction in the small college town along the Tygart River. There is also the limb amputation.

In June 1861, a minor skirmish took place in Philippi, identified by some as the first land battle of the Civil War. The Federal troops routed the Confederates who retreated so fast the battle has been called the "Philippi Races." Among the few wounded was James Hanger of Virginia.

Dr. James Robinson of Ohio amputated Hanger's cannonball shattered leg that fateful day in June. It was the first limb amputation of the Civil War. Hanger made himself an artificial leg of wood, then began fashioning them for other amputees. The Confederate army kept Hanger busy, eventually contracting with him to manufacture artificial limbs. After the war, he invented an organization to continue producing the wooden limbs. Today, J.E. Hanger Inc. is one of the world's largest manufacturers of artificial limbs. A plaque on Crim Memorial Church just off the main square of Philippi recognizes its macabre beginning.

Mystery Hole

Since the early '70s, the **Mystery Hole** has been the paramount eccentricity for many visitors. The tiny roadside gift shop covered with signs encouraging you to come in had a gorilla mounted on top and a pre-revival VW bug smashed into its side. On the other side, stairs led you down into the main attraction—the Mystery Hole. For those who ventured into the narrow hallway lined with fun house mirrors and weird posters, the dollar admission bought creator

Don Wilson's tour hustle, a tilted room and berserk gravity tricks. It was virtual reality before the concept was invented, liberally mixed with hillbilly taste and humor.

The gift shop, rated ultimate on the trashy scale, was open to everyone whether they paid for the tour or not.

In early 1998, Don Wilson, visionary founder and tour guide extraordinaire, died. Many despaired that his 25-year creation hugging the side of US 60 just west of Hawks Nest State Park would become one of those wonders that used to be there. Fate stepped in and the following year Sandy and Will Morrison turned their mid-life crises into a quest, relocating from Michigan to Fayette County where Will's granny lived. "We lived near a place called Mystery Hill," said Will. "I used to joke that someday I'll have to buy one."

The vertigo inducing tour is still a bargain and Will has added a few new gravity tricks including water that flows uphill. He is not open year 'round because spending too much time in the wacky gravity affected his stability.

The gorilla disappeared soon after Wilson's death. It resurfaced in mid-2001 and the story goes that the owner rescued it from a contractor who received it in payment for debts from Wilson's widow. The big question now is whether it will ever find its way back to the Mystery Hole.

Nature Training

The **National Conservation Training Center** in Shepherdstown, completed in 1997, is the best of its kind in the world. In fact, it may be the only one of its kind. Developed by the Fish and Wildlife Service of the U.S. Government, it is working on the future of education by offering a civic version of temple training for environmental servants.

Hidden on 125 acres of the 538-acre former Hendrix Farm, the campus view is filled with giant hay biscuits, rather than the upscale housing developments crowding the area near Shepherd College. Mrs. Hendrix still lives on a five-acre life estate near the entrance of the facility.

Former governor Gaston Caperton built a showplace home next-door.

The architecture of the training center is a successful example of ecological resonance, both physical and cultural. A dozen buildings with the look of barns on steroids are linked by walkways through sycamore groves rather than parking lots. Low maintenance design favored stonewalls, recycled steel roofs and brick floors. Concern for "outdoor" folk who spend more time with trees than people dictated lots of light and single rooms with private baths for housing.

The Commons offers a cafeteria dining room that compares with the Greenbrier's facility at Tamarack, minus the arty tabletops. There's even a wine pub with the only mounted head in the place—a rare Tule elk shot by poachers and captured by Fish and Wildlife cops who tracked the evildoers down.

Walls in all the buildings are shrines to conservation heritage displaying countless pictures of Fish and Wildlife employees and other conservation professionals doing the sacred work—saving rivers, forests and animals. A memorial wall displays plaques with the names of Fish and Wildlife employees killed in the line of duty.

The long list of "gee whiz" items at the Center includes both education and technology wonders. In the Geographical Information Systems lab, digital maps with varying information overlays are created on drafting tables that are in reality, computer screens. Production facilities are state-of-the-art including television and audio studios, a digital editing suite and satellite uplink. Live distance learning to the field is planned, although the facility is designed to be a training "home" for the Fish and Wildlife Service's far-flung employees; a place where they return every three years for "touchstone" courses and "roots" development through re-exposure to the Center.

The facility is equipped for development of conservation education materials with a professional design staff and a special hands-on lab where kids can come in and play with the stuff that turns into classroom courses. For outdoor studies, they move just outside the large glass doors to a pond that hatched literally millions of frogs one day. "The frogs poured out of that pond for hours," said my tour guide. I asked what happened. "They headed for the woods," he replied.

An existing storehouse of public domain conservation film footage and still images for information use by anyone, anywhere, is being expanded daily.

Folks who go to lots of training sessions obviously had a hand in designing the education space. Informal breakout areas are flooded with light and pastoral views, and abundant techie toys fill each of the 19 classrooms. There are four state-of-the-art labs—two "wet" and two "dry"—for training state and local officials in testing standards and techniques. The labs are wired so individual students can watch the teacher from their own video screen.

Conservation professionals are the student body—men and women working for the government on every level from federal to local, or for their corporate and private sector organization partners in the work of conserving the Earth's resources. The 90-page training catalog outlines more than 150 classes including Principles and Techniques of Electrofishing, Advanced Land Acquisition, Oil Spill Response, and Habitat Planning for Endangered Species. Field personnel teach most of the offerings.

For the Fish and Wildlife Service, the National Conservation Training Center is a prize, a source of pride for the often-overlooked bureau. Conservation officials from all over the planet clamor to train at the facility. Biotech conferences bring international CEOs to the conservation table and corporate jets to Martinsburg airport. In late 2000, the center hosted delegates from 152 countries for the first U.S. meeting on the world's oldest environmental treaty regulating endangered species. After the terrorist bombings on September 11, 2001, the center was a safe house of choice for several Cabinet level officials.

The world-class working laboratory of continuous education is also a good neighbor, preserving farmland and boosting educational opportunities for Shepherd College students. With an unusual financial deal that will allow NCTC to pay its own way, the facility is a shining example of how well spent $134 million can be.

Palace Of Gold

It is the most startling view in the state.

Traveling north to Moundsville, there's a small sign indicating the turn onto a typical back road — narrow, rough, twisting repeatedly around tree-covered hills. Suddenly, after one more curve, the **Palace of Gold** appears, beamed down directly from a Himalayan village. Gold encrusted domes peek over the red and pink brick colonnade; a wide brick thoroughfare leads down from the Palace to the temple, lodge and lake. Krishna's pet peacocks strut around the lake, paying homage at the feet of 30-foot-tall statues representing Hindu aspects of divinity. Ritual swan boats nestle in an elaborately domed boathouse or skim the lake with blissful passengers. Redwood chalets surround the lake putting visitors in mind of a surreal state park that happens to have larger-than-life elephant and sacred cow sculptures.

In fact, the scene is the 3,000-acre mountaintop home of the **New Vrindaban** community of **Hare Krishnas**, largest of their farm communities in the world, and the location of America's largest goshalla (cow shelter) at its Govardhan Dairy. The sign by the lodge spells out its unique destiny: "You are entering a sacred place. No smoking, intoxicants. No non-vegetarian foods. Please keep grounds clean."

The sacred complex was the brainchild of Srila Prabhupada, who came to America in 1965. He invented the Hare Krishnas with their signature chanting as a path to higher consciousness. America, the world and countless airport travelers have felt the impact of Prabhupada's vision.

According to the New Vrindaban party line, the head swami selected Bhaktipada, a young American he met in New York, to create a special Hare Krishna center on an abandoned farm outside Moundsville. It was named after the place in India where Lord Krishna reportedly spent his childhood. When Prabhupada visited the West Virginia site in 1969, there were a dozen or so devotees living in primitive conditions, walking groceries in two miles from the county road. The guru left his disciples with a vision of seven temples built on seven hills.

Prabhupada was a humble teacher who died before the splendor of the Palace of Gold was completed. He never lived in the east gallery, where ornately paneled and inlaid rooms are described as his study and living rooms. He never turned on the gold plated fixtures with rosy quartz handles on the marble sink in "his" bathroom. He never saw the lifelike idol of himself, mounted on a golden throne under a crystal dome, dressed luxuriously in a way the live saint would never have allowed. He never sat through the homage paid to his idol in a daily ceremony called "worshipping the guru."

In its heyday of the mid 1980s, when more than 600 devotees called the huge compound home and more than 200,000 visitors passed through, the *New York Times* dubbed New Vrindaban and its Palace of Gold "America's Taj Mahal." Built specifically to attract public attention to the teachings of Krishna, the Palace is a wonder of West Virginia appropriately located in an area selected by the ancients for one of their largest mounds, and by the state for its Gothic prison.

Bhaktipada's devotion drove unskilled devotees to do-it-yourself books where they learned to cut marble, mix cement, landscape and assemble crystal chandeliers. Masters appeared to carve, sculpt, paint and create stained glass. For seven years they struggled in the hills and the result is stunning—a tribute to the power of devotion.

The Palace of Gold is 8,000 square feet, with ten rooms of rare materials inside a shining black and gold trimmed structure, framed by two levels of extensive terraces. A 25-foot dome has 4,200 crystals in a ceiling mural of Lord Krishna. There are 31 stained glass windows, including four of peacocks glowing and shimmering in tones of blue and gold. Other windows have ornate scrollwork under a halo of colored glass jewels. Antique French chandeliers illuminate elaborate hand painted murals. More than 52 varieties of imported marble and onyx decorate walls, floors and ceilings. Intricately carved teakwood doors lead to the main hall, which is dazzling with gold marble pillars and more than 20,000 polished pieces of marble. All the gold leaf tracery, inside and out, is 22 carat—and it covers thousands of square feet of surface. A vegetarian restaurant, lounge and gift shop complete the floor plan. Chatras—elaborately painted and inlaid open domes that are covered sitting places for prayer—mark the corners of the lower terrace interspersed with flowers, lions and fountains. Ornate gardens tumble across the landscape from the palace terraces culminating in huge sitting statues.

Where the Indian holy man Prabhupada envisioned New Vrindaban as a tribute to Lord Krishna, the renamed American follower, Bhaktipada, built it to honor Prabhupada. The hubris proved lethal. As guru, Bhaktipada eventually was consumed by the dangerous doctrine that the position made him all-powerful.

Bhaktipada began altering the traditional rituals and practices of the Hare Krishnas and earned New Vrindaban expulsion from the international organization in 1987. By 1994, the community was in near total collapse, with resources drained by legal trials and fines. The life of a cow was held sacred at New Vrindaban; unfortunately for its development, the lives of its members were not. After two trials, Bhaktipada received a 20-year federal jail sentence for racketeering in 1996; his henchmen were convicted of murder.

One of his appeals was handled by noted attorney Alan Dershowitz. Because of the ongoing hostility of Moundsville residents and officials, he compared the case to a "witchcraft trial."

Having severed ties to Bhaktipada, the community struggles to return from near destruction. Current plans chart the path back through selling off more than 2,000 acres to member families, and revitalizing New Vrindaban as a resort community with a spiritual flavor. In 2000, the community was accepted back into the Hare Kirshna international organization. Bhaktipada died in 2011.

Fewer than a hundred devotees currently live at New Vrindaban, where they sustain the intricate daily rituals of worshipping Krishna and maintaining the farm and school. Yet some tasks do not get done. On hot summer days, the holding pond method of sewage treatment lends an aroma to the place that even incense cannot hide.

Introducing the culture to visiting tourists remains a major part of the project, and the complex is open for tours or just to wander around at will. The Palace of Gold still gleams in its gardens and terraces, with domes outlined against the mountains of three states, and signature chanting filling the air. Whatever else is true, the Hare Krishnas have always had the best beat.

World Favorite

Mention rich, famous and luxury in one sentence in West Virginia and you have to be talking about the **Greenbrier.** A historic landmark before the Civil War, the Greenbrier has dominated the "best resorts in the world" list for the past century and a half. There are thousands of pristine acres and expansive gardens, a European style spa, the luxury of more staff than guests, and matchless food. Guests once shared the three golf courses with the Greenbrier's famous pro, Sam Snead, and come for unique diagnostic vacations at the hotel's medical clinic.

In 2009, the august resort passed from the hands of CSX railroad after 99 years and acquired a West Virginia owner, Jim Justice.

Unlike any other five-star resort in America, the Greenbrier had contingency plans for nuclear Armageddon. The U.S. Government built and maintained a secret bunker for Congress under the West Virginia wing, to which they would escape when "the big one" dropped. Even when the bunker was decommissioned, Congress continued to escape to the Greenbrier. Since 2000, it ranks as the second most visited resort among members of Congress trailing only Manhattan, which hardly qualifies as a resort, so we like to think the Greenbrier is first. *See* "Tours" for more about the bunker.

History reigns supreme at the Greenbrier, bestowing a timeless quality on "Old White." Annual pilgrimages for the 400 ruling families of the South were the order of the day in antebellum times when the Greenbrier was White Sulphur Springs, Virginia and Henry Clay was its unofficial host. After the war, as part of the new state of West Virginia, railroads blended the prevailing southern society with northern wealth for a new sparkling society that lasted through the rest of the century. Revered as a summer retreat, Old White was a must for Europeans on the "American Grand Tour."

The Treadmill, invented at the resort, defined the primary purpose of 19th century visitors and it was not health. Every evening, splendidly dressed guests indulged in a fashion and matchmaking parade around the huge dining room, which could seat 1,200! Being on display at the Greenbrier virtually guaranteed a young girl a husband. Irene Langhorne was a Greenbrier belle who became immortalized as The Gibson Girl by her husband, artist Charles Dana Gibson.

Greenbrier's tenure as America's premier resort was broken only twice in its long history. It served as a military hospital, first for the Confederacy then later for Union forces, after a Captain Du Pont of Delaware persuaded his general from burning it to the ground. During World War II, the U.S. Army commandeered it to serve as Ashford General Hospital for military personnel.

Following both interruptions, private owners recovered the resort and it continued with undiminished reputation. The post-World War II grand reopening was marked by a famed party of the time, hosted by the Duke and Duchess of Windsor. It was a nostalgic return for the Windsors. She had been there for her first honeymoon, he for a holiday while King of England. Other notables included the Kennedy family with their son, John, the young Congressman from Massachusetts. Bing Crosby broke a lifetime rule for the party and sang for his fellow guests.

During the 1950s and '60s when the historic hotel industry was at its lowest, the Greenbrier hosted guests like Dwight D. Eisenhower, Princess Grace and the Kennedys in luxury suites. The sumptuous Presidential Suite is a virtual private residence in the Virginia wing of the hotel with a grand piano, large dining room and curved stairs that lead to seven bedrooms on the suite's second floor. Outside the main hotel, the Colonnade Estate House dates to 1838 when it was President Martin Van Buren's summer retreat.

That legends beget legends is commonplace wisdom at the Greenbrier. Royalty, movie stars, 26 U.S. Presidents, millionaires and celebrities have visited creating memories that are the stuff of legend. Countless thousands of obscure guests, including this author, have their own magical Greenbrier stories.

It was an improbable trip from the beginning. A friend and I had been hired to "tell fortunes" at a '60s party planned for the Blockbuster video store convention. We negotiated a minimal fee and lodging at the Greenbrier. It was the opportunity of a lifetime. We recruited my pilot-husband and arrived like

many of the rich and famous do—flying into the sophisticated, jet-accepting Greenbrier Valley Airport.

As we checked in, the improbable ascended to mythic. Juliana was at the front desk. She recognized my name, knew our purpose, and was waiting for us. "Read my cards," she said, "and we'll upgrade you at no charge to a Paradise Row Cottage." A free, $650 a night room was impossible to decline.

Cottages are the most traditional housing available at the Greenbrier, which began its life as a cottage resort in the first decade of the 19th century. Paradise Row cottages were among the first built at the resort and long served as honeymoon lodging hence their name. Renovated in the 1980s, they offer the amenities common to all the 69 guesthouses: privacy, comfort, fireplaces, and complimentary limo service to the main hotel, an easy stroll away. Our cottage in Paradise Row had the biggest bed in the largest bedroom I've ever seen, let alone slept in. The porch had a stunning view of the historic main hotel framed by green West Virginia mountains and acres of flowers and manicured lawns attended to constantly by armies of garden workers.

Beginning life as a Georgian antebellum masterpiece, today's main hotel has been altered and rebuilt nearly half a dozen times, currently reflecting its colonial Virginia roots and having more than 500 rooms and 50 suites. A Gilbert Stuart painting of George Washington hangs in the entrance and the staff historian is on hand for tours and lectures.

Along with social position, health has always been a primary commodity at the Greenbrier. As with everything else about the Greenbrier, they elevated health care to a five star level. In 1948, the Greenbrier Clinic was site for the country's first executive health program. It was founded by Franklin Delano Roosevelt's former Secretary of State and has evolved to the exclusive Greenbrier Diagnostic Clinic. Development of a new Medical Institute is underway. Plans include facilities and a focus on sports medicine and performance as well as cosmetic surgery.

Golf and spa activities are enhanced by fly-fishing, outdoor and indoor tennis courts. For those seeking more unusual recreation, falconry is available with both instruction and demonstrations. Romantics enjoy tea in the Wisteria Room and carriage or sleigh rides around the resort.

For more on special aspects of the Greenbrier, *see* "Fast Living", "Local Food", "Great Plumbing", "Amazing Architecture", "Superlatives" and "Tours".

Mothman Lives! In Stainless Steel And On The Big Screen

From 1965-68, more than 100 people in and around Point Pleasant described encounters with a giant winged creature. They generally agreed that it had red, saucer-shaped eyes. On December 15, 1967, the collapse of Point Pleasant's Silver Bridge and the resultant deaths of 46 people brought the town to the attention of the world. It was the worst bridge disaster in U.S. history. A simulation can be seen at the **River Museum.** Soon after the collapse, Mothman sightings ceased in the area, leading many to link the creature to the bridge collapse, either causing it or warning of it. Others pointed to Shawnee Chief Cornstalk's curse.

Mothman's notoriety increased dramatically in 2002 with the release of *Mothman Prophecies,* a spooky major motion picture starring Richard Gere, and based on John Keel's book of that name. Although *Mothman Prophecies*

In 2003, Point Pleasant erected a locally sculpted seven-foot stainless steel statue of Mothman complete with wings and glowing red eyes cast by Blenko.

was not filmed in the state, devotees in Point Pleasant have capitalized on the fame trickling down from the film.

Visitors come from around the world to be photographed with Mothman. Across the street, is the **Mothman Museum** with a large collection of props and memorabilia from the movie. Centerpiece of the collection is the Death List that includes all the strange deaths linked with Mothman. More than 100 handwritten eyewitness accounts are also a major attraction. There are shirts, dolls, ornaments, multiple websites and a menu's worth of Mothman themed drinks, sandwiches and pizzas. The annual **Mothman Festival** draws thousands in September. So far, no one has been able to book the monster for a return appearance.

Cosmic Ears And Ancient Rocks

The time continuum from ancient past to unforeseeable future runs south through the West Virginia mountains from **Seneca Rocks** to the **National Radio Astronomy Observatory** in Green Bank. The connection was made astonishingly obvious by two extraordinary events between October 1987 and November 1988.

At 3:27 pm on October 22, 1987, the 20 ton third prong of the great rock fell.

For the past 400 million years or so, natural forces have eroded away a geologic fold so nothing but the root of the mountain remains. As long as anyone knew, the root was three-pronged. Called Seneca Rocks after the native tribes who introduced the place to early settlers, it is over 900 feet of Tuscarora sandstone jutting up from the North Fork River. The 25-foot chimney of hard rock named the Gendarme gave no warning. Its disappearance will forever divide Seneca Rocks time into before and after.

John Maxwell, founder of the **Gendarme Climbing School and Store**, characterized the event as "the peak of fall and fall of peak." The astrological position of the stars indicates that the fall took place at a moment of almost pure balance and harmony, under the Libra New Moon.

No discernible pattern, no harsh weather or measureable earth changes linked the fall of the rock with the fall of a telescope so close in time and space. Postulating a cosmic message, both could have been affected by the Harmonic Convergence, claimed by millions around the world in August 1987 as the beginning of a new cosmic vibration.

Thirty miles south and a year later, at 9:43pm on November 15, 1988, one of the world's largest radio telescopes—300 feet—crashed to the ground in an instant. The cause cited was sudden failure of a key structural item. Its collapse tore a hole in the fabric of the astronomical community.

Walking around the array of scientific ears in the form of giant white telescopic dishes listening to outer space at the National Radio Astronomy Observatory, I could feel the remarkable confluence of unusual energy. Intent listening seemed to be drawing cosmic force to the spot surrounded by friendly, spruce-covered mountain peaks in remote West Virginia. If the Harmonic Convergence, derived from Mayan calendars, depicted an actual shift in the fabric of time, they would have heard about it in Green Bank. That's the type of pattern in the space chatter they're listening for as the telescopes focus cosmic radio waves. Sometimes too much focus on too strong a force can knock a giant telescope down it seems. The theory is easy to accept when you feel the energy and hear the hum of the radio waves drawn to Green Bank.

The 2,700-acre depression on top of a mountain—a natural bowl for listening—was selected by officialdom in 1954 for its isolation from man-made interference with radio waves. Even to the naked eye, the uncluttered West Virginia night sky provides almost unmatchable opportunities to view the stars. On satellite maps of light pollution, there's a black hole over much of the state. A facility of the National Science Foundation, the Observatory was in place by 1958. It is one of only four in the world, and is part of a global array of radio telescopes that observe quasars and measure the motion of continents. In addition, the telescopes here are responsible for keeping the official time for the United States.

For a place where such astounding work is being done, the site is remarkably open. It is an extraordinary experience to walk up and touch the huge mechanical wonders and hear them hum. Wandering along the roads and paths is permissible as long as you move on foot. Only special vehicles without the common motorized systems that disturb the telescopes' energy field are allowed to drive beyond a gate on the road. The staff uses bicycles.

The 485-foot, 17 million pound replacement for the fallen telescope is the largest, most advanced and fully steerable radio telescope on Earth. The 2.3-acre receiving dish has a unique surface that can be adjusted to maintain a perfect shape for focusing radio waves, while its jagged perimeter makes it look perpetually out of focus. Able to listen in on a much wider band of waves in its work of mapping both planets and distant stars, the new Robert C. Byrd Green Bank Telescope is revolutionizing radio astronomy.

Old jokes about the satellite dish being West Virginia's state flower fade when confronted with the array of enormous telescope dishes tucked along a typical

In 2003, a state-of-the-art Science Center opened on the complex filled with interactive exhibits about the arcane task of seeking messages from outer space.

twisting mountain road, which draw astronomers and space scientists from across the globe. By listening to the universe, the scientists of Green Bank explore the profound truths of the structure of space, nature of time and eternal radio hiss. They are taking an ongoing census of cosmic noise. Any aliens who follow the radio tracking back to its source will be perplexed as they glide into the 3,500-foot Green Banks airstrip, which leads directly to the giant telescope. Their main obstacle will be the deer on the strip; their biggest question will be—how did those four-legged creatures build that telescope with those hooves?

In addition to the gargantuan **Green Bank Telescope**, there are other notable instruments to be seen in the compound. The 200 foot high, 140-foot dish is the largest equatorially mounted radio telescope in the world. The 85-foot Tatel Telescope is the oldest built at the Observatory. In 1960, the OZMA Project that became the now nearly mythical search for extraterrestrial intelligence (SETI) was launched from here. A 40-foot telescope is used for student projects.

Green Bank is also the center of the world's only Radio Quite Zone, approximately 13,000 square miles where any mechanisms that could interfere with the cosmic ears are strictly regulated. Although it is an unfounded rumor that using a cell phone is a capital offense, the Quiet Zone demarcation shows up in numerous fictional television shows and movies.

There are even historic landmark instruments, including an exact replica of the antenna used in 1933 to discover radio waves from space, as well as the backyard-built original parabolic radio telescope used in the 1940s to produce the first maps of the radio sky.

The big boys at Green Bank have a little cousin at the **Morgan County**

Observatory which houses a rare Cassegrain telescope in a gem of a building with a rotating and openable dome. Once certified, folks can officially discover planets, stars and asteroids from a ridge top outside Berkeley Springs.

While Green Bank is listening for extraterrestrials, the Etam Earth Station in Preston County and one at Sugar Grove in Pendleton County are part of "good guy" snooping operations worldwide picking all types of electronically transmitted communications from the air.

From space aliens roaming along the Ohio in the western part of the state (*see* "Remarkable Collections") to the scientific world listening to space chatter in the east, West Virginia has an assured place in a galactic community.

Suspended Between Past And Present

Matewan is more than the scene of America's bloodiest gunfight in May 1920; it is a cool place waiting to happen. I could feel it ready to burst into bloom. When it was built in the 1890s, the railroad was so important that all the buildings had two facades: one facing the main street, one facing the railroad. Now only coal trains roar past every half hour, and sitting facing the track feels like sitting backwards. The tiny town, scarcely six blocks square, is sandwiched between the railroad and the river, with the rails back against the mountain; the river against Kentucky. Once Matewan was a fiercely independent town in the midst of the world's largest coal field.

The lovely brick former Post Office is on the Historic Register and waiting for a new tenant. The Hatfield Building includes the Matewan Development Center and its shop, as well as a cafe that serves breakfast anytime and is decorated with train photos. Bullet holes in the Old Matewan National Bank on the corner where the Matewan Massacre took place can still be seen. Repeated destructive flooding was endured due to the lack of flood-free land near the booming coalfield. Beginning in 1992, a 2,350-foot floodwall that ranges in height from six to 29 feet was constructed along the Tug Fork of the Big Sandy River. The wall has been used as a backdrop for graphics showing Matewan's geological, historical and economic history.

"Here for Life"

Grown-up potbelly pigs, feral cats and handicapped dogs share the space at **PIGS,** a 55-acre farm sanctuary for more than 400 unwanted and unadoptable animals. Threatened by encroaching high-end development and spiraling costs, sheltering the creatures no one else wants is a true act of love. The animals create art to sell, the place is rented for kids' parties and weddings, and many donate to PIGS support. Tours can be arranged but watch your heartstrings.

Center Of The Boy Scout Universe

When travelers arrive by train at the **Summit Bechtel Boy Scout** center, they'll use a one-of-a-kind railway station in Prince. The art deco prototype for a generation of train stations never built has been saved by the Boy Scout adventure. For more *see* "Superlatives."

CHAPTER SEVENTEEN

Unusual Places to Stay

The ads promoting West Virginia to potential visitors inevitably feature the state's matchless natural beauty or outdoor adventure possibilities. Strangers can be forgiven if they think there's no place to sleep except under the stars. What a surprise it is to find more than enough lodging, some of it quite unforgettable.

Forest Fantasy

Tricking a trout is the ultimate experience at the **Cheat Mountain Club**, a formerly exclusive Victorian hunting club at the top of the West Virginia world. The century-old red spruce lodge with hemlock siding still offers Spartan rooms and gender-separated gang bathrooms. Monogrammed towels and bathrobes are kept in the closet of each guest room to guarantee that guests are prepared for the middle-of-the-night walk down the hall. Boar and deer heads adorn the walls of the Great Room and a collection of autographed shelf fungus decorates the mantle of the huge stone fireplace.

Various odd touches pay tribute to CMC's prime purpose of outdoor adventure.

On one side of the front entrance a line of stakes protrudes from the wall designed to hang waders. The other side has an odd line of clips that turn out to be holders for fly fishing rods that, according to those who know, can never be leaned or laid down.

There's more than a mile of Shavers Fork riverfront for fishing or simply lounging in the romantic circle of deck chairs at the edge of the lawn. A working beaver pond highlights one hiking trail. A short walk along another trail leads to a 100-foot-long parabolic suspension footbridge with a distinctive swell and sway movement and a stunning view of Shavers Creek rushing beneath the floor. The invisible cloud of attitude-enhancing negative ions is an added bonus.

Three family-style meals a day come with the room, served at posted times and announced by the ringing of a giant brass hand bell. All meals are made to order in the club's kitchen, often staffed by a cook who drives over two mountains daily to cook for guests. Spring water is piped in from the mountain, there's an honor bar for evening cocktails and the wine rack displays about 70 bottles with an ingenious bottle opener mounted on the wall.

When we visited we were charmed by a stripling of a young man, Jason Means, who is CMC's outfitter, night manager and late night fly tyer. He's an all-around bonus the club offers its guests—along with free use of necessary equipment ranging from fly-fishing rods and waders to snowshoes and mountain bikes. "I would give anything for your job," Jason's been told by CEOs with six figure salaries and stratospheric stock options who regularly gather at the club for business meetings and pleasure trips.

Cheat Mountain Club has always been prized for its fly-fishing. The original trout hatcheries and runs are now used as holding tanks for fish brought in from various trout ranches. Once upon a time the daily catch limit was 300 fish. Today, it's catch and release fishing for brook, brown and rainbow trout. If a group pays to have the river stocked especially for them, they can keep the fish they catch; the lodge will even cook them.

Cradled at about 4,000 feet in an elevated indentation on Shavers Mountain, CMC has a unique weather universe all its own. Pack a season-spanning wardrobe to allow for hiking in warm sunshine one afternoon then waking the next morning to several inches of snow.

Unlike the weather, some things never change. In 1918, a quartet of noted traveling companions who called themselves the Vagabonds, arrived at the lodge which was then maintained by the Sportsmen Association of Cheat Mountain. According to the entry Thomas Edison made in the guest register, he and his friends—Henry Ford, Harvey Firestone and naturalist, John Burroughs, found the club "a beautiful spot."

Only Tell Your Friends

Originating as a pre-war summer resort—that's pre-Civil War—the family-operated **Capon Springs** wants prospective guests to understand what the cultural environment is. The fashionable 19th century resort with a huge hotel and bathing colonnade is gone. The current incarnation boasts first-rate Victorian buildings in excellent condition and a pre-war—this time World War II—family orientation.

At **Capon Springs and Farms**, the farms are real. Organic strawberries and tomatoes are grown by resort staff and find their way onto dining room tables where they are joined by Capon Springs eggs and resort-raised and cured ham and bacon. There's an 11 p.m. curfew, a volunteer flag raising each morning, regular songfests and talent shows in the activities hall. Guests can even add their own slides and films to evening programs. Alcoholic beverages are BYO and confined to guest rooms and porches.

There is no town at Capon Springs in modern terms—no post office, courthouse, mini-mart or other hallmarks of town life. Instead, you find a registered historic district filled with gracious cottages and the main hotel where guests are lodged; it was all built in the 1880s. Monumental cliffs and eccentric shaped rock outcroppings frame the 5,000-acre scenic resort.

Once a country getaway for presidents and notables, Capon Springs stood in virtual ruins during the 1920s from fire, flood and hard economic times. Lou Austin revived it as an offshoot of his quest to bottle the spring water, which contains lithia. Today, Austin grandkids, known as the "Thirds," manage Capon Springs with an enduring dedication to the face-to-face charm of the place. The deep narrow valley where the springs bubble forth is now filled with hammocks, water fountains, tennis, badminton, golf course, pools, hiking trails and children with grandparents. A spa was added in 2006. *See* "Great Plumbing"

Life is casual and reminiscent of a big family camp that happens to have grown up around noted springs. When the hundred rooms are full, 250 guests of all ages dine family-style in a light-filled dining room, called there three times a day by an old iron bell. Ties and dress-up clothes are considered unfashionable, and there are no limits placed on appetites, which is fortunate when the homemade bread and baked goods emerge fresh from huge, coal powered, brick ovens. Hotel chefs can often be cajoled into following the tradition of cleaning and cooking a guest's catch for breakfast, and outdoor barbecues happen regularly. There's a rack of black umbrellas at the ready and a free place to do the laundry.

People know each other here. Summertime finds a list of all guests coming for the week posted at the desk for all to see. Many names are familiar. Guests return each year, same time, same rooms, and same fellow guests. "Sometimes they call to let us know," chuckled Jonathan Bellingham, an Austin grandson. Some guests haven't missed a year in half a century and more than 50 families have annual reunions there. Newcomers are quickly absorbed into the extended resort family of the moment.

As befits a unique place, there are unique souvenirs to take home along with memories. Lou Austin was a philosopher, who transmitted his understanding of personal responsibility and the spiritual connection both through the resort, and through his books and "Little Me/Great Me" dolls. Former U.S. Labor Secretary Willard Wirtz is a longtime regular who wrote **Capon Valley Sampler** about the region. The books and dolls are available at the resort shop; the day-to-day experience of an honorable life is available to all who visit. Water is free for the taking.

Summer is traditionally the most active time, when the resort is filled with families and served by more than 120 staff members. Open from May 1 to November 1, spring and fall offer an almost idyllic private getaway into a genteel past where the sound of playing children is replaced by the near silence of the stream. Never are there sounds of traffic.

Tradition is not exorbitantly priced at Capon Springs and best of all, there are no nickel and dime annoyances. One personal check at the end of a guest's stay covers everything. The memories are up to you. The resort joins Berkeley Springs and the Greenbrier as the only remaining operative springs resorts in West Virginia.

It's a tough act to balance—being friendly but reclusive. So, don't scream Capon Springs to the world, share it as a special secret.

No Elvis Sightings At This Graceland

Stylish Grace Davis was her father's Washington hostess for the years **Henry Gassaway Davis** served as the first elected U.S. Senator from West Virginia. The lavish Victorian summer house Davis built overlooking Elkins was named in her honor and often filled with famous guests. Restored as an inn by Davis & Elkins College, **Graceland** has been renting rooms to the public since late 1996.

Walking out of a guest room suite in the middle of the night onto wide halls, sweeping staircases with seating areas on the landings, and a wide-angle view of the Great Hall and massive fireplace on the floor below, I felt like I was staying in Grace Davis' Victorian mansion. The lights of Elkins twinkled through large windows decorated with opulent tieback drapes. Soft shadows gleamed in the corners of elegant West Virginia hardwood floors and walls.

Railroads and timber made Henry Davis rich. Political power accompanied the wealth and in 1904, Davis lived up to his title of Grand Old Man and became the oldest man to ever run for U.S. Vice President. He was 80 and ran on the unsuccessful Democratic ticket against Teddy Roosevelt.

The Queen Anne style mansion with turrets and wrap-around porches was the height of style in 1893, filled with every innovation Davis could find. He

and son-in-law Steven Elkins, who built the twin mansion of Halliehurst, put in electricity and maintained their own power generating plant. The exterior of Graceland was local sandstone; the roof, red Vermont slate. The family last occupied the house in 1939 (*see* "Amazing Architecture".)

After Graceland was used for 30 years as a fraternity house and a few years more for storage, the college had plans to tear the mansion down. Fate, private supporters and Senator Robert Byrd intervened.

It took three years and $2 million to restore Graceland to its Victorian splendor, and it was done to the highest standards of excellence. One father and son team spent nearly a year properly hanging more than 90 doors; most were original with reconfigured hardware. Sliding counterweighted pocket doors were refurbished and original shutters, with wall insets where the shutters "disappear," were remounted on floor to ceiling windows. In the two-story entry hall a huge original painting of Blackwater Falls once again hangs.

Heirloom treasures are mostly in wood. There's cherry wood in the library, a floor-to-ceiling wood billiard room, and a music room entirely of birds eye maple, including the cabinets. The inn's restaurant in the Mingo Dining Room is red oak with a glass conservatory. All the original fireplaces have hand carved mantles.

Fabulous stained glass windows dominate the front of the house. They were saved from destruction and hidden away by folks at the Augusta Heritage Center when there was talk of demolition. When the restoration began, the windows were revealed. They've been totally reconstructed to last another century or two.

I stayed in Ellen Bruce Lee's room, now a luxurious guest suite. The lace canopy bed was a climb and Oriental throw rugs were strewn on original wood floors. Along with her husband, journalist John Kennedy, Bruce traveled the world. Later she lived at Sunrise in Charleston, the notable mansion of former Governor MacCorkle.

Bruce apparently loved a soak. Her deep claw foot tub with a thick gray marble cap around the top edge and gleaming chrome fixtures is set in a small bathroom lined with original marble.

Grace's Suite was in the turret and is now filled with lush, rich furnishings. Every guest room is different, but all are filled with period furnishings, and have a private bath.

The magnificent oak at the entrance to Graceland grew from an acorn Grace Davis picked up at a party in the Emperor's garden in Japan while on her honeymoon.

www.avalon-nude.com

Clothing is optional on the lawn, at volleyball games, Saturday night dances (usually only the band is clothed) or in the dining room. It's forbidden in the hot tub and swimming pool. **Avalon** is a family-style naturalist resort tucked away in the hills of Hampshire County near Paw Paw on the site of a former church camp. Undistinguished from other members of the local Chamber of Commerce at group meetings, the folks from Avalon don't recruit.

There's an aquatic and fitness center with pool and two heated spas, 18-room lodge, dance barn, private homes and campgrounds on the 250-acre site. Proud of their food quality, Avalon's public dining room was featured on the cable television show, *Extreme Cuisine*. One female diner was quoted as explaining that she simply did not want anything coming between her and her food. There was a towel between her and her chair however, a standard naturalist resort rule.

Although nudism is growing in America by leaps and bounds, and has its own Washington action committee, the average age remains way above nubile. Avalon memberships are available although non-members may visit. More than 90 people attend weekend dances and music festivals draw far more.

According to one Avalon neighbor, skinny-dipping is nothing new in these hills. Still others engage in affectionate jokes. Responding to a fire call at the resort's laundry room, one fireman wondered why they had a laundry since they didn't wear clothes.

. . . it's like a big family picnic with lots of nice people except nobody wears clothes.

There are local dissenters. When the Berkeley Springs newspaper ran a thoughtful feature on the nearby resort, it sparked three times as many column inches in responding letters including one calling it "the shame of Hampshire County."

How could I resist when the folks from Avalon asked me to come do a book signing? Being about 20 years and 50 pounds too late for clothing optional, I showed my respect by wearing a costume. My husband willingly volunteered to accompany me. Our ride over was punctuated with burning questions like where would they keep their money—in a fanny pack? We noticed that the nudity was almost never total. There were body piercings, hats, socks and tattoos. Visors were a favorite spot to attach the Nude Recreation Week pin. At the end of my talk and signing, we watched the pudding throw competition outside the wall of glass in the dining room and realized some sports are meant to be played in the nude.

Afford To Feel Rich

The horse barn was more enticing than many highway motels with its thick sawdust floors and twenty-two individual solid-door stalls equipped with dumbwaiters for hay. **Glade Springs Resort's** lodging choices run the gamut from a new hotel to the cutting edge Chestnut Hill Lodges, showpieces for comfort and flexibility. Multi-level houses with more bathrooms than bedrooms, they can also be cut and pasted into single oversized rooms, suites or the whole facility. Bring along all the cousins since the cottages offer a ten-bed bunkroom on the top floor. You'll never know the kids are there, but if you need to reach them, there are phones in every bathroom.

Along with the allure of 4,100 acres, an eighteen-hole golf course, free shuttles to the nearby Winterplace ski slopes and several fishing ponds, Glade Springs has indoor tennis and swimming as well as an equestrian program worthy of its palatial barn. To satisfy the true thrill seekers, Glade Springs created an exclusive outfitter to custom plan your outdoor adventures from white water rafting and sporting clays to mountain biking and fly fishing.

Built near Beckley in the early 1970s as a private resort for in-state coal barons with money to burn, Glade Springs has made the leap to a full-service paradise for the rest of us.

Century Old Beds

There are ghosts, old time water fountains in the halls, corkscrews mounted on bathroom walls and no bed less than a century old at the **General Lewis Inn.**

We checked in with a lovely woman at the tiny front desk. Both Patrick Henry and Thomas Jefferson reportedly stood and checked in at that same hand-built desk in its previous incarnation at the once-grand Sweet Chalybeate Springs Hotel nearby. We were directed to wander the halls and select from any room with the door open. We tried a few beds and checked the view. We selected a corner room with windows on two sides, from which we could see both the rooftops of historic Lewisburg and folks playing croquet on the inn's clipped lawns.

Gardens more than 70 years old surround a little playhouse that began life as a 19th century "necessary" and now serves as a tiny museum of children's playthings.

There are antiques everywhere indoors as well. Many of the furnishings were handcrafted in the region, authentic remnants of the frontier Lewisburg once was. An enormous but organized collection of antique tools and household items—many made from covered wagon parts—hang on the walls in Memory Hall. Other caches are tucked away in old cupboards throughout the inn. The comfortable parlor has games, puzzles and a lovely fire in season.

Breakfast was served in the dining room, located on what was the first floor of the original 1834 home. Sunlight flooded the windows and baroque music played. The breakfast potatoes were an abundant assemblage that included mushrooms, scallions, tomatoes, banana peppers, cheese, salsa and sour cream. Belgian waffles with real maple syrup and delicious omelets held their own with the potatoes.

As for the ghosts—those in the know ask for rooms 206 and 208, both part of the original house. The ghosts are an adult and two children. Innkeeper Jim Morgan was skeptical as befits a former research scientist for Du Pont and inventor of one segment of the Polaroid process. He attributed the reports to mistaken identity. Steam heat dries out the wood and causes thumps and groans. "No one ever sees the ghosts in summer," said Jim.

Lowe's in Point Pleasant also claims ghosts listing rooms 311 and 312 as favorite haunts. Like the General Lewis, Lowe's is unapologetically old but irresistible especially with its prime location. Out front is the Mothman statue, around back is the Riverwalk. Signed Tiffany glass panels ring the lobby and dining room. Lowe's telephone switchboard is the last one operating in the Bell System.

Cabin Fever

A remote location did not protect the nearly 10,000 mountainous acres of **Kumbrarow State Forest** from being stripped of their fine hemlock and spruce forests early in the 20th century. The excessively wet climate—the wettest place around even in the last Ice Age—accelerated the second growth forest, which now envelops the small clearing where the park's five rustic cabins sit around a central courtyard near a picturesque well house.

Built by the Civilian Conservation Corps in the late 1930s, the cabins have no electricity or running water. They do have a fireplace, gas appliances, pit toilets and the well. Light is provided by Coleman-type lanterns, including one ingeniously rigged as a five-pod chandelier. The screened porch backs up to the very loud, rock-strewn Mill

Creek, noted as a native brook trout stream. Lush vegetation and abundant rhododendron are everywhere along the walking trails. One direction leads easily downstream to a series of falls, riffles and rapids. Although it is the state's highest forest at 3,855 feet, the area around the cabins is the relatively flat Mill Creek streambed.

A favorite with hunters, each cabin is equipped out back with hanging racks for game.

Room with a Ride

There's only one way down and up at **Mountain Creek Lodge**—an aerial tram that connects the 30-room hideaway deep in the Bluestone Gorge to Pipestem State Park's main hotel on the rim. Rooms are undistinguished except for the balcony overlooking the rock-strewn Bluestone River. Easy walks along the riverbank may stir up over-friendly wildlife. I was shadowed for miles by a fawn that didn't get it that I consider all deer potential garden wreckers and candidates for the road kill bill. *See* "Tours" and "Local Food" for more on Pipestem.

Millennium Lodging

Adventure-based camps like **Elk River Touring Center** are the evolving face of West Virginia lodging. There are 12 rooms available in an inn and farmhouse that come with breakfast, as well as four cabins and a campground. The Restaurant at Elk River offers a cooked-from-scratch menu that changes daily and include tasty treats like whole wheat French bread and griddle fried pound cake. Established in 1985 as one of the first mountain bike touring companies in the United States, Elk River is an outfitter for day, weekend and week-long guided trips mostly through the Monongahela National Forest. They rent an assortment of camping gear, tents, sleeping bags and sports equipment as well as arrange for meals in wilderness. They also offer mountain bike riding camps, fly fishing trips and cross-country skiing. More than 200 miles of trails spoke-out from the Touring Center hub.

The Inn at Mountain Quest in Frost was created as a conference center and is also open to the getaway public. It sits on 450 acres, has a 14,000-volume library and tower for scenic viewing. There are a dozen guests rooms that are distinctively themed and a resident chef. You can start each morning greeting the animals ranging from horses to llamas.

Notable Bed Time

★ I spotted the five-story rounded corner bay as we approached the **Blennerhassett Hotel's** modest entrance on Parkersburg's main thoroughfare, and immediately began plotting how to get whatever room was hidden there. One-of-a-kind guest quarters are a trait of old hotels and examining the outside is an almost infallible way of discovering where those special rooms may be. What I found in the turret at the Blennerhassett was room 315, oversized, with a view from the curved window of the Smoot, an historic vaudeville theater. It became my room of choice.

Built in 1889, the historic hotel doubled its size and re-opened in 1986. Its rooms have the distinction of frontage on a tropical atrium filled with sunlight and a jungle of greenery. The street-level lounge is dark and inviting; the dining room is dress-up with white linen. Ghost tours are conducted regularly from its lobby.

★ Once the site of an important stagecoach stop on the old Kanawha Turnpike, the **Glen Ferris Inn** (*right*) is famous for its spectacular view of Kanawha Falls, especially from an executive suite and the river side rooms. The building dates from 1853.

★ Two state parks—**Tomlinson Run** and **Twin Falls**—make camping easy. Their rent-a-camp sites come complete with all equipment but the sleeping bags. At **Camp Creek State Forest and Park** you can bring your own horse and stay on an equestrian campsite with plenty of trails in the adjacent forest. **Seneca State Forest** may be the #1 contender for best pillow view in the east. Its unusual fire tower perched on a platform 55 feet above the top of a 3,415-foot peak is now a prime backcountry pillow although a primitive one. Seneca also has pioneer cabins that come with a canoe.

★ Home to a rare sanctuary for the largest native cat in the US—the cougar—you can pay extra to see them fed at **Mountain Creek Cabins**, and extra for a breakfast basket in your cabin.

★ You could always stay in a former company house built when **Cass** was a booming timber town. Now, you can sleep in a caboose located at Cass' three rail stations, all high on the mountain. There's a coal stove for heat, no electricity and bring-your-own bedding but you do get to ride the train up and back. **Mountain Rail Adventures** provides a ride to a secluded wilderness spot along the Greenbrier where guests learn what the Castaway Caboose means: room for six, a full shower and wood for the stove.

No Ogres In This Bavarian Fable

A visit to the **Bavarian Inn** is certain to stir childhood memories of *Grimm's Fairy Tales*, one with a beautiful princess and a happy ending. Chalets of distinctive stucco, dark timbered Alpine architecture and individual balconies perched high above the rushing Potomac River recall Hansel and Gretel's town before they were lost in the woods. Our room behind the balcony had a high four-poster canopied bed and a gilded mirror above the whirlpool bath. I was Sleeping Beauty, fantasy floating in a nobleman's castle high above the Danube.

Time shifted back to reality. I was a guest with my husband at the Bavarian Inn. And the cliffs of the Potomac at the edge of Shepherdstown marked the rise of the Alleghenies not the Alps. Still, I remembered *Snow White* and wondered about the gleaming red apples on the table.

The entry road marked "Bavarian Inn" curves up to an unexpected world of tidy Alpine structures outlined against the forested mountain across the river. The subdued hum of historic Shepherdstown seems far away.

Authentic Old World charm intensified at dinner in the original gray stone mansion. We ate near the stone fireplace in the hardwood-trimmed Hunt Room. A three-foot chandelier of twisted deerhorn lit our table; matching antler sconces were scattered around the handsome room. The extensive menu featured an entire column of schnitzels and wursts, an unpronounceable selection of German cordials and an invitation to slip downstairs to the Rathskeller. Casual and comforting, the Rathskeller offers the welcoming closeness of a richly paneled hideaway—with benches before the fireplace ready for comrades sipping brandy or clicking steins of German beer.

The Alpine setting comes naturally for "the Bavarian man with an English wife and two blond boys in liederhosen," as Erwin Asam and his wife Carol were described when they first arrived in the late 1970s. Both are dapper, courtly, and obviously the European spirits that inhabit the place and generate its flavor. And it is just as natural for the rustic 11-acre spot above the Potomac to be where 200 years earlier there had been a thriving German community known as Mecklenburg.

The chalets were built using the images on Bavarian postcards as models. Rounded bathrooms fill the turrets in one chalet, and each building has several private entrances for clusters of rooms. Foundations were blasted from the solid rock cliffs on which they sit. An appealing gallery of Alpine frescoes is featured on the exterior walls of chalets and the outdoor garden wall of the new lodge.

The Bavarian Inn was one of the first places in the area to have rooms with fireplaces and private whirlpools. Most of the 70 guest rooms are equipped with both, as well as European bidets.

The senior Asams have proven to be champs in succession planning. The towheads in liederhosen are now young men, college educated and back home with their families to begin the second generation at the Bavarian Inn.

From Derelict to Diva

Hotel Morgan was the grande dame of Morgantown society when it opened in 1925. The tallest building in town, its chandeliered ballroom was the site of memorable events including the visit of President John F. Kennedy. Eventually, the hotel fell on hard times. In October 1999, the historic hotel reopened after a major restoration that transformed 150 antique rooms into 76 business class mini-suites.

Grandeur marks the hotel from top to bottom. You walk into a lobby paneled in original stained oak. The main floor ballroom glitters with alternate panels of oak and mirrors. Huge oak pillars support the 24-foot ceiling. The 8th floor penthouse has been transformed into the Pinnacle Club. The cozy lounge boasts a working fireplace, sunken bar and giant, overstuffed swivel chairs masquerading as bar stools. There are young bellhops anxious to satisfy your every whim especially when it allows them to travel the original antique elevator.

Ideally located in the center of the award winning downtown, Hotel Morgan is an easy walk from both the West Virginia University campus and the newly developed waterfront area. While it may no longer be the tallest building in town, its glowing red neon rooftop sign is visible from all directions.

The happy ending of the Hotel Morgan is touched with tragedy. Innovative businessman, Ted Brandt, passionately pursued the historic restoration. Less than a year after the hotel reopened, Brandt died suddenly. Today, the hotel's elegant boardroom bears his name.

Swank Wilderness

The ski and summer resort at Snowshoe can sleep more than 9,000 people in standard condos and lodge rooms. The most daring of visitors may choose the **Wilderness Hut** for overnight stays or simply for dinner. The six room, log construction cabin sits on the rim of Cheat Mountain Ridge overlooking the Greenbrier River; the view includes nothing created by man. A wind generator and rechargeable batteries provide power. The three-mile journey—twisting, turning, plunging and climbing—can be hiked in summer, skied in winter or taken in the motorized Hydrotaxx—a six-wheeled, all terrain, amphibious vehicle. The Hutmaster, who doubles as the chef, stays in residence and guarantees that strangers sharing the space hang out together. The food is not rustic and a set menu ranges from pecan crusted salmon to crab stuffed New York strips. Mind your manners; it's a long walk back.

Rooms Plus

★ There is no dinner but plenty of time for enlightenment at the **Bhavana Society Forest Monastery** and Retreat Center where the sight of saffron-robed, shaved head power walkers is not strange to their rural neighbors. Accommodations are single-bed cottages or gender-specific dormitories and silence is the rule.

★ Always worried about where to park your plane when you go camping? There's a manicured backcountry grass airstrip complete with B&B rooms, cabins and a campground at **Heaven's Landing Retreat.**

Appendix — Way Out by County

The best place to contact for detailed information is the local convention and visitors bureau in each area. They are listed below with the county or counties they serve. For West Virginia in general call 1-800-CALL WVA. They will send *West Virginia, Wild and Wonderful!*, a glossy gold mine of useful travel information. Or you can check the extensive state travel website at www.wvtourism.com

Towns/cities

Beckley—*see* Raleigh
Berkeley Springs—*see* Morgan
Bluefield—*see* Mercer
Buckhannon—*see* Upshur
Charleston—*see* Kanawha
Clarksburg—*see* Harrison
Elkins—*see* Randolph
Fayetteville—*see* Fayette
Harpers Ferry—*see* Jefferson

Huntington—*see* Cabell
Lewisburg—*see* Greenbrier
Martinsburg—*see* Berkeley
Morgantown—*see* Monongalia
Parkersburg—*see* Wood
Philippi—*see* Barbour
Romney—*see* Hampshire
Shepherdstown—*see* Jefferson
Wheeling—*see* Ohio

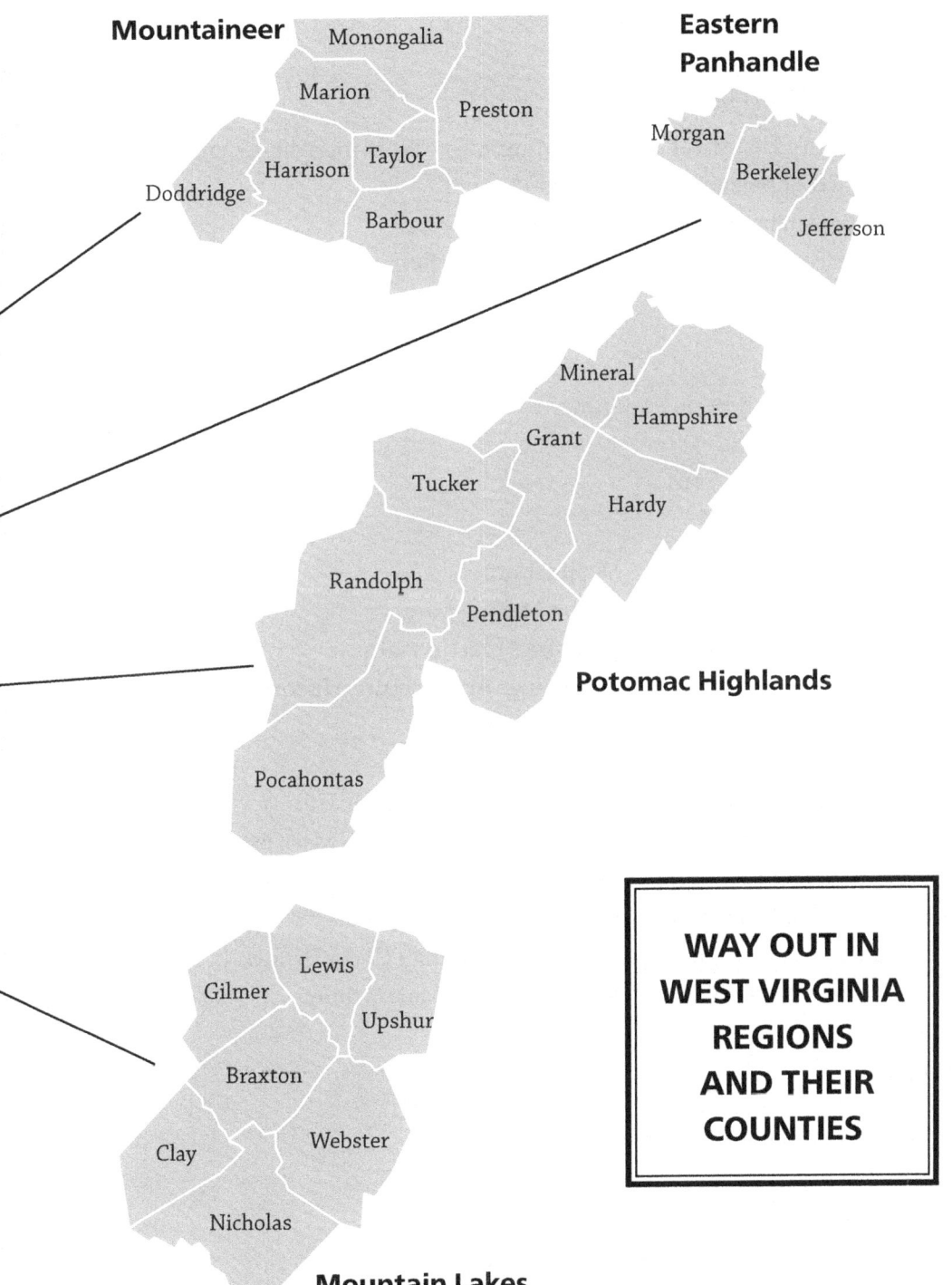

Barbour

City of Philippi CVB
304-457-3700

Barbour County Historical Museum/Mummies • Truly Incredible • Philippi
Carrollton CB • Amazing Architecture • Philippi
Philippi CB • Amazing Architecture • Philippi
Valley Furnace • Things That Used To Be There • Philippi

Berkeley

Martinsburg-Berkeley County CVB
126 E. Race St.
Martinsburg 25401
800-4WVA-FUN

Apollo Theater • Art Wonders • Martinsburg
Belle Boyd House • Historic Oddities • Martinsburg
Blue Ridge Bank • Amazing Architecture • Martinsburg
B&O Roundhouse Complex • Amazing Architecture/Historic Oddities • Martinsburg
Buck's Hill • Million Dollar Views
Bunker Hill Mill • Things That Used To Be There • Bunker Hill
Carriage House @ Hartwood Mansion • Great Plumbing • Martinsburg
De Fluri's Chocolates • Local Food • Martinsburg
Martinsburg Public Library • Art Wonders • Martinsburg
Peacemaker National Training Center • Fast Living • Gerrardstown
Vanmetre Ford Bridge • Amazing Architecture • Martinsburg

Boone

1st coal discovered in US • Superlatives • Racine

Braxton

>Braxton County Convention and Visitors Bureau
>245 Skidmore Ln.
>Sutton 26601
>304-765-6533

Burnsville Lake and Dam • Superlatives • Burnsville
Elk River Water Trail • Mother Nature's Wonders
Flatwoods Monster • Remarkable Collections • Flatwoods

Brooke

>Top of WV CVB
>3393 Main St.
>Weirton 26062
>877-723-7114

Bethany • Superlatives
Grimes Golden • Mother Nature's Wonders • Wellsburg

Cabell

>Cabell/Huntington CVB
>210 11th St.
>Huntington 25708
>800-635-6329

Blenko Glass • Shopping Treasures • Milton
East Huntington Bridge • Amazing Architecture • Huntington
Frost-Top Drive-in • Art Wonders • Huntington
Heiner's Bakery • Tours • Huntington
Heritage Farm Museum and Village • Remarkable Collections • Huntington
Hillbilly Hot Dog • Local Food • Lesage
Hot Dog Festival • Far-Out Festivals • Huntington
Huntington Mall • Shopping Treasures • Huntington
Huntington Memorial Arch • Amazing Architecture • Huntington
Huntington Museum • Amazing Architecture/Remarkable Collections • Huntington

Keith Albee Theater • Art Wonders • Huntington
Milton Maize Maze • Far-Out Festivals • Milton
Mud River CB • Amazing Architecture • Milton
Museum of Radio and Technology • Remarkable Collections • Huntington
Old Central City • Shopping Treasures • Huntington
Pullman Plaza Hotel • Historic Oddities • Huntington
Red Cross • Art Wonders • Huntington
Ritter Park • Superlatives • Huntington
Stewart's Original Hot Dogs • Local Food • Huntington
Summerfest • Fast Living • Huntington
Touma Medical Museum • Remarkable Collections • Huntington
West Virginia Biological Survey Museum • Remarkable Collections • Huntington

Calhoun

Albert's Chapel • Amazing Architecture • Sand Ridge
Grantsville • Adventure Driving
Heartwood in the Hills • Art Wonders • Five Forks
Mike Fink's Grave • Historic Oddities • Minora

Clay

Ramps • Local Food • Clay
Solomon's Secret • Far-Out Festivals • Clay

Doddridge

Center Point CB • Amazing Architecture
Middle Island Creek • Superlatives
North Bend Trail • Adventure Driving

Fayette

> Fayetteville Convention and Visitors Bureau
> 310 N. Court St.
> Fayetteville 25840
> 888-574-1500

Ace Adventure Center • Great Plumbing • Oak Hill
Adventures on the Gorge • Fast Living • Lansing
Bridge Day • Far-Out Festivals
Camp Washington Carver • Amazing Architecture/Superlatives
Canyon Rim Visitors Center • Million Dollar Views/Mother Nature's Wonders
Cathedral Cafe • Art Wonders • Fayetteville
Country Road Cabins • Great Plumbing • Hico
Glade Creek Grist Mill • Things That Used To Be There • Clifftop
Glen Ferris Inn • Unusual Places to Stay • Glen Ferris
Hawks Nest Diversion Tunnel • Historic Oddities • Ansted
Hawks Nest State Park • Million Dollar Views • Ansted
Jet boats @ Hawks Nest • Fast Living • Ansted
Kaymoor Mine Trail • Things That Used To Be There
Midland Trail Scenic Highway • Adventure Driving
Mill Creek Cabins • Great Plumbing • Lansing
Mountain Chalets • Great Plumbing • Fayetteville
Mystery Hole • Truly Incredible • Ansted
New River/New River Gorge • Fast Living/Festivals/Mother Nature's Wonders
New River Gorge Bridge—US 19 • Amazing Architecture/Festivals
Smokey's on the Gorge • Local Food • Lansing
Thurmond • Adventure Driving/Things That Used To Be There

Gilmer

Glenville State College • Superlatives • Glenville
West Virginia State Folk Festival • Far-Out Festivals • Glenville

Grant

>Grant County Convention and Visitors Bureau
>126 S. Main St.
>Petersburg 26847
>304-257-9266

Country Store Opry • Art Wonders
Fort Mulligan • Superlatives • Petersburg
Harman's North Fork Cottages and Cabins • Great Plumbing • Petersburg
Heaven's Landing Retreat • Unusual Places to Stay • Medley
Mount Storm Lake • Fast Living
Mount Storm Wind Farm • Superlatives
North Fork Mountain Inn • Great Plumbing
Petersburg Fish Hatchery • Superlatives • Petersburg
Petersburg Wave Camp • Adventure Driving • Petersburg
Smoke Hole Cabins • Great Plumbing • Petersburg
Smoke Hole Caverns • Superlatives/Mother Nature's Wonders • Petersburg
Smoke Hole Road • Adventure Driving

Greenbrier

>Greenbrier County Convention and Visitors Bureau
>200 W. Washington St.
>Lewisburg 24901
>800-833-2068

Alderson • Historic Oddities
Carnegie Hall • Art Wonders • Lewisburg
General Lewis Inn • Great Plumbing/Unusual Places to Stay • Lewisburg
Greenbrier • Truly Incredible/Superlatives/Great Plumbing/Unusual Places to Stay • White Sulphur Springs
Greenbrier Bunker Tour • Tours • White Sulphur Springs
The Greenbrier Christmas Shop at the Depot • Shopping Treasures • White Sulphur Springs
Greenbrier River • Superlatives
Greenbrier River Trail • Adventure Driving/Superlatives

Herns Mill CB • Amazing Architecture
Hokes Mill CB • Amazing Architecture • Ronceverte
Jeff's Breads • Local Food • Renick
Lake Sherwood • Mother Nature's Wonders
Lay over roads • Adventure Driving
Lewisburg • Great Plumbing/Mother Nature's Wonders
Livery Tavern • Local Food • Lewisburg
Lost World Caverns • Mother Nature's Wonders • Lewisburg
Midland Trail Scenic Highway • Adventure Driving
Oakhurst Links • White Sulphur Springs
Old Stone Presbyterian Church • Superlatives • Lewisburg
Organ Cave • Historic Oddities/Mother Nature's Wonders • Ronceverte
Savannah Lane Shooting Association • Fast Living • Lewisburg
Shanghai Parade • Far-Out Festivals • Lewisburg
Smooth Ambler Distillery • Local Food • Maxwelton
Sunshine Farm • Mother Nature's Wonders • Renick

Hampshire

Hampshire County Convention and Visitors Bureau
91 S. High St.
Romney 26757
304-822-7477

Avalon • Unusual Places to Stay
Bhavana Society • Unusual Places to Stay
Bloomery • Things That Used To Be There
Capon Springs and Farms • Great Plumbing/Unusual Places to Stay/ Things That Used To Be There • Capon Springs
Fort Mill Ridge Trenches • Historic Oddities • Romney
Ice Mountain • Mother Nature's Wonders
Indian Mound Cemetery • Historic Oddities • Romney
Potomac Eagle • Tours • Romney
Raven Rocks • Million Dollar Views

Hancock

Top of WV CVB
3393 Main St.
Weirton 26062
877-723-7114

Hilltop Drive-in Theater • Art Wonders • Newell
Homer Laughlin • Shopping Treasures/Tours • Newell
Line of the Seven Ranges • Historic Oddities • Chester
Mountaineer Racetrack and Gaming Resort • Fast Living • Chester
Peter Tarr Iron Furnace • Things That Used To Be There • Weirton
Tomlison Run • Unusual Places to Stay
World's Largest Teapot • Superlatives • Chester

Hardy

Hardy County CVB
122 N. Main St.
Moorefield 26826
304-897-8700

Hanging Rocks • Mother Nature's Wonders • Baker
Lee White Sulphur Springs • Things That Used To Be There • Mathias
Lost River Artisans Cooperative • Shopping Treasures • Lost River
Lost River State Park • Mother Nature's Wonders • Wardensville
South Branch Inn • Great Plumbing • Moorefield
Trout Pond • Mother Nature's Wonders

Harrison

Greater Bridgeport Convention and Visitors Bureau
164 W. Main St.
Bridgeport 26330
800-368-4324

Greater Clarksburg Convention and Visitors Bureau
208 Court St.
Clarksburg 26301
304-662-2157

Bice-Ferguson Museum • Remarkable Collections • Shinnston
Bonnie Belle Bakery • Local Food • Nutter Fort
Clarksburg • Adventure Driving
D'Annunzio's Health Bread Company • Local Food • Clarksburg
Fletcher CB • Amazing Architecture • Wolf Summit
Gray Barker UFO Collection • Remarkable Collections • Clarksburg
Italian Heritage Festival • Far-Out Festivals • Clarksburg
Julio's • Local Food • Clarksburg
Lagniappe Cafe • Local Food • Clarksburg
North Bend Trail • Adventure Driving • Wood/Ritchie/Doddridge/Harrison
Oak Mound • Historic Oddities • Clarksburg/Harrison
Peter Dye Golf Club • Superlatives • Bridgeport
Scottish Festival and Celtic Gathering • Far-Out Festivals • Bridgeport
Simpson Creek CB • Amazing Architecture • Bridgeport/Harrison
Sunset Drive-in Theater • Art Wonders • Shinnston
Tomaro's • Local Food • Clarksburg

Jackson

Jackson County Chamber of Commerce
104 Miller Dr.
Ripley 25271
304-373-1117

Mountain State Art and Craft Fair • Far-Out Festivals • Ripley
Sarvis Fork CB • Amazing Architecture • Sandyville
Staats Mill CB • Amazing Architecture • Ripley
Washington Western Lands Museum • Historic Oddities • Ravenswood

Jefferson

> Jefferson County CVB
> 37 Washington Ct.
> Harpers Ferry 25425
> 866-HELLO-WV

Bavarian Inn & Lodge • Great Plumbing/Unusual Places to Stay • Shepherdstown
Charles Town • Historic Oddities/Mother Nature's Wonders
Charles Town Post Office • Superlatives • Charles Town
Contemporary American Theater Festival • Art Wonders • Shepherdstown
Crazy House • Amazing Architecture • Harpers Ferry
George Tyler Moore Center for the Study of the Civil War • Historic Oddities • Shepherdstown
German Street • Amazing Architecture • Shepherdstown
Ghost Tours of Harpers Ferry • Tours • Harpers Ferry
Harpers Ferry National Historical Park • Amazing Architecture/Historic Oddities/ Things That Used To Be There • Harpers Ferry
Hillbrook Inn • Historic Oddities • Charles Town
Hollywood Casino at Charles Town Races • Fast Living • Charles Town
Jefferson County Courthouse • Amazing Architecture/Historic Oddities • Charles Town
Jefferson County House and Garden Tour • Historic Oddities
Jefferson Rock • Million Dollar Views • Harpers Ferry
John Brown's Fort • Amazing Architecture • Harpers Ferry
McMurran Hall • Superlatives • Shepherdstown
Morgan's Grove Park • Superlatives • Shepherdstown
Mountain Heritage Arts and Crafts Festival • Shopping Treasures • Harpers Ferry
National Conservation Training Center • Truly Incredible • Shepherdstown
O'Hurley's General Store • Great Plumbing/Shopping Treasures • Shepherdstown
PIGS, a Sanctuary • Truly Incredible • Shepherdstown
Presidential Election of 1860 • Far-Out Festivals • Harpers Ferry
River Riders • Fast Living • Harpers Ferry

Rumsey Boathouse • Historic Oddities • Shepherdstown
Rumsey Monument • Historic Oddities • Shepherdstown/Jefferson
Shannondale Springs • Things That Used To Be There • Charles Town
Shepherdstown Bakery • Local Food • Shepherdstown
Shepherdstown Opera House • Art Wonders • Shepherdstown
Storer College • Historic Oddities • Harpers Ferry
Summit Point Raceway • Fast Living • Summit Point
Thomas Shepherd Gristmill • Things That Used To Be There • Shepherdstown
Virginius Island • Things That Used To Be There • Harpers Ferry
West Virginia Breeders Classic • Fast Living • Charles Town
Zion Episcopal Church Cemetery • Historic Oddities • Charles Town

Kanawha

Charleston CVB
200 Civic Center Dr.
Charleston 25301
800-733-5469

S. Charleston CVB
301 D. St.
South Charleston 25303
800-238-9488

Cabela's • Shopping Treasures • Charleston
Capitol Market • Shopping Treasures • Charleston
Capitol Theater • Art Wonders • Charleston
Carriage Trail • Tours • Charleston
Center for National Response WV Memorial Tunnel • Superlatives • Standard
Charleston Boulevard Rod Run and Doo Wop • Far-Out Festivals • Charleston
Clay Center • Art Wonders • Charleston
Dutch Hollow Wine Cellar Park. • Historic Oddities • Dunbar
East End Yard Sale • Shopping Treasures • Charleston
Festivall • Far-Out Festivals • Charleston
Fret 'n Fiddle • Shopping Treasures • St. Albans
Kanawha State Forest Braille Trail • Tours • Charleston
Mountain Stage • Art Wonders • Charleston

Soho's • Local Food • Charleston
South Charleston Mound • Historic Oddities • South Charleston
Spring Hill Pastry Shop • Local Food • Charleston
State Capitol • Superlatives • Charleston
Trace Fork Canyon Trail • Mother Nature's Wonders • South Charleston
Vandalia Festival • Art Wonders/Far-Out Festivals • Charleston
West Virginia Archives and History Library • Remarkable Collections • Charleston
West Virginia Music Hall of Fame • Art Wonders • Charleston
West Virginia State Museum • Historic Oddities/Remarkable Collections/Superlatives • Charleston
Yeager Airport • Adventure Driving • Charleston
Yeager Monument • Adventure Driving • St. Albans

Lewis

Lewis County CVB
499 US 33
Weston 26452
304-269-7328

Appalachian Glass • Tours • Weston
Citizens Bank • Amazing Architecture • Weston
Irish Spring Festival • Far-Out Festivals • Ireland
Jackson's Mill • Superlatives/ Things That Used To Be There • Weston
Lambert's Vintage Wines • Local Food • Weston
Mountaineer Military Museum • Remarkable Collections • Weston
Stonewall Jackson State Park • Tours • Roanoke
Walkersville CB • Amazing Architecture • Walkersville
Weston Episcopal Church • Amazing Architecture • Weston
Trans-Allegheny Lunatic Asylum • Amazing Architecture/Superlatives/Tours • Weston
West Virginia Museum of American Glass • Remarkable Collections • Weston

Lincoln

Spencer's Taxidermy • Shopping Treasures • West Hamlin

Logan

Hatfield-McCoy Convention and Visitors Bureau
214 Stratton St.
Logan 25601
304-752-1324

Battle of Blair Mountain • Historic Oddities • Blair Mountain
Chief Logan State Park • Historic Oddities
Devil Anse Hatfield statue • Historic Oddities • Sarah Ann
Morrison's Drive-in • Local Food • Stollings

Marion

Marion County CVB
110 Adams St.
Fairmont 26554
800-843-7365

Barrackville CB • Amazing Architecture • Barrackville
Biselli's Pasta • Local Food • Fairmont
Colasessano's • Local Food • Fairmont
Country Club Bakery • Local Food • Fairmont
Prickett's Fort • Superlatives • Fairmont
Round Barn • Amazing Architecture • Mannington
Three Rivers Festival • Local Food • Fairmont
Valley Falls State Park • Million Dollar Views • Fairmont

Marshall

>Moundsville Economic Development
>818 Jefferson St.
>Moundsville 26041
>304-845-6200

Cameron City Pool • Amazing Architecture • Cameron
Cresap Mound • Historic Oddities • Marshall
Grand Vue Park • Fast Living • Moundsville
Grave Creek Mound • Historic Oddities/Superlatives • Moundsville
Ohio River Islands Wildlife Refuge • Mother Nature's Wonders
Palace of Gold • Truly Incredible • Moundsville
Strand Theater • Art Wonders • Moundsville
Undo's • Local Food • Benwood
West Virginia Penitentiary Tours • Tours • Moundsville

Mason

>Mason County CVB
>210 Viand St.
>Point Pleasant 25550
>304-675-6788

Cornstalk • Historic Oddities • Point Pleasant
Lowe's • Unusual Places to Stay • Point Pleasant
Mothman Museum & Statue/Festival • Things That Used To Be There/Truly Incredible • Point Pleasant
Riverwalk murals • Art Wonders • Point Pleasant
Robert Byrd Locks Visitor Center • Million Dollar Views
TNT area • Things That Used To Be There • Point Pleasant
Tu-Endie-Wei State Park • Historic Oddities • Point Pleasant
West Virginia State Farm Museum • Remarkable Collections • Point Pleasant

McDowell

> City of Welch
> 88 Howard St.
> Welch 24801
> 304-436-3113

Carswell • Things That Used To Be There
Cinder Bottom • Things That Used To Be There • Keystone
Elkhorn Inn and Theater • Art Wonders • Keystone
Gary • Superlatives
October Sky • Art Wonders • Coalwood
Kimball Memorial • Superlatives
McDowell County Courthouse • Amazing Architecture • Welch
Panther State Forest • Mother Nature's Wonders

Mercer

> Mercer County Convention and Visitors Bureau
> 704 Bland St.
> Bluefield 24701
> 800-221-3206

Bluefield • Amazing Architecture/Mother Nature's Wonders
Bramwell • Amazing Architecture/ Things That Used To Be There
Camp Creek State Forest and Park • Unusual Places to Stay • Camp Creek
Chicory Square Park • Art Wonders • Bluefield
Concord United Methodist Church • Art Wonders • Athens
Cooper House • Amazing Architecture • Bramwell
Corner Shop • Things That Used To Be There • Bramwell
East River Mountain Overlook • Million Dollar Views • Bluefield
East River Mountain Tunnel • Adventure Driving • Bluefield
Eastern Regional Coal Archives • Remarkable Collections • Bluefield
Gary Bowling's House of Art • Art Wonders • Bluefield
Marsh Carillion • Art Wonders • Athens
Pinnacle Rock State Park • Mother Nature's Wonders

Pocahontas Coal Fields • Mother Nature's Wonders/Superlatives
Ramsey School • Amazing Architecture • Bluefield
Shamrock • Superlatives • Bluefield

Mingo

Tug Valley Chamber of Commerce
73 East 2nd Ave.
Williamson 25661
304-235-5240

Coal House • Amazing Architecture • Williamson
Dingess Tunnel • Adventure Driving
Hatfield and McCoy Reunion Festival • Far-Out Festivals • Williamson
Laurel Lake Wildlife Management Area • Lenore
Matewan flood wall • Amazing Architecture • Matewan
Matewan • Historic Oddities/Truly Incredible • Matewan
Old Matewan National Bank • Historic Oddities • Matewan
Twisted Gun Golf Club • Superlatives • Wharncliffe
Williamson • Adventure Driving • Williamson

Mineral

Mineral County CVB
1 Grand Central Park
Keyser 26726
304-788-2513

Allegany Ballistics Lab • Fast Living
Cumberland Airport • Adventure Driving
Fort Ashby • Historic Oddities/ Things That Used To Be There • Keyser
Rock-n-Wood Heaven • Amazing Architecture • New Creek
Saddle Mountain • Adventure Driving/Million Dollar Views
Waffle Rock • Mother Nature's Wonders • Elk Garden

Monongalia

>Greater Morgantown CVB
>68 Donley St.
>Morgantown 26501
>800-458-7373

Core Arboretum • Superlatives • Morgantown
Dents Run CB • Amazing Architecture
Gabriel Brothers • Shopping Treasures • Morgantown
Hotel Morgan • Unusual Places to Stay • Morgantown
The Met • Fast Living • Morgantown/Monongalia
Mannette Steel Drums • Tours • Morgantown
Mario's Fishbowl • Local Food • Morgantown
Metropolitan Billiard Parlor • Fast Living • Morgantown
Metropolitan Theater • Art Wonders • Morgantown
West Virginia Geological Survey Museum • Remarkable Collections • Morgantown
West Virginia and Regional History Collection • Remarkable Collections • Morgantown
Woodburn Hall • Amazing Architecture • Morgantown

Monroe

>Travel Monroe County
>866-677-3003 ext 11

A Taste of Eggcellence • Local Food • Gap Mills
Alderson • Historic Oddities
Cheese n' More • Adventure Driving/Local Food • Gap Mills
Hanging Rock Observatory • Adventure Driving/Million Dollar Views
Indian Creek CB • Amazing Architecture • Salt Sulphur Springs
Laurel Creek CB • Amazing Architecture
Marie Road • Adventure Driving
Monroe County Confederate Monument • Historic Oddities • Union
Monroe County Quilt Trail • Art Wonders
Peter's Mountain • Adventure Driving/Great Plumbing

Reeds Mill • Things That Used To Be There • Second Creek
Rehobeth Church and Museum • Superlatives • Union
Salt Sulphur Springs • Things That Used To Be There
Scott Hollow Cave • Mother Nature's Wonders • Sinks Grove
Sweet Springs • Adventure Driving/ Things That Used To Be There • Sweet Springs
Union • Adventure Driving/Amazing Architecture

Morgan

Travel Berkeley Springs
127 Fairfax St.
Berkeley Springs 25411
800-447-8797

Apple Butter Festival • Far-Out Festivals • Berkeley Springs
Atasia Spa • Great Plumbing • Berkeley Springs
Berkeley Castle • Amazing Architecture • Berkeley Springs/Morgan
Berkeley Springs • Great Plumbing/Historic Oddities/Superlatives/ Things That Used To Be There • Berkeley Springs
Berkeley Springs International Water Tasting • Far-Out Festivals • Berkeley Springs
Berkeley Springs State Park • Historic Oddities/Great Plumbing
The Country Inn • Great Plumbing • Berkeley Springs
Eddie's Tires • Shopping Treasures • Berkeley Springs
Exline's Iris Garden • Mother Nature's Wonders • Berkeley Springs
Highlawn Inn • Great Plumbing • Berkeley Springs
Hunters Hardware • Shopping Treasures • Berkeley Springs
Ice House • Shopping Treasures • Berkeley Springs
Lot 12 Public House • Local Food • Berkeley Springs
Midas Muffler Man • Art Wonders • Unger
Morgan County Observatory • Truly Incredible • Berkeley Springs
Museum of the Berkeley Springs • Remarkable Collections • Berkeley Springs
Panorama Overlook • Million Dollar Views • Berkeley Springs
Paw Paw Tunnel • Amazing Architecture • Paw Paw
ragtime's 1000 Points of Peace • Art Wonders • Berkeley Springs

Ridersville Cycle • Adventure Driving • Berkeley Springs
Star Theatre • Art Wonders • Berkeley Springs
SR 9 • Adventure Driving
Tari's Premier Cafe • Local Food • Berkeley Springs
Tony's Butcher Block • Local Food • Berkeley Springs
Troubadour Lounge • Art Wonders • Berkeley Springs

Nicholas

>Summersville CVB
>3 Armory Way
>Summersville 26651
>866-716-0448

Brier Run Farm • Local Food • Birch River
Feast of the Ransom • Far-Out Festivals • Richwood
Isaiah Morgan Distillery/Kirkwood Wineries • Local Food • Summersville
Mt. Nebo Tractor Bar • Fast Living • Mt. Nebo
Summersville Lake & Dam • Fast Living/Superlatives • Summersville

Ohio

>Wheeling CVB
>1401 Main St.
>Wheeling 26003
>800-828-3097

"The Aviator" • Superlatives • Wheeling
Cabela's • Shopping Treasures • Tridelphia
Capitol Theatre • Art Wonders • Wheeling
Carriage House Glass • Shopping Treasures • Wheeling
Centre Market • Amazing Architecture • Wheeling
Coleman's • Local Food • Wheeling
DiCarlo's Pizza • Local Food • Wheeling
Festival of Lights • Far-Out Festivals • Wheeling
Imperial Teacher's Store • Shopping Treasures • Wheeling/Ohio
Jebbia's Market • Shopping Treasures • Wheeling

Kruger Street Toy and Train Museum • Remarkable Collections • Wheeling
Oglebay Institute • Art Wonders • Wheeling
Oglebay Institute's Glass Museum • Remarkable Collections/Superlatives • Wheeling
Oglebay Resort • Superlatives • Wheeling
Ohio River Islands Wildlife Refuge • Mother Nature's Wonders
St. Joseph's Cathedral • Amazing Architecture • Wheeling
Stifel Fine Arts Center • Art Wonders • Wheeling
Stages • Shopping Treasures • Wheeling
Victorian Wheeling Landmarks Foundation • Amazing Architecture • Wheeling
Wheeling Airport Terminal/Stifel Field • Remarkable Collections • Wheeling
Wheeling Island Racetrack and Gaming Center • Fast Living • Wheeling Island
Wheeling Island • Superlatives
Wheeling Jamboree • Art Wonders • Wheeling Island
Wheeling Jesuit University • Superlatives • Wheeling
Wheeling Suspension Bridge •Amazing Architecture • Wheeling
Wymer's General Store and Museum • Remarkable Collections • Wheeling
Ziegenfelder Company • Local Food • Wheeling

Pendleton

Pendleton County Chamber of Commerce
605 N. Main St.
Franklin 26807
304-358-3884

Gendarme and Seneca Rocks Climbing School • Million Dollar Views/Shopping Treasures • Seneca Rocks
Nelson Rocks Preserve • Million Dollar Views • Judy Gap
Seneca Caverns • Mother Nature's Wonders/Superlatives
Seneca Rocks • Truly Incredible/Million Dollar Views/Mother Nature's Wonders
Seneca Rocks Discovery Center • Million Dollar Views • Seneca Rocks
Spruce Knob • Mother Nature's Wonders
Yokum's Stables • Million Dollar Views • Seneca Rocks

Pleasants

>Pleasants County Development Authority
309 2nd St.
St. Mary's 26170
304-684-1220

Grave in the Rock • Historic Oddities • Belmont
Ohio River Islands Wildlife Refuge • Mother Nature's Wonders

Pocahontas

>Pocahontas County Convention and Visitors Bureau
700 Fourth St.
Marlinton 25954
800-336-7009

Beartown State Park • Mother Nature's Wonders • Droop
Brazenhead Inn • Local Food • Mingo
Cass Scenic Railroad State Park • Tours/ Things That Used To Be There • Cass
Cranberry Glades • Mother Nature's Wonders
Droop Mountain Battlefield State Park • Superlatives
Elk River Touring Company • Unusual Places to Stay • Slatyfork
Falls of Hill Creek • Mother Nature's Wonders
Gaudineer State Forest • Mother Nature's Wonders • Randolph
Greenbrier River • Superlatives
Greenbrier River Trail • Adventure Driving/Superlatives • Greenbrier
Highland Scenic Highway • Adventure Driving
Inn at Mountain Quest • Unusual Places to Stay • Frost
Locust Creek CB • Amazing Architecture • Hillsboro
Marlinton • Superlatives
Mountain Quest Inn • Places to Stay • Marlinton
National Radio Astronomy Observatory • Truly Incredible • Green Bank
Opera House • Amazing Architecture • Marlinton
Pearl Buck Birthplace • Remarkable Collections • Hillsboro
Roadkill Cook-off • Far-Out Festivals • Marlinton
Seneca State Forest • Unusual Places to Stay • Dunmore

Sharpe's Country Store • Shopping Treasures • Slatyfork
Snowshoe Mountain Resort • Fast Living/Tours/Unusual Places to Stay • Snowshoe

Preston

Preston County
200 W Main St. # A
Kingwood 26537
304-329-4660

Arthurdale • Superlatives • Kingwood
Buckwheat Festival • Far-Out Festivals • Kingwood
Cathedral State Park • Mother Nature's Wonders • Aurora
Henry Clay Iron Furnace • Things That Used To Be There
Cool Springs Park • Remarkable Collections • Fellowsville
Coopers Rock State Forest • Million Dollar Views
Green Glades Creamery • Local Food • Terra Alta
Luminaria • Far-Out Festivals
Mountain Creek Cabins • Unusual Places to Stay • Bruceton Mills
Our Lady of the Pines • Amazing Architecture/Superlatives • Silver Lake
Tunnelton • Amazing Architecture • Preston
Vicki's Part of Heaven • Art Wonders • Arthurdale
Virginia Furnace • Things That Used To Be There • Albright
World War II Museum in Szilagyi Center • Remarkable Collections • Rowlesburg

Putnam

Putnam County CVB
3 Valley Park Rd.
Hurricane 25526
304-562-0518

Citywide Garage Sale • Shopping Treasures • Hurricane
Harrah's Symphonic Organ • Superlatives • Hurricane
Hurricane Fire Hall • Art Wonders • Hurricane
Maiden of the Rock petroglyph • Historic Oddities • Hurricane
Village site • Historic Oddities • Buffalo

Raleigh

> Beckley Raleigh Convention and Visitors Bureau
> 1406 Harper Rd.
> Beckley 25801
> 304-252-2244

Beckley Exhibition Coal Mine • Tours • Beckley
Country Inn and Suites • Great Plumbing • Beckley
Glade Springs Resort • Unusual Places to Stay • Daniels
Howard Johnson Express Inn • Great Plumbing • Beckley
King Tut Drive-In • Local Food • Beckley
Peace Totem • Art Wonders • Beckley
Tamarack • Local Food/Art Wonders/Shopping Treasures/Truly Incredible • Beckley

Randolph

> Randolph County CVB
> 1035 N. Randolph Ave.
> Elkins 26241
> 800-422-3304

Augusta Heritage Center • Art Wonders/Remarkable Collections • Elkins
Beverly Cemetery • Superlatives • Beverly
Cheat Mountain Club • Unusual Places to Stay
Cheat River Lodge • Great Plumbing • Elkins
Darby Prehistoric and Pioneer Collection • Remarkable Collections • Elkins
Fasnatch • Far-Out Festivals • Helvetia
Gaudineer State Forest • Mother Nature's Wonders • Randolph
Graceland • Amazing Architecture/Unusual Places to Stay • Elkins
Halliehurst • Amazing Architecture • Elkins
Hutte Restaurant • Local Food • Helvetia
Kumbrabow State Forest • Unusual Places to Stay
Maple Syrup Festival • Far-Out Festivals • Pickens
Mountain Rail Adventures • Tours/Unusual Places to Stay • Elkins
Mountain State Forest Festival • Far-Out Festivals • Elkins

The Old Mill at Harmon • Things That Used To Be There • Harmon
Pickin' in the Park • Art Wonders • Elkins
International Ramp Cook-Off and Festival • Elkins
Ramps • Far-Out Festivals • Helvetia
Richters Maplehouse • Local Food • Pickens
Sinks of Gandy • Mother Nature's Wonders • New Italy

Ritchie

> Ritchie County Tourism and Visitors Bureau
> Historic Bank Building
> Cairo 26337
> 888-379-7873

Berdines • Shopping Treasures • Harrisville
Country Trails Bikes • Adventure Driving • Cairo
Natural Wonder Wild Food Weekend • Far-Out Festivals • Harrisville
North Bend Trail • Adventure Driving
West Virginia Marble Festival • Far-Out Festivals • Cairo

Roane

Roane County Chamber of Commerce
207 Court St.
Spencer 25276
304-927-1780

Charles Fork Lake • Adventure Driving • Spencer
Robey Theater • Art Wonders • Spencer
Spencer Heritage Park • Things That Used To Be There • Spencer

Summers

> Summers County CVB
> 206 Temple St.
> Hinton 25951
> 304-466-5420

Alderson • Historic Oddities
Barger Springs • Adventure Driving
Bluestone Canyon • Mother Nature's Wonders
Graham House • Superlatives
John Henry Collection • Remarkable Collections
John Henry Statue and Park • Historic Oddities
Pence Springs Hotel • Amazing Architecture/Great Plumbing/Unusual Places to Stay • Pence Springs
Pipestem Drive-in Theater • Art Wonders • Athens
Pipestem Resort State Park and Observation Tower • Million Dollar Views/Tours/Unusual Places to Stay • Pipestem
Ritz Theater • Art Wonders • Hinton
Sandstone Falls • Million Dollar Views • Hinton
St. Patrick's Church • Art Wonders • Hinton
Star House • Amazing Architecture • Hinton
State Water Festival • Fast Living • Hinton

Taylor

> Grafton/Taylor CVB
> 214 W. Main St.
> Grafton 26354
> 304-265-3938

Grafton National Cemetery • Superlatives • Grafton
Anna Jarvis Birthplace Museum • Superlatives • Grafton
Mother's Day Shrine • Superlatives • Grafton
Tygart Dam • Superlatives • Grafton

Tucker

> Tucker County CVB
> W. Main St.
> Davis 26260
> 800-782-2775

Black Bear Resort • Great Plumbing • Canaan Valley
Blackwater Falls State Park • Million Dollar Views
Canaan Valley • Mother Nature's Wonders/Superlatives
Davis • Superlatives
Dolly Sods • Mother Nature's Wonders
Fairfax Stone • Historic Oddities
Purple Fiddle • Fast Living • Thomas
Sirianni's • Local Food • Davis

Tyler

Sistersville City Hall
200 Diamond St.
Sistersville 26175
304-652-6361

Ben's Run Fortifications • Historic Oddities • Ben's Run
The Jug of Middle Island Creek • Mother Nature's Wonders • Middlebourne
Marble King • Shopping Treasures • Paden City
Ohio River Islands Wildlife Refuge • Mother Nature's Wonders
Sistersville Ferry • Things That Used To Be There • Sistersville
Tyler County Museum • Remarkable Collections • Middlebourne

Upshur

Buckhannon-Upshur Convention and Visitors Bureau
16 South Kanawha St.
Buckhannon 26201
304-473-1400

Donut Shop • Local Food • Buckhannon
Fish Hawk Acres Farm • Local Food • Rock Cave
Lascaux Micro-Theater • Art Wonders • Buckhannon
Pringle Sycamore • Things That Used To Be There • Buckhannon
West Virginia Weslyan • Amazing Architecture • Buckhannon
West Virginia Wildlife Center • Mother Nature's Wonders • French Creek

Wayne

Austin's Homemade Ice Cream • Local Food • Ceredo
Camden Park • Historic Oddities/Superlatives • Huntington
Ceredo Petroglyph • Superlatives • Ceredo
Heritage Farm Museum and Village • Remarkable Collections • Wayne
Pumpkin House • Far-Out Festivals • Kenova

Webster

> Webster County Tourism
> 139 Baker St.
> Webster Springs 26288
> 304-847-2145

The Custard Stand • Local Food • Webster Springs
Holly River State Park • Historic Oddities
International Bergoo Cook-Off • Far-Out Festivals • Webster Springs
Jerry Run Summer Theater • Art Wonders
Tecumseh • Historic Oddities
Webster County Woodchopping Festival • Far-Out Festivals • Bakers Island

Wetzel

> Wetzel County CVB
> 136 Main St.
> New Martinsville 26155
> 304-398-4910

Choo Choo's • Local Food • New Martinsville
Fish Creek CB • Amazing Architecture • Hundred
New Martinsville • Amazing Architecture
Ohio River Islands Wildlife Refuge • Mother Nature's Wonders
Quinet's Court Restaurant • Local Food • New Martinsville
Thistledew Farms • Far-Out Festivals • Proctor

Wirt

Burning Springs • Things That Used To Be There
Ruble Church • Amazing Architecture

Wood

>Greater Parkersburg Convention and Visitors Bureau
>350 Seventh St.
>Parkersburg 26101
>800-752-4982

Artsbridge • Art Wonders • Parkersburg
Blennerhassett Hotel • Unusual Places to Stay • Parkersburg
Blennerhassett Island State Park • Historic Oddities • Parkersburg
Blennerhassett Museum • Historic Oddities/Remarkable Collections • Parkersburg
Blennerhassett Island Tour • Tours • Parkersburg
Fenton Glass • Tours • Williamstown
Henderson Hall • Historic Oddities/Remarkable Collections • Williamstown
Holls Chocolates • Local Food • Vienna
Julia-Ann Square Historic District • Amazing Architecture • Parkersburg
North Bend Trail • Adventure Driving
Ohio River Islands Wildlife Refuge • Mother Nature's Wonders
Oil and Gas Museum • Remarkable Collections • Parkersburg
Point Park • Historic Oddities/Tours • Parkersburg
Quaker State Windmill • Amazing Architecture • Parkersburg
Sixth Street Railroad Bridge • Amazing Architecture • Parkersburg
Smoot Theater • Art Wonders • Parkersburg
West Virginia Honey Festival • Far-Out Festivals • Parkersburg
WV Motor Speedway • Fast Living • Mineral Wells

Wyoming

Pineville 24874
304-732- 8030

R.D. Bailey Lake & Dam • Superlatives
Castle Rock • Mother Nature's Wonders • Pineville
Lilydale runes • Historic Oddities • Lilydale
Mullens murals • Art Wonders • Mullens
Pineville Drive-in Theater • Art Wonders • Pineville
SR 97 • Adventure Driving • Pineville
Twin Falls State Park • Amazing Architecture/Million Dollar Views/Mother Nature's Wonders/Unusual Places to Stay

Way Out Index

A

A Taste of Eggcellence • Local Food • Gap Mills/Monroe • 5510 Sweet Springs Valley Rd • 304-772-4253

ACE Adventure Center • Fast Living/Great Plumbing • Oak Hill/Fayette • Along New River two miles from Oak Hill • 800-787-3982

Adventures on the Gorge • Fast Living • Lansing/Fayette • 1 Ames Heights Rd • 888-650-1932

Alberts Chapel • Amazing Architecture • Sand Ridge/Calhoun • US 33 & 119

Alderson • Historic Oddities • Summers/Greenbrier/Monroe • I-64, Alta exit then south on SR 12

Appalachian Glass • Tours • Weston/Lewis • 499 US 33 E • 304-269-1030

Apple Butter Festival • Far-Out Festivals • Berkeley Springs/Morgan • Columbus Day weekend • 800-447-8797

Apollo Theater • Art Wonders • Martinsburg/Berkeley • 128 E Martin St • 304-263-6766

Arthurdale • Superlatives • Kingwood/Preston • SR 92 • Driving tour/Visitor Center • 304-864-3959

Artsbridge • Art Wonders • Parkersburg/Wood • 935 Market St • 304-428-3988

Atasia Spa • Great Plumbing • Berkeley Springs/Morgan • 206 Congress St • 304-258-7888

Augusta Heritage Center • Art Wonders/Remarkable Collections • Elkins/Randolph • 100 Campus Drive • 304-637-1209

Austin's Homemade Ice Cream • Local Food • Ceredo/Wayne • 1103 C St • 304-453-2071

Avalon • Art Wonders/Unusual Places to Stay • Hampshire • Critton Hollow Rd • 304-947-5600

"The Aviator" • Superlatives • Wheeling/Ohio • Linsly School/Leatherwood Lane • 304-233-3260

B

R.D. Bailey Lake & Dam • Superlatives • Justice/Mingo & Wyoming • US 52 • 304-664-3229

Barbour County Historical Museum • Truly Incredible • Philippi/Barbour • 200 N Main St

Barger Springs • Adventure Driving • Summers • Marie Rd @ junction of SR 122 and SR 12

Barrackville CB • Amazing Architecture • Barrackville/Marion County • US 250/CR 32

Battle of Blair Mountain • Historic Oddities • Blair Mountain/Logan • SR 17 east of Logan • 304-369-9800

Bavarian Inn and Lodge • Great Plumbing/Unusual Places to Stay • Shepherdstown/Jefferson • 164 Shepherd Grade Rd • 304-876-2551

Beartown State Park • Mother Nature's Wonders • Droop/Pocahontas • US 219 • 304-653-4254

Beckley Exhibition Coal Mine • Tours • Beckley/Raleigh • 513 Ewart Ave • 304-256-1747

Belle Boyd House • Historic Oddities • Martinsburg/Berkeley • 126 E Race St • 304-267-4713

Ben's Run Fortifications • Historic Oddities • Ben's Run/Tyler County • SR 2

Berdines • Shopping Treasures • Harrisville/Ritchie • 106 Court St • 9-5, closed Sundays • 304-643-2217

Berkeley Castle • Amazing Architecture • Berkeley Springs/Morgan • SR 9 W • 304-258-4000

Berkeley Springs International Water Tasting • Far-Out Festivals • Berkeley Springs/Morgan • Saturday of last full weekend in February • 800-447-8797

Berkeley Springs State Park • Great Plumbing • Berkeley Springs/Morgan • Washington and Fairfax Sts • 304-258-2711

Bethany College • Superlatives • Bethany/Brooke

Beverly Cemetery • Superlatives • Beverly/Randolph • US 219/250

Bhavana Society • Unusual Places • High View/Hampshire • Back Rd • 304-856-3241

Bice-Ferguson Museum • Remarkable Collections • Shinnston/Harrison • 400 Pike St • 304-677-6650

Black Bear Resort • Great Plumbing • Davis/Tucker • 55 Cortland Rd • 304-866-4391

Blackwater Falls State Park • Million Dollar Views • Tucker • SR 32/CR29 • 304-259-5216

Blenko Glass • Shopping Treasures • Milton/Cabell • 9 Bill Blenko Rd • 304-743-9081

Blennerhassett Hotel • Unusual Places to Stay • Parkersburg/Wood • 320 Market St • 800-262-2536

Blennerhassett Island State Park • Historic Oddities • Parkersburg/Wood • 304-420-4800

Blennerhassett Museum • Historic Oddities/Remarkable Collections • Parkersburg/Wood • 137 Juliana St • 304-420-4800

Blennerhassett Island Tour • Tours • Parkersburg/Wood • Leave Point Park off SR 68 in downtown Parkersburg • 304-420-4800

Bloomery • Things That Used To Be There • Hampshire • SR 127

Bluefield • Mother Nature's Wonders • Mercer • US 52 W • 800-221-3206

Blue Ridge Bank • Amazing Architecture • Martinsburg/Berkeley • 420 S Raleigh St • 304-264-4510

Bluestone Canyon • Mother Nature's Wonders • Summers • 304-466-5420

B&O Roundhouse Complex • Amazing Architecture/Historic Oddities • Martinsburg/Berkeley • 100 E Liberty St • 304-260-4141

Bonnie Belle's Pastries • Local Food • Nutter Fort/Harrison • 1520 Buckhannon Pike • 304-622-7471

Bramwell • Amazing Architecture/Things That Used To Be There • Mercer • 304-248-7114

Brazenhead Inn • Local Food • Mingo/Pocahontas • US 219 • 304-339-6917

Bridge Day • Far-Out Festivals • Fayette • US 19 • Third Sat in October • 800-927-0263

Brier Run Farm • Local Food • Birch River/Nicholas • HC 32, Box 73 • 304-649-2975

Buck's Hill • Million Dollar Views • Berkeley • SR 45 & 51

Buckwheat Festival • Far-Out Festivals • Kingwood/Preston • 304-379-2203

Bunker Hill Mill • Things That Used To Be There • Bunker Hill/Berkeley • SR 26

Burning Springs • Wirt • Things That Used To Be There • SR 5 south of Elizabeth

Burnsville Lake and Dam • Superlatives • Burnsville/Braxton • 2550 S Main St • 304-853-2371

C

Cabela's • Shopping Treasures • Tridelphia/Ohio • 304-238-0120 • Charleston/Kanawha • 304-400-6000

Camden Park • Historic Oddities/Superlatives • Huntington/Wayne • US 60 • 866-8CAMDEN

Cameron City Pool • Amazing Architecture • Cameron/Marshall • Park St • 304-686-2366

Camp Creek State Forest and Park • Unusual Places to Stay • Camp Creek/Mercer • Exit 20 off I-77 • 304-425-9481

Camp Washington Carver • Amazing Architecture/Superlatives • Clifftop/Fayette • 304-438-3005

Canaan Valley • Fast Living/Mother Nature's Wonders/Superlatives • Tucker • SR 32 • 800-622-4121

Canyon Rim Visitors Center • Million Dollar Views/Mother Nature's Wonders • Fayette • US 19 north of Beckley • 304-465-0508

Capitol Market • Shopping Treasures • Charleston/Kanawha • 800 Smith St • 304-344-1905

Capitol Theatre • Art Wonders • Wheeling/Ohio • 1015 Main St • 304-233-4470

Capitol Theater • Art Wonders • Charleston/Kanawha • 123 Summers St • (officially: WV State University Capitol Theater)

Capon Springs and Farms • Great Plumbing/Unusual Places to Stay/Things That Used To Be There • Capon Springs/Hampshire • CR 16 • 304-874-3695

Carnegie Hall • Art Wonders • Lewisburg/Greenbrier • 105 Church St • 304-645-7917

Carriage House Glass • Shopping Treasures • Wheeling/Ohio • Oglebay Resort • SR 88 • 304-243-4058

Carriage Trail • Tours • Charleston/Kanawha

Carrollton CB • Amazing Architecture • Philippi/Barbour • CR 36 1mi. from US 119 south of Philippi

INDEX

Carswell • Things That Used To Be There • McDowell County • US 52

Cass Scenic Railroad State Park • Tours/Things That Used To Be There/Unusual Places to Stay • Cass/Pocahontas • 304-456-4300

Cast-Iron Cook-Off • Local Food

Castle Rock • Mother Nature's Wonders • Pineville/Wyoming

Cathedral Cafe • Art Wonders • Fayetteville/Fayette • 134 S Court St • 304-574-0202

Cathedral State Park • Mother Nature's Wonders • Aurora/Preston • US 50 • 304-735-3771

Center for National Response WV Memorial Tunnel • Superlatives • Standard/Kanawha • Paint Creek Rd

Center Point CB • Amazing Architecture • Doddridge • SR 23

Centre Market • Amazing Architecture • Wheeling/Ohio • Market St between 22nd and 24th • 304-234-3878

Ceredo Petroglyph • Superlatives • Ceredo/Wayne • Ceredo Museum • 601 Main St • 304-453-3025

Challenger Learning Center/Wheeling Jesuit University • Superlatives • Wheeling/Ohio • 304-243-4325

Charles Fork Lake • Adventure Driving • Spencer/Roane • SR 36

Charleston Boulevard Rod Run and Doo Wop • Far-Out Festivals • Charleston/Kanawha • Kanawha Blvd • 888-436-6967

Charles Town • Historic Oddities/Mother Nature's Wonders • Jefferson • US 340 & SR 115 • 304-535-2627

Charles Town Post Office • Superlatives • Charles Town/Jefferson • 101 W Washington St

Cheat Mountain Club • Local Food/Unusual Places to Stay • Randolph • Off US 250 on Shavers Creek • 304-456-4627

Cheat River Lodge • Great Plumbing • Elkins/Randolph • Stuarts Recreation Park then 1.5 mi • 304-636-2301

Cheese n' More • Adventure Driving/Local Food • Gap Mills/Monroe • 5521 Sweet Springs Valley • 304-772-5211

Chicory Square Park • Art Wonders • Bluefield/Mercer • Federal or Bland at Raleigh

Chief Logan State Park • Historic Oddities • Logan • SR 10 • 304-792-7125

Choo Choo's • Local Food • New Martinsville/Wetzel • 155 Vine St • 304-455-4768

Cinder Bottom • Things That Used To Be There • Keystone/McDowell

Citizens Bank • Amazing Architecture • Weston/Lewis • 201 Main Ave • 304-269-2862

Citywide Garage Sale • Shopping Treasures • Hurricane/Putnam • Main St. • 304-562-5896

Clarksburg • Adventure Driving • Harrison • US 50 downtown exit

Clay Center • Art Wonders • Charleston/Kanawha • 1 Clay Square • 304-561-3570

Henry Clay Iron Furnace • Things That Used To Be There • Preston • Coopers Rock State Forests • 304-594-1561

Coal House • Amazing Architecture • Williamson/Mingo • 2nd & Court • Tug Valley Chamber of Commerce • 304-235-5240

Coffindaffer Cross Clusters • Adventure Driving • statewide

Colasessano's • Local Food • Fairmont/Marion • 141 Middleton Cir. • 304-363-0571

Coleman's Fish Market • Local Food • Wheeling/Ohio • Centre Market/2226 Market St • 304-232-8510

Concord United Methodist Church • Art Wonders • Athens/Mercer •109 Vermillion St • 304-384-7922

Contemporary American Theater Festival • Art Wonders • Shepherdstown/Jefferson • Shepherd University • 800-999-2283

Cool Springs Park • Remarkable Collections • Rowlesburg/Preston • 12696 George Washington Hwy • 304-454-9511

Cooper House • Amazing Architecture • Bramwell/Mercer County • SR 120/Main Street • 304-248-7114

Coopers Rock State Forest • Million Dollar Views • Bruceton Mills/Preston • I-68 • 304-594-1561

Core Arboretum • Superlatives • Morgantown/Monongalia • Monongahela Blvd • 304-293-0387

Corner Shop • Things That Used To Be There • Bramwell/Mercer • 171 Main St • 304-248-7632

Cornstalk • Historic Oddities • Point Pleasant/Mason • Tu-endie-wei State Park/1 Main St

Country Club Bakery • Local Food • Fairmont/Marion • 1211 Country Club Rd • 304-363-5690

The Country Inn • Great Plumbing • Berkeley Springs/Morgan • 110 S Washington St • 304-258-1200

Country Inn and Suites • Great Plumbing • Beckley/Raleigh • 2120 Harper Rd • 304-252-5100

Country Road Cabins • Great Plumbing • Hico/Fayette • 888-712-2246

Country Store Opry • Art Wonders • Grant/Hampshire/Pendleton • 304-358-7771 •

Country Trails Bikes • Adventure Driving • Cairo • 304-628-3100

Corner Shop • Things That Used To Be There • Bramwell/Mercer • 171 Main St • 304-248-7632

Cranberry Glades • Mother Nature's Wonders • Pocahontas • Off SR 39/55 • 304-653-4826

Crazy House • Amazing Architecture • Harpers Ferry/Jefferson • Ridge St

Cresap Mound • Historic Oddities • Marshall • SR 2, 6m south

The Custard Stand • Local Food • Webster Springs/Webster • 364 Webster Rd • 304-847-7774

D

Dancing Outlaw • Art Wonders

D'Annunzio's Health Bread Company • Local Food • Clarksburg/Harrison • 1909 Williams Ave • 304-622-3492

Darby Prehistoric and Pioneer Collection • Remarkable Collections • Elkins/Randolph • Myles Center for the Arts/Davis and Elkins College

Davis • Superlatives • Tucker • SR 32

Dee Jay's BBQ Ribs & Grille • Local Food • Weirton/Hancock • 380 Three Springs Dr • 304-748-1150

De Fluri's Chocolates • Local Food • Martinsburg/Berkeley • 130 N Queen St • 304-264-3698

Dents Run CB • Amazing Architecture • Monongalia • Just off US 19 and CR 43 near Morgantown

Devil Anse Hatfield statue • Historic Oddities • Sarah Ann/Logan • Off SR 44

DiCarlo's Pizza • Local Food • Wheeling/Ohio • 1311 Main St • 304-233-0730

Dingess Tunnel • Adventure Driving • Mingo County • SR 65

Dolly Sods • Mother Nature's Wonders • Grant/Randolph/Tucker • 304-257-4488

Donut Shop • Local Food • Buckhannon/Upshur • 19 N. Locust St • 304-472-9328

Droop Mountain Battlefield State Park • Superlatives • Hillsboro/Pocahontas • US 219 • 304-653-4254

Dutch Hollow Wine Cellar Park • Historic Oddities • Dunbar/Kanawha • SR 25 Follow signs • 304-766-0223

E

East End Yard Sale • Shopping Treasures • Charleston/Kanawha • 304-767-9800

East Huntington Bridge • Amazing Architecture • Huntington/Cabell • Connects SR 2 and US 60 with Ohio SR 7

East River Mountain Overlook • Million Dollar Views • Bluefield/Mercer • US 460 to SR 598 to top of mountain

East River Mountain Tunnel • Adventure Driving • Bluefield/Mercer • I-77

Eastern Regional Coal Archives • Remarkable Collections • Bluefield/Mercer • Craft Memorial Library • 600 Commerce St • 304-325-3943

Eddie's Tires • Shopping Treasures • Berkeley Springs/Morgan • US 522 south of Berkeley Springs • 304-258-1368

Elkhorn Inn and Theater • Art Wonders • Landgraff/McDowell • US 52 • 800-708-2040

Elk River Touring Company • Unusual Places to Stay • Slatyfork/Pocahontas • US 219 • 304-572-3741

Elk River Water Trail • Mother Nature's Wonders • Braxton • 304-765-6533

Exline's Iris Garden • Mother Nature's Wonders • Berkeley Springs/Morgan • Follow the signs from River Rd or WV 9 E • 301-988-6175

F

Fairfax Stone • Historic Oddities • Tucker • About 2 mi from US 219 north of Thomas (not where mile marker is) 4-acre park • 304-259-5315

Fall Color Map • Tours • 1-800-CALLWVA

Falls of Hill Creek • Mother Nature's Wonders • Pocahontas • SR 55/39 • 304-653-4826 •

Fasnacht • Far-Out Festivals • Helvetia/Randolph • Saturday before Ash Wednesday • SR 46 • 304-924-6435

Fenton Glass • Tours • Williamstown/Wood • 700 Elizabeth St • 304-375-6122

Festivall • Art Wonders • Charleston/Kanawha • http://festivallcharleston.com

Festival of Lights • Far-Out Festivals • Wheeling/Ohio • SR 88 • 800-624-6988

Mike Fink's Grave • Historic Oddities • Minora/Calhoun • CR 13

Fish Creek CB • Amazing Architecture • Hundred/Wetzel • CR 13 off US 250

Fish Hawk Acres Farm • Local Food • Rock Cave/Upshur • 1 Fish Hawk Dr • 304-473-7741

$5 Frank • Things That Used To Be There • Fayetteville/Fayette • Fayette Airport • US 19 2 mi. SW of city

Flatwoods Monster • Remarkable Collections • Flatwoods/Braxton • US 19 • 304-765-6533

Fletcher CB • Amazing Architecture • Wolf Summit/Harrison • CR 5/29

Flying • Adventure Driving

Fort Ashby • Historic Oddities/Things That Used To Be There • Keyser/Mineral • SR 28 • 301-697-9292

Fort Mill Ridge Trenches • Historic Oddities • Romney/Hampshire • US 50/Fort Mill Ridge WMA sign

Fort Mulligan • Superlatives • Petersburg/Grant

Fret 'n Fiddle • Shopping Treasures • St. Albans/Kanawha • 809 Pennsylvania Ave • 304-729-8013

Frostop Drive-in • Art Wonders • Huntington/Cabell • 1449 Hal Greer Blvd • 304-523-6851

G

Gabriel Brothers • Shopping Treasures • Morgantown/Monongalia • 55 Scott Ave • 304-292-6965

Gary Bowling's House of Art • Art Wonders • Bluefield/Mercer • 500 Bland St • 304-324-4242

Gaudineer Scenic Area • Mother Nature's Wonders • Randolph/Pocahontas • FR 27

Gendarme and Seneca Rocks Climbing School • Million Dollar Views/Shopping Treasures • Seneca Rocks/Pendleton • SR 33 & 55 • 800-548-0108

George Tyler Moore Center for the Study of the Civil War • Historic Oddities • Shepherdstown/Jefferson • German and Church Sts • 304-876-5429

General Lewis Inn • Great Plumbing/Unusual Places to Stay • Lewisburg/Greenbrier • 301 E Washington St • 304-645-2600

German Street • Amazing Architecture • Shepherdstown/Jefferson • SR 45

Ghost tours of Harpers Ferry • Tours • Harpers Ferry/Jefferson • 100 Church St • 304-725-8019

Glade Creek Grist Mill • Things That Used To Be There • Clifftop/Fayette • Babcock State Park • 304-438-3004

Glade Springs Resort • Unusual Places to Stay • Daniels/Raleigh • 200 Lake Drive • 800-634-5233

Glen Ferris Inn • Unusual Places to Stay • Glen Ferris/Fayette • US 60 • 304-632-1111

Glenville State College • Superlatives • Glenville/Gilmer • 200 High St • 304-462-7361

Graceland • Amazing Architecture/Unusual Places to Stay • Elkins/Randolph • Davis & Elkins College • 800-624-3157

Grafton National Cemetery • Superlatives • Grafton/Taylor • US 119

Graham House • Superlatives • Summers • 304-716-6430

Grand Vue Park • Fast Living • Moundsville/Marshall • 250 Trail Dr • 304-845-9810

Grave Creek Mound Historic Site • Historic Oddities/Superlatives • Moundsville/Marshall • 801 Jefferson Ave • 304-843-4128

Grave in the Rock • Historic Oddities • Belmont/Pleasants • Schultz Rd off SR 2

Gray Barker UFO collection • Remarkable Collections • Clarksburg/Harrison • 404 W Pike St • 304-627-2236

Greenbrier • Fast Living/Great Plumbing/Local Food/Superlatives/Truly Incredible/Unusual Places to Stay • White Sulphur Springs/Greenbrier • 800-624-6070 •

Greenbrier Bunker Tour • Tours • White Sulphur Springs/Greenbrier • 300 W Main St • 855-453-4858

The Greenbrier Christmas Shop at the Depot • Shopping Treasures • White Sulphur Springs/Greenbrier • 300 W Main St • 304-536-1110

Greenbrier River • Superlatives • Greenbrier/Pocahontas

Greenbrier River Trail • Adventure Driving/Superlatives • Greenbrier/Pocahontas

Green Glades Creamery • Local Food • Terra Alta/Preston • 304-789-6511

Grimes Golden • Mother Nature's Wonders • Wellsburg/Brooke

H

Halliehurst • Amazing Architecture • Elkins/Randolph • Davis & Elkins College • 800-624-3157

Hanging Rock Observatory • Adventure Driving/Million Dollar Views • Monroe • CR 15, Waiterville Rd. Allegheny Trail parking area at crest of Peter's Mountain • 540-552-4641

Hanging Rocks • Mother Nature's Wonders • Baker/Hardy • SR 55 east of Baker

Harman's North Fork Cottages & Cabins • Great Plumbing • Petersburg/Grant • SR 55 • 304-257-2220

Harpers Ferry National Historical Park • Amazing Architecture/Historic Oddities/Things That Used To Be There • Harpers Ferry/Jefferson • 304-535-6371

Harrah Symphonic Organ • Superlatives • Hurricane/Putnam • Forest Burdette United Methodist Church • 2848 Putnam Ave • 304-562-5903

Hatfield and McCoy Reunion Festival • Far-Out Festivals • Matewan and Williamson/Mingo • 304-235-5240

Hatfield and McCoy Trail • Adventure Driving • 800-592-2217

Hawks Nest State Park • Historic Oddities/Million Dollar Views • Ansted/Fayette • US 60 • 304-658-5212

Heartwood in the Hills • Art Wonders • Big Bend/Calhoun • Lovada Rd • 304-354-7874

Heavens Landing Retreat • Unusual Places to Stay • Medley/Grant • 304-703-5898

Heiner's Bakery • Tours • Huntington/Cabell • 1300 Adams Ave 304-523-8411

Henderson Hall • Historic Oddities/Remarkable Collections • Williamstown/Wood • 517 Old River Rd • 304-375-2129

Heritage Farm Museum and Village • Remarkable Collections • Huntington/Wayne • 3300 Harvey Rd • 304-522-1244

Herns Mill CB • Amazing Architecture • Greenbrier • CR 40/Muddy Creek Mountain Rd

Highland Scenic Highway • Adventure Driving • Pocahontas • SR 55 from Richwood to US 219 north of Hillsboro • 304-636-1800

Highlawn Inn • Great Plumbing • Berkeley Springs/Morgan • 171 Market St • 304-258-5700

Hillbilly Hot Dogs • Local Food • Lesage/Cabell • 6951 Ohio River Road/SR 2

Hillbrook Inn • Historic Oddities • Charles Town/Jefferson • 4490 Summit Point Rd • 304-725-4223

Hilltop Drive-in Theater • Art Wonders • Newell/Hancock • SR 8 • 304-387-1611

Hokes Mill CB • Amazing Architecture • Ronceverte/Greenbrier • CR 62 off US 219 S

Holls Chocolates • Local Food • Vienna/Wood • 2001 Grand Central Ave • 800-842-4512

Holly River State Park • Historic Oddities • Hacker Valley/Webster • SR 20 • 304-493-6353

Hollywood Casino at Charles Town Races • Fast Living • Charles Town/Jefferson • US 340/SR 51 • 800-795-7001

Homer Laughlin • Shopping Treasures/Tours/Superlatives • Newell/Hancock • 672 Fiesta Dr • 800-452-4462

Hot Dog Festival • Far-Out Festivals • Huntington/Cabell • Pullman Square • Last Saturday in July • 304-525-7788

Hotel Morgan • Great Plumbing/Unusual Places to Stay • Morgantown/Monongalia • 127 High St • 304-292-8200

Howard Johnson Express Inn • Great Plumbing • Beckley/Raleigh • I-77 & 64 • 304-255-5900

Hunters Hardware • Shopping Treasures • Berkeley Springs/Morgan • 115 Independence St • 304-258-2442

Huntington Mall • Shopping Treasures • Huntington/Cabell • 500 Mall Rd and I-64 @ Barboursville • 304-733-0492

Huntington Memorial Arch • Amazing Architecture • Huntington/Cabell • Memorial Blvd and 11th Avenue W

Huntington Museum • Amazing Architecture/Remarkable Collections • Huntington/Cabell • 2033 McCoy Rd • 304-529-2701

Hurricane Fire Hall • Art Wonders • Hurricane/Putnam • Main St

Hutte Restaurant • Local Food • Helvetia/Randolph • 1 Main St SR 20 to French Creek then SR 46 or US 250 S then Mill Creek & 46 to Helvetia. • 304-924-6435

I

Ice House • Shopping Treasures • Berkeley Springs/Morgan • Independence and Mercer Sts • 304-258-2300

Ice Mountain • Mother Nature's Wonders • Hampshire • Nature Conservancy Tours • 304-637-0160

Imperial Teacher's Store • Shopping Treasures • Wheeling/Ohio • 2347 Main St • 304-233-0711

Indian Creek CB • Amazing Architecture • Salt Sulphur Springs/Monroe • US 219

Indian Mound Cemetery • Historic Oddities • Romney/Hampshire • In cemetery on US 50 at western edge of Romney

Inn at Mountain Quest • Unusual Places to Stay • Frost/Pocahontas • SR 92 • 304-799-7267

International Burgoo Cook-off • Far-Out Festivals • Webster Springs/Webster • Bakers Island • 304-847-7291

Irish Spring Festival • Far-Out Festivals • Ireland/Lewis • US 19

Isaiah Morgan Distillery • Local Food • Summersville/Nicholas • 45 Winery Lane • 888-498-9463

Italian Heritage Festival • Far-Out Festivals • Clarksburg/Harrison • Fri-Sun of Labor Day weekend • 304-622-7314

J

Jackson's Mill • Superlatives/Things That Used To Be There • Weston/Lewis • CR 12 • 800-287-8206

Anna Jarvis Birthplace Museum • Superlatives • Grafton/Taylor • US 250/119 • 304-265-5549

Jebbia's Market • Shopping Treasures • Wheeling/Ohio • 2600 Chapline St • 304-233-0280

Jefferson County Courthouse • Historic Oddities • Charles Town/Jefferson • N George & Washington Sts • 304-725-9761

Jefferson County Museum • Charles Town/Jefferson • 200 E Washington St • 304-728-8628

Jefferson Rock • Million Dollar Views • Harpers Ferry/Jefferson • US 340 @ WV/MD/VA border. Steps past St. Peter's Church

Jeff's Breads • Local Food • Renick/Greenbrier• US 219 • 304-497-2768

Jerry Run Summer Theater • Art Wonders • Hacker Valley/Webster • SR 20 • 304-493-6574

Jet boats @ Hawks Nest • Fast Living • Ansted/Fayette • Hawks Nest State Park • US 60 • 304-640-0924

John Brown's Fort • Amazing Architecture • Harpers Ferry/Jefferson • Harpers Ferry Historical Park • US 340 @ WV/MD/VA border • 304-535-6371

John Henry Collection • Remarkable Collections • Hinton/Summers • Summers County Visitors Center • 206 Temple St • 304-466-5420

John Henry Statue and Park • Historic Oddities • Talcott/Summers • SR 3

The Jug of Middle Island Creek • Mother Nature's Wonders • Middlebourne/Tyler

Julia-Ann Square Historic District • Amazing Architecture • Parkersburg/Wood

Julio's • Local Food • Clarksburg/Harrison • 501 Baltimore Ave • 304-622-2592

K

Kanwaha State Forest Braille Trail • Tours • Charleston/Kanawha • 7500 Kanawha State Forest Dr • 304-558-3500

Kaymoor Mine Trail • Things That Used To Be There • Fayette • Fayette Station Rd, 1 mi on right is railhead

Keith Albee Theater • Art Wonders • Huntington/Cabell • 925 4th Ave • 304-696-6656

Kimball World War I Memorial • Superlatives • Kimball/McDowell • 178 One Way Street • 304-585-7789

King Pizza • Local Food • Martinsburg/Berkeley • 313 Rock Cliff Dr • 304-262-0155 •

King Tut Drive-In • Local Food • Beckley/Raleigh • 301 N Eisenhower Dr • 304-252-6353

Kirkwood Wineries • Local Food • Summersville/Nicholas • US 19 north of Summersville to CR 8 • 304-872-7332

Kruger Street Toy and Train Museum • Remarkable Collections • Wheeling/Ohio • 144 Kruger St • 304-242-8133 • http://www.toyandtrain.com

Kumbrabow State Forest • Unusual Places to Stay • Randolph/Huttonsville • CR 219-16 • Closed January through late April • 304-335-2219 • http://www.kumbrabow.com

L

Lake Sherwood • Mother Nature's Wonders • Greenbrier • CR14-1 N

Lambert's Vintage Wines • Local Food • Weston/Lewis • 190 Vineyard Dr • 304-269-4903

Lascaux Micro-Theater • Art Wonders • Buckhannon/Upshur • 29 E Main St • 304-473-1818

Laurel Creek CB • Amazing Architecture • Monroe • CR 219/11-Lilydale Rd

Laurel Lake Wildlife Management Area • Lenore/Mingo • 304-475-2823 • CR 3/5

Lay over roads • Adventure Driving • Pocahontas/Greenbrier

Lee White Sulphur Springs • Things That Used To Be There • Mathias/Hardy

Lewisburg • Great Plumbing • Greenbrier • I-64, exit 169 or US 219 • 800-833-2068

Lilydale Celtic Runes • Historic Oddities • Lilydale/Wyoming • 5th St to railroad tracks. Go about 200 yards to left along tracks

Line of the Seven Ranges • Historic Oddities • Chester/Hancock • SR 39

Livery Tavern • Local Food • Lewisburg/Greenbrier • 217 E Washington St • 304-645-9836

Locust Creek CB • Amazing Architecture • Hillsboro/Pocahontas • CR 31/near the entrance of Calvin Price State Forest

Lost River Artisans Cooperative • Shopping Treasures • Lost River/Hardy • SR 259 • 304-897-7242

Lost River State Park • Superlatives • Mathias/Hardy • CR 12/park at swimming pool and walk up trail. • 304-897-5372

Lost World Caverns • Mother Nature's Wonders • Lewisburg/Greenbrier • Fairview Road/CR 32 • 304-645-6677

Lot 12 Public House • Local Food • Berkeley Springs/Morgan • 117 Warren St • 304-258-6264

Lowe's Hotel • Unusual Places to Stay • Point Pleasant/Mason • 401 Main St • 304-675-2260

Luminaria • Far-Out Festivals • Bruceton Mills/Preston • SR 26

M

Maiden of the Rock petroglyph • Historic Oddities • Hurricane/Putnam • Main St • 304-562-5896

Manette Steel Drums • Tours • Morgantown/Monongalia • 166 Dents Run Rd

Maple Syrup Festival • Far-Out Festivals • Pickens/Randolph • Main St • 304-924-5509

Marble King • Shopping Treasures • Paden City/Tyler • S 4th St • 304-337-2264

Marie Rd • Adventure Driving • Monroe • SR 12 to CR 20 then CR 17

Marlinton • Superlatives • Pocahontas • US 219 • 800-336-7009

Mario's Fishbowl • Local Food • Morgantown/Monongalia • 704 Richwood Ave • 304-292-2511

Marsh Carillon • Art Wonders • Athens/Mercer • Concord College Campus • 1000 Vermillion St • 304-384-5271

Martinsburg Public Library • Art Wonders • Martinsburg/Berkeley • 101 W King St • 304-267-8933

Matewan • Historic Oddities/Truly Incredible • Matewan/Mingo • Located on Tug Fork River. Slow and twisty ride along SR 52 • 304-235-5240

McDowell County Courthouse • Amazing Architecture • Welch/McDowell • US 52 west from Bluefield/Court & Wyoming Sts • 304-436-3113

McMurran Hall • Superlatives • Shepherdstown/Jefferson • German Street

Memorial Arch • Amazing Architecture • Huntington/Cabell • 11th Avenue and Memorial Boulevard

Metropolitan Billiard Parlor • Fast Living • Morgantown/Monongalia • 371 High St in the basement • 304-362-9518

The Metropolitan Theater • Art Wonders • Morgantown/Monongalia • 363 High St • 304-291-4884

Midas Muffler Man • Art Wonders • Unger/Morgan • Winchester Grade Rd 13/1 mi south of Unger Store

Midland Trail National Scenic Byway • Adventure Driving • Greenbrier-Kanawha • US 60

Mill Creek Cabins • Great Plumbing • Lansing/Fayette • Milroy Grose Rd • 800-692-5005

Milton Maize Maze • Far-Out Festivals • Milton/Cabell • Start at Milton Middle School on US 60 • 304-634-MAZE

Mister Bee Potato Chips • Local Food • Parkersburg/Wood • 512 W Virginia Ave • 304-428-6133

Monroe County Confederate Monument • Historic Oddities • Union/Monroe • US 219/SR 3 • 304-772-3003

Monroe County Quilt Trail • Art Wonders • Monroe • 304-772-3003

Morgan County Observatory • Truly Incredible • Berkeley Springs/Morgan • Winchester Grade Rd 13 • 304-258-1013

Morgan's Grove Park • Superlatives • Shepherdstown/Jefferson • WV 480

Morgantown • Art Wonders • Monongalia • I-68 & 79 • 800-458-7373

Morrison's Drive-in • Local Food • Stollings/Logan • 126 Stolling Ave • 304-752-9872

Mother's Day Shrine • Superlatives • Grafton/Taylor • St. Andrew's Methodist Episcopal Church • 11 E Main St • 304-265-1589

Mothman Festival • Truly Incredible • Point Pleasant/Mason • 304-812-5211

Mothman Legend and Museum • Things That Used To Be There/Truly Incredible • Point Pleasant/Mason • 411 Main St

Mountain biking • Adventure Driving • 800-CALL WVA

Mountain Creek Cabins • Unusual Places to Stay • Bruceton Mills/Preston

Mountain Heritage Arts and Crafts Festival • Shopping Treasures • Harpers Ferry/Jefferson • Sam Michaels Park/1516 Job Corps Rd • 304-725-2055

Mountain Rail Adventures • Tours/Unusual Places to Stay • Elkins/Randolph • 304-636-9477

Mountain Stage • Art Wonders • Charleston/Kanawha • Cultural Center, 1900 Kanawha Blvd E

Mountain State Art and Craft Fair • Far-Out Festivals • Ripley/Jackson • Cedar Lakes/CR 25 • 304-372-3247

Mountain State Forest Festival • Far-Out Festivals • Elkins/Randolph • 304-636-1824

Mountaineer Military Museum • Remarkable Collections • Weston/Lewis • 345 Center Ave • 304-472-3943

Mountaineer Racetrack and Gaming Resort • Fast Living • Chester/Hancock • SR 2 • 304-804-0468

Mt. Nebo Tractor Bar • Fast Living • Mt. Nebo/Nicholas • 546 Wilderness Highway • 304-872-8100

Mt. Storm • Fast Living/Superlatives • Grant

Mud River CB • Amazing Architecture • Milton/Cabell • CR 25 off US 60

Mullens • Art Wonders • Wyoming • SR 54 and 16 Howard Ave

Mummies • Truly Incredible • Philippi/Barbour • Barbour County Historical Museum • 200 N Main St

Museum of the Berkeley Springs • Berkeley Springs/Morgan • 2nd floor Roman Bath House • Remarkable Collections • 800-447-8797

Museum of Radio & Technology • Remarkable Collections • Huntington/Cabell • 1640 Florence Ave • 304-525-8890

Mystery Hole • Truly Incredible • Ansted/Fayette • 16724 Midland Trail • 304-658-9101

N

National Conservation Training Center • Truly Incredible • Shepherdstown/Jefferson • 698 Conservation Way • 304-876-7200

National Radio Astronomy Observatory • Truly Incredible • Green Bank/Pocahontas • SR 92/28 • 304-456-2150

Natural Wonder Wildfood Weekend • Far-Out Festivals • Harrisville/Ritchie • North Bend State Park • Third weekend in September • 304-643-2931

Nelson Rocks Preserve • Million Dollar Views • Judy Gap/Pendleton • Nelson Gap Rd

New Deal Homestead Museum • Superlatives • Arthurdale/Preston • SR 92, 10 miles west of Kingwood • 304-864-3959

New River/New River Gorge/New River Gorge Bridge • Amazing Architecture/Fast Living/Festivals/Mother Nature's Wonders • Fayette • 304-465-0508

North Bend Trail • Adventure Driving • Wood/Ritchie/Doddridge/Harrison • Headquarters in Cairo • 304-643-2931

North Fork Mountain Inn • Great Plumbing • Smoke Hole/Grant • 304-257-1108

O

Oak Mound • Historic Oddities • Clarksburg/Harrison • US 19 2 mi south of Clarksburg on a hill near Veterans Hospital

Oakhurst Links • Superlatives • White Sulphur Springs/Greenbrier • 800-624-6070

Oglebay Institute • Art Wonders • Wheeling/Ohio • SR 88 • 304-242-4200

Oglebay Institute's Glass Museum • Remarkable Collections/Superlatives • Wheeling/Ohio • SR 88 • 304-242-7272

Oglebay Resort • Superlatives • Wheeling/Ohio • SR 88 • 800-624-6988 • http://www.oglebay-resort.com

Ohio River Island Wildlife Refuge • Mother Nature's Wonders • Wood/Pleasants/Tyler/Wetzel/Marshall/Ohio • 304-375-2923

O'Hurley's General Store • Art Wonders/Great Plumbing/Shopping Treasures • Shepherdstown/Jefferson • 205 E Washington St • 304-876-6907

Oil and Gas Museum • Remarkable Collections • Parkersburg/Wood • 119 Third St • 304-485-5446

Old Central City • Shopping Treasures • Huntington/Cabell • W 14th St from Madison to Washington Sts

Old Matewan National Bank • Historic Oddities • Matewan/Mingo • along the railroad tracks

The Old Mill at Harmon • Things That Used To Be There • Harmon/Randolph • SR 32

Old Stone Presbyterian Church • Superlatives • Lewisburg/Greenbrier • 200 Church St • 304-645-2676

Organ Cave • Historic Oddities/Mother Nature's Wonders/Tours • Ronceverte/Greenbrier • SR 63 • 304-645-7600

Our Lady of the Pines • Amazing Architecture/Superlatives • Silver Lake/Preston • US 219 • Mass celebrated by mission priests in season

P

Palace of Gold • Truly Incredible • Moundsville/Marshall • 3759 McCreary's Ridge Rd • Can wander at will. Tours available • 304-843-1600

Panorama at the Peak • Local Food • Berkeley Springs/Morgan • SR 9 W • 304-258-0050

Panorama Overlook • Million Dollar Views • Berkeley Springs/Morgan • SR 9, 3 miles west of Berkeley Springs • 800-447-8797

Panther State Forest • Mother Nature's Wonders • Panther/McDowell • CR 3-2 • 304-938-2252

Paw Paw Tunnel • Amazing Architecture • Paw Paw/Morgan • SR 29. Cross Potomac River .5 mi on right

Peacemaker National Training Center • Fast Living • Gerrardstown/Berkeley • 1624 Brannons Ford Rd • 304-229-4867

Peace Totem • Art Wonders • Beckley/Raleigh • Youth Museum of Southern West Virginia • 509 Ewart Ave

Pearl Buck Birthplace • Art Wonders/Remarkable Collections • Hillsboro/Pocahontas • US 219 • 304-653-4430

Pence Springs Hotel • Amazing Architecture/Great Plumbing/Things That Used To Be There • Pence Springs/Summers • SR 3 & 12

Peter Dye Golf Club • Superlatives • Bridgeport/Harrison • 801 Aaron Smith Dr • 304-842-2801

Petersburg Fish Hatchery • Superlatives • Petersburg/Grant • 220/Fish Hatchery/Airport Rd • 304-257-4014

Petersburg Wave Camp • Adventure Driving • Petersburg/Grant • Grant County Airport/Johnson Run Rd • March

Peter's Mountain • Adventure Driving/Great Plumbing • Gap Mills/Monroe • CR 15/Waiterville Rd. Allegheny Trail parking area at crest of Peter's Mountain • 304-772-3003

Peter Tarr Iron Furnace • Things That Used To Be There • Weirton/Hancock • Kings Creek Rd

Philippi CB • Amazing Architecture • Philippi/Barbour • US 250

Pickin' in the Park • Art Wonders • Elkins/Randolph • Elkins City Park • 304-637-1209

PIGS, a Sanctuary • Truly Incredible • Shepherdstown/Jefferson • 1112 Persimmon Lane • 833-257-7447

Pinnacle Rock State Park • Mother Nature's Wonders • Bramwell/Mercer • US 52 • 304-425-9481

Pipestem Drive-in Theater • Art Wonders • Athens/Summers • SR 20/Speedway • 304-384-7382

Pipestem Resort State Park & Observation Tower • Fast Living/Million Dollar Views/Tours/Unusual Places to Stay • Pipestem/Summers • SR 20 • 304-466-1800

Pocahontas Coal Fields • Mother Nature's Wonders/Superlatives • Bluefield/Mercer • 800-221-3206

Pocahontas Opera House • Amazing Architecture • Marlinton/Pocahontas • 818 Third Ave • 304-799-6645

Point Park • Historic Oddities/Tours • Parkersburg/Wood • 2nd St/confluence of Little Kanawha and Ohio Rivers

Potomac Eagle • Tours • Romney/Hampshire • SR 28 • 304-822-3595

Presidential Election of 1860 • Far-Out Festivals • Harpers Ferry/Jefferson • Saturday of Columbus Day weekend. Harpers Ferry National Historic Park • 304-535-6029

Prickett's Fort • Superlatives • Fairmont/Marion • Exit 139/I-79 • 304-363-3030

Pringle Sycamore • Things That Used To Be There • Buckhannon/Upshur • Pringle Tree Park Rd • 304-473-1400

Pullman Plaza Hotel • Historic Oddities • Huntington/Cabell • 1001 Third Ave • 304-525-1001

Pumpkin House • Far-Out Festivals • Kenova/Wayne • 748 Beech St

Purple Fiddle • Fast Living • Thomas/Tucker • 21 E Ave • 304-463-4040

Purple Iris @ Hartwood • Great Plumbing • Martinsburg/Berkeley • 304-262-6110

Q

Quaker State Windmill • Amazing Architecture • Parkersburg • 800 Murdoch Ave

Quinet's Court Restaurant • Local Food • New Martinsville/Wetzel • 217 Main St • 304-455-2110

R

ragtime's 1000 Points of Peace • Art Wonders • Berkeley Springs/Morgan • to order a peace sign: www.1000pointsofpeace.com

Ramps/Feast of the Ransom • Far-Out Festivals • Mid-April when first ramps peek out • Richwood/Nicholas • Richwood High School • 304-846-6790

Ramsey School • Amazing Architecture • Bluefield/Mercer • 300 Ramsey St

Raven Rocks • Million Dollar Views • Hampshire • Culmination of Nature Conservancy tours to Ice Mountain

Red Cross • Art Wonders • Huntington/Cabell • 1111 Veteran's Memorial Blvd • 304-526-2900

Reeds Mill • Things That Used To Be There • Second Creek/Monroe • CR 219/1

Rehobeth Church and Museum • Superlatives • Union/Monroe • SR 3 • 304-772-3003

INDEX

Richters Maplehouse • Local Food • Pickens/Randolph • Pickens Rd • 304-924-5404

Ridersville Cycle • Adventure Driving • Berkeley Springs/Morgan • US 522 S • 304-258-1449

Ritter Park • Superlatives • Huntington/Cabell • Near 12th St/Rose Garden • 304-696-5954

Ritz Theater • Art Wonders • Hinton/Summers • 211 Ballengee St • 304-466-6700

River Riders • Fast Living • Harpers Ferry/Jefferson • 408 Alstadts Hill Road • 800-326-7238

Roadkill Cook-off • Far-Out Festivals • Marlinton/Pocahontas • September • 304-646-8940

Robert Byrd Locks Visitor Center • Million Dollar Views • Apple Grove/Mason • SR 2 • 304-576-2272

Robey Theater • Art Wonders • Spencer/Roane • 318 Main St • 304-927-1390

Rock-n-Wood Heaven • Amazing Architecture • New Creek/Mineral • US 50 just east of SR 972

Round Barn • Amazing Architecture • Mannington/Marion • Flaggy Meadow Rd • 304-986-7053

Ruble Church • Amazing Architecture • Elizabeth/Wirt County • SR 5

Rumsey Boathouse • Historic Oddities • Shepherdstown/Jefferson behind Entler Hotel/Shepherdstown Museum • 129 E German St • 304-261-6710

Rumsey Monument • Historic Oddities • Shepherdstown/Jefferson • End of N Mill St

S

Saddle Mountain • Adventure Driving/Million Dollar Views • Mineral • US 50

Salt Sulphur Springs • Things That Used To Be There • Monroe • US 219/3 mi. south of Union • 304-772-3003

Sandstone Falls • Million Dollar Views • Hinton/Summers • SR 20 • 304-466-0417

Sarvis Fork CB • Amazing Architecture • Sandyville/Jackson • CR 21

Savannah Lane Shooting Association • Fast Living • Maxwelton/Greenbrier • 304-667-1035

Scott Hollow Cave • Mother Nature's Wonders • Sinks Grove/Monroe • 800-814-5218

Scottish Festival and Celtic Gathering • Far-Out Festivals • Bridgeport/Harrison • Bridgeport Park • 304-667-6245

Seneca Caverns • Mother Nature's Wonders/Superlatives • Riverton/Pendleton • 3328 Germany Valley Rd • 800-239-7647

Seneca Rocks/Seneca Rocks Discovery Center • Truly Incredible/Million Dollar Views/Mother Nature's Wonders • Seneca Rocks/Pendleton • SR 33 • 304-567-2827

Seneca State Forest • Unusual Places to Stay • Dunmore/Pocahontas • SR 28 • 304-799-6213

Shamrock Bar • Superlatives • Bluefield/Mercer

Shanghai Parade • Far-Out Festivals • Lewisburg/Greenbrier • January 1 • 800-833-2068

Shannondale Springs • Things That Used To Be There • Charles Town/Jefferson • CR 9/5 • 304-822-3551

Sharpe's Country Store • Shopping Treasures • Slatyfork/Pocahontas • US 219

Shepherdstown Sweet Shop Bakery • Local Food • Shepherdstown/Jefferson • 100 W German St • 304-876-2432

Shepherdstown Opera House • Art Wonders • Shepherdstown/Jefferson • 131 W German St

Simpson Creek CB • Amazing Architecture • Bridgeport/Harrison • CR 24/2

Sinks of Gandy • Mother Nature's Wonders • Osceola/Randolph • CR 29

Sirianni's • Local Food • Davis/Tucker • William Ave • 304-259-5454

Sistersville Ferry • Things That Used To Be There • Sisterville/Tyler • 900 Riverside Dr •

Sixth Street Railroad Bridge • Amazing Architecture • Parkersburg/Wood

Smoke Hole Cabins • Great Plumbing • Petersburg/Grant • SR 28 • 800-828-8478 •

Smoke Hole Caverns • Superlatives/Mother Nature's Wonders • Petersburg/Grant • SR 55/28 • 800-828-8478 • http://www.smokehole.com

Smoke Hole Rd • Adventure Driving • Grant • SR 55/28

Smokey's on the Gorge • Local Food • Lansing/Fayette • Ames Heights Rd • 304-574-4905

Smoot Theater • Art Wonders • Parkersburg/Wood • 213 5th St • 304-422-7529

Smooth Ambler Distillery • Local Food • Maxwelton/Greenbrier • 745 Industrial Park Rd • 304-497-3123

Snowshoe Resort • Fast Living/Tours/Unusual Places to Stay • Snowshoe/Pocahontas • 1 Snowshoe Drive • 304-572-1000

Soho's • Local Food • Charleston/Kanawha • 800 Smith St • 340-720-7646

Solomon's Secret • Far-Out Festivals • Clay/Clay • JG Bradley Campground

South Charleston Mound • Historic Oddities • South Charleston/Kanawha • US 60/ MacCorkle Ave • 304-746-5552

Spencer Heritage Park • Things That Used To Be There • Spencer/Roane • 116 Court St • 304-927-1640

Spencer's Taxidermy • Shopping Treasures • West Hamlin/Lincoln • 200 Virginia St • 304-824-3745

Spring Hill Pastry Shop • Local Food • South Charleston/Kanawha • 600 Chestnut St • 304-768-7397

Spruce Knob • Mother Nature's Wonders/Superlatives • Judy Gap/Pendleton • US 33, 10 mi past Seneca Rocks, right on Briery Gap Rd, 12 mi. graveled forest road to summit and observation tower • 304-567-2827

St. Joseph's Cathedral • Amazing Architecture • Wheeling/Ohio • 1300 Eoff St • 304-233-4121

St. Patrick's Church • Art Wonders • Hinton/Summers • 309 2nd Ave • 304-466-3966

Stages • Shopping Treasures • Wheeling/Ohio • 1063 Main St • open M-Sa 10-5 • 304-232-1106

Star House • Amazing Architecture • Hinton/Summers • Union and James Sts

Star Theatre • Art Wonders • Berkeley Springs/Morgan • corner Washington and Congress Sts • 304-258-1404

State Capitol • Historic Oddities/Superlatives • Charleston/Kanawha • Capitol Complex/ Kanawha Blvd

State Fair of West Virginia • Far-Out Festivals • Lewisburg/Greenbrier • US 219 • 304-645-1090

State Water Festival • Fast Living • Hinton/Summers • Bluestone Lake • July/August • 304-466-5420

Stewart's Original Hot Dogs • Local Food • Huntington/Cabell • 2445 5th Ave (US 60) • 304-529-3647

Stifel Fine Arts Center • Art Wonders • Wheeling/Ohio • 1330 National Rd • 304-242-7700

Stages • Shopping Treasures • Wheeling/Ohio • 1063 Main St • 304-232-1107

Strand Theater • Art Wonders • Moundsville/Marshall • 811 5th St • 304-845-3009

Stonewall Jackson Lake State Park and Resort • Tours • Roanoke/Lewis • US 19/940 Resort Dr • 888-278-8150

Storer College • Historic Oddities • Harpers Ferry/Jefferson • Harpers Ferry Historical Park • 304-535-6371

Summersville Lake & Dam • Fast Living/Superlatives • Summersville/Nicholas • US 19 to SR 129

Summerfest • Fast Living • Huntington/Cabell • Tri-State Fair & Regatta • July • Riverfront Park • 304-525-7333

Summit Bechtel National Scout Reserve • Superlatives • Mount Hope/Fayette

Summit Point Raceway • Fast Living • Summit Point/Jefferson • 2026 Summit Point Rd • 304-725-8444

Sunset Drive-in Theater • Art Wonders • Shinnston/Harrison • SR 19 • 304-592-3909

Sunshine Farm and Garden • Mother Nature's Wonders • Renick/Greenbrier • 304-497-2208

Sweet Springs • Adventure Driving/Things That Used To Be There • Sweet Springs/Monroe • SR 3 • 304-772-3003

T

Tamarack • Local Food/Art Wonders/Shopping Treasures/Truly Incredible • Beckley/Raleigh • I-77, exit 45 • 1-88-TAMARACK

Tari's Premier Cafe • Local Food • Berkeley Springs/Morgan • 33 N Washington St • 304-258-1196

Tecumseh • Historic Oddities • Hacker Valley/Webster • Tenshwatawa Falls at Holly River State Park • SR 20 • 304-493-6353

Thistledew Farm • Far-Out Festivals • Proctor/Wetzel • SR 2 • 304-455-1728

Thomas Shepherd Gristmill • Things That Used To Be There • Shepherdstown/Jefferson • N Mill St

Those Shoes • Art Wonders • Weston/Lewis • 304-269-9782

Three Rivers Festival • Local Food • Fairmont/Marion • 1694 Fairmont Ave • 304-366-5084

Thurmond • Adventure Driving/Things That Used To Be There • Fayette • CR 25

TNT area • Things That Used To Be There • Point Pleasant/Mason • Adjacent to Mason County Fairgrounds • SR 62 east to Fairgrounds Rd

Tomlinson Run • Unusual Places to Stay • New Manchester/Hancock • SR 8 • 304-564-3651

Tomaro's • Local Food • Clarksburg/Harrison • 411 N 4th St • 304-622-0691

Tony's Butcher Block • Local Food • Berkeley Springs/Morgan • 2880 Valley Rd • 304-258-4770

Touma Medical Museum • Remarkable Collections • Huntington/Cabell • 9th Street Plaza • by appointment only • 304-696-5787

Trace Fork Canyon Trail • Mother Nature's Wonders • South Charleston/Kanawha • Little Creek Park • Spring Hill Ave

Trans-Allegheny Lunatic Asylum • Amazing Architecture/Superlatives/Tours • Weston/Lewis • US 19 • 304-269-5070

Troubadour Lounge • Art Wonders • Berkeley Springs/Morgan • Troubadour Lounge • Highland Ridge Rd

Trout Pond • Mother Nature's Wonders • Hardy • CR16 south of Wardensville • 540-984-4101

Tu-Endie-Wei State Park • Historic Oddities • Point Pleasant/Mason • 1 Main St • 304-675-0869

Tunnelton • Amazing Architecture • Preston • US 50 to SR 26 at Fellowsville

Twin Falls State Park • Amazing Architecture/Mother Nature's Wonders/Unusual Places to Stay • Mullins/Wyoming • SR 97 • 304-294-4000

Twisted Gun Golf Club • Superlatives • Wharncliffe/Mingo • 202 Twisted Gun Rd • 304-687-1514

Tygart Dam • Superlatives • Grafton/Taylor • CR 44 • 304-265-1760

Tyler County Museum • Remarkable Collections • Middlebourne/Tyler • Dodd St • 304-758-4288

U

Undo's • Local Food • Benwood/Marshall • 753 Main St • 304-233-0560

Union • Adventure Driving/Amazing Architecture • Monroe • SR 3 & US 219

V

Valley Falls State Park • Million Dollar Views • Fairmont/Marion • SR 310 • 304-367-2719

Valley Furnace • Things That Used To Be There • Philippi/Barbour • SR 38

Vandalia Festival • Art Wonders/Far-Out Festivals • Charleston/Kanawha • Capitol Complex/Kanawha Blvd • Memorial Day weekend • 304-558-0220

Vanmetre Ford Bridge • Amazing Architecture • Martinsburg/Berkeley • E Burke St • Berkeley County Historic Society • 304-267-4713

Vickie's Part of Heaven • Art Wonders • Arthurdale

Victorian Wheeling • Amazing Architecture • Wheeling/Ohio • 832 Main St • 304-233-1600

Village site • Historic Oddities • Buffalo/Putnam • US 35

Virginia Furnace • Things That Used To Be There • Albright/Preston • SR 26

Virginius Island • Things That Used To Be There • Harpers Ferry/Jefferson • Harpers Ferry Historical Park • US 340 @ WV/MD/VA border • 304-535-6371

W

Waffle Rock • Mother Nature's Wonders • Elk Garden/Mineral • Jennings Randolph Lake • US 50 • 304-355-2346

Walkersville CB • Amazing Architecture • Walkersville/Lewis • US 19

Washington Western Lands Museum • Historic Oddities • Ravenswood/Jackson • Lockhouse 22 @ Riverfront Park • 304-273-2621

Washington Heritage Trail National Scenic Byway • Berkeley/Jefferson/Morgan counties

Webster Woodchopping Festival • Far-Out Festivals • Webster Springs/Webster • Baker's Island Recreation Area • Memorial Day weekend/May • 304-847-7666

West Virginia and Regional History Collection • Remarkable Collections • Morgantown/Monongalia • Colson Hall, West Virginia University • 304-293-3536

West Virginia Archives and History Library • Remarkable Collections • Charleston/Kanawha • Cultural Center, Kanawha Blvd • 304-558-0230

West Virginia Breeders Classic • Fast Living • Charles Town/Jefferson • 304-725-0709

WV Crafts Map • Art Wonders • 800-CALL WVA

West Virginia Biological Survey Museum • Remarkable Collections • Huntington/Cabell • Science Building/Marshall University • 800-642-3463

West Virginia Geological Survey Museum • Remarkable Collections • Morgantown • Cheat Lake exit I-68 • 304-594-2331

West Virginia Historic Theater Trail • Art Wonders

West Virginia Honey Festival • Far-Out Festivals • Parkersburg/Wood • Wood County 4-H campgrounds • mid-September • 800-752-4982

West Virginia Hot Dog Festival • Huntington/Cabell • Pullman Square

West Virginia Marble Festival • Far-Out Festivals • Cairo/Ritchie • 1st Sat in May • 304-628-3321

West Virginia Motor Speedway • Fast Living • Mineral Wells/Wood • I-77 • 304-771-5051

INDEX

West Virginia Museum of American Glass • Remarkable Collections • Weston/Lewis • 230 Main Ave • 304-269-5006

West Virginia Music Hall of Fame • Art Wonders • Charleston/Kanawha • 1427 Lee St • 304-342-4412

West Virginia Penitentiary Tours • Tours • Moundsville/Marshall • 818 Jefferson Ave • 304-845-6200

West Virginia State Farm Museum • Remarkable Collections • Point Pleasant/Mason • 1458 Fairground Rd • 304-675-5737

West Virginia State Folk Festival • Far-out Festivals • Glenville/Gilmer • 3rd weekend in June

West Virginia State Museum • Historic Oddities/Remarkable Collections • Charleston/Kanawha • Cultural Center, Kanawha Blvd • 304-558-0220

West Virginia Wesleyan • Amazing Architecture • Buckhannon/Upshur • 59 College Ave • 304-473-8000

West Virginia Wildlife Center • Mother Nature's Wonders • French Creek/Upshur • SR 20 • 304-924-6211

Weston Episcopal Church • Amazing Architecture • Weston/Lewis • 206 E Second St

Wheeling Airport Terminal/Stifel Field • Adventure Driving/Historic Oddities/Remarkable Collections/Superlatives • Wheeling/Ohio • CR 2 • 304-234-3865

Wheeling Island Racetrack and Gaming Center • Fast Living • Wheeling Island/Ohio • 877-WIN-HERE

Wheeling Island • Superlatives • Wheeling/Ohio • I-70, exit 0

Wheeling Jamboree • Art Wonders/Fast Living • Wheeling/Ohio • Wheeling Island Casino • 304-907-0306

Wheeling Suspension Bridge • Amazing Architecture • Wheeling/Ohio • I-70, exit 1A, south to 10th and Main St

White water rafting • Fast Living • 1-800-CALLWVA for a list of outfitters

Wilderness Hut • Unusual Places to Stay • Snowshoe/Pocahontas • 1 Snowshoe Dr • 304-572-1000

Williamson • Adventure Driving • Williamson/Mingo

Woodburn Hall • Amazing Architecture • Morgantown/Monongalia • West Virginia University Campus

World's Largest Teapot • Superlatives • Chester/Hancock • SR 2 & 30 intersection north of Chester

World War II Museum in Szilagyi Center • Remarkable Collections • Rowlesburg/Preston • SR 72 • 304- 329-1240

Wymer's General Store and Museum • Remarkable Collections • Wheeling/Ohio • 1400 Main St • 304-232-1810

Y

Yann Hot Dogs • Local Food • Fairmont/Marion • 300 Washington St • 304-366-8660

Yeager Airport • Adventure Driving • Charleston/Kanawha • 100 Airport Rd • 304-344-8033

Yeager Monument • Adventure Driving • St. Albans/Kanawha • US 60 west of Charleston

Yokum's Stables • Million Dollar Views • Seneca Rocks/Pendleton • 304-567-2466

Z

Ziegenfelder Company • Local Food • Wheeling/Ohio • 87 18th St • 304-232-6360

Zion Episcopal Church Cemetery • Historic Oddities • Charles Town/Jefferson • 301 E Congress St • 304-725-5312

Bibliography

All That Remains, 2nd Edition Robert L. Pyle. Archeological discoveries in the state. 1998. Archeology Archives Inc, 1964 Negley Ave. Morgantown, WV 26505

Bath, That Seat of Sin. Fred Newbraugh. History of Berkeley Springs' raunchy past.

Best of Hillbilly. Jim Comstock. Collection of articles from Comstock's *Hillbilly* newspaper. Droke House. 1968.

Bicycle West Virginia Adventure Guide

Charleston Gazette. Daily paper has done a credible job of documenting some of the oddities included here. Check their archives and on line. • 800-982-6397

50 Hikes in West Virginia. Leonard Adkins. Countryman Press • 800-245-4151

Goldenseal...More in depth looks at traditional West Virginia and its oddities. Published 4 times/year by Division of Culture & History, State of WV. Cultural Center, 1900 Kanawha Blvd E. Charleston, 25305 • 304-558-0220

Graffiti...Inspiration for the book and source of in-depth looks at many of the oddities listed here by editor and journalist, Michael Lipton

Historic Springs of the Virginias. Stan Cohen. Quarrier Press

Historic West Virginia, the National Register of Historic Places. 2000. WV Division of Culture and History. Charleston, WV

The History of the Greenbrier, America's Resort. Robert Conte. Pictorial Histories

History of the Valley of Virginia. Samuel Kercheval

Last Sleep: Battle of Droop Mountain. Terry Lowry.

The Mothman Prophecies. John Keel.

Mountain Biking in West Virginia. Frank Hutchins. Quarrier Press.

The New West Virginia One-Day Trip Book. Colleen Anderson. 1998.

Rail Trails along the Greenbrier River. Jim Hudson. Quarrier Press.

Roadside Markers in West Virginia. Charles Adams.

Shaman's Story. West Virginia Petroglyphs. Dean Braley. St. Albans Publishing.

David Hunter Strother: "One of the best draughtsman the country possess." Published in conjunction with the exhibition of the Strother Collection. WVU Press.

Travel Through Time. David Hunter Strother. Historic drawings and writings of Porte Crayon • Porte Crayon & Co.

West Virginia: A History for Beginners. John Alexander Williams.

West Virginia Atlas and Gazetteer. DeLorme.

West Virginia's Covered Bridges. Stan Cohen. Pictorial Histories Publishing Co.

West Virginia Encyclopedia. edited by Ken Sullivan. A project of the WV Humanities Council. 1310 Kanawha Blvd E. Charleston, 25301. 2006

West Virginia Heritage compiled and edited by Jim Comstock and Bronson McClung. West Virginia Heritage Foundation. Richwood, WV. 1969.

West Virginia Heritage Encyclopedia edited and published by Jim Comstock. Richwood. 1976. 25 volumes plus 25 volume Supplement.

West Virginia History Database

West Virginia, Wild and Wonderful—State's official travel guide. Everything you need to know to tour the state. 1-800-CALL-WVA

West Virginia Off-the-Beaten-Path. Stephen and Stacy Soltis. The Globe Pequot Press

West Virginia UFOs, Close Encounters in the Mountain State. Bob Teets. Headline Books.

Where People and Nature Meet, A History of the West Virginia State Parks. Pictorial Publishing, Charleston, WV. 1988

Wildwater West Virginia

Wonderful West Virginia magazine. West Virginia Department of Natural Resources. 1-800-CALL WVA.

About the Author

Jeanne Mozier, until her much-bereaved death on Thanksgiving Day of 2020, lived in historic Berkeley Springs where, for forty-three years, she and her husband owned and operated the unique vintage movie house, the Star Theatre, as well as a commercial apple and peach orchard. A sparkplug for several local cultural and economic development organizations, she also served on the state Arts Commission. She was the recipient of many awards for her contributions to state economic development and arts and culture. She was an award-winning writer of both fiction and nonfiction.

Way Out in West Virginia was voted Best Book about West Virginia and Mozier was voted Best West Virginia author by statewide readers. She wrote the text for two volumes of Steve Shaluta photographs: *West Virginia Beauty: Familiar and Rare* and *Wonders of West Virginia*.

Mozier co-authored the historical compendium *Images of Berkeley Springs* with Betty Lou Harmison.

She was also author of *Panhandle Paradise*, the sole lifestyle guide to West Virginia's Eastern Panhandle.

Her short stories are included in three volumes of *Tales from the Springs*, and three of her plays have been staged. She was a contributor to the *West Virginia Encyclopedia*, and was a regular contributor of travel and lifestyle articles to a variety of regional and national publications.

Her novel is called *Senate Magic*.

Jeanne was a popular speaker, receiving numerous awards for arts, tourism, business and volunteer activities including being named a Distinguished West Virginian. She was one of five women in America honored by *Traditional Home* magazine as a Classic Woman in 2006. She chose to make West Virginia her home in 1977. Mozier was a graduate of Cornell and Columbia universities.

Made in the USA
Monee, IL
19 May 2023